ISBN 0-8240-6999-4

Published by Garland Publishing, Inc.
136 Madison Avenue, New York, N.Y. 10016

Printed in the United States of America
10   9   8   7   6   5   4   3   2   1

Apple, Atari, IBM, Commodore, TI 99/4A,
and TRS-80 are trademarks of:

    Apple Computer, Inc.
    Atari, Inc.
    IBM Corporation
    Commodore Business Machines, Inc.
    Texas Instruments, Inc.
    Tandy Corporation

National Education Association
Educational Computer Service's

The Yellow Book

A Parent's Guide to Teacher-Tested Educational Software

teacher certified
NEA™

Garland Publishing, Inc.

This expanded edition of *The Yellow Book of Computer Products for Education* has been developed for the home user. The NEA Educational Computer Service recognizes that many parents, students, and others in the general public need to identify and select microcomputer software for use with their own personal computers. The software industry itself has recognized this need from the beginning. For example, most educational software was originally developed for the home and later adapted for school.

Many of these programs have been improved as a direct result of the reviews provided by the NEA Educational Computer Service. Publishers frequently have made changes in the programming and/or the documentation to improve the quality of their products following our evaluations. The result is of equal benefit to you, the home user as it is to the teacher.

Only those products that have successfully passed our assessment process are listed and described in the catalog. You can therefore choose "NEA Teacher Certified" products with confidence that they will perform as described in *The Yellow Book*.

L. J. Fedewa, Ph.D.
L. J. Fedewa, Ph.D.
Executive Director

About the NEA Educational Computer Service...

The NEA Educational Computer Service was formed in 1983 to help teachers, students, and schools benefit from the "computer revolution" now occurring throughout American education. Our function is to identify "schoolworthy" software products from among the thousands of software programs being marketed today. The published criteria are used by carefully selected and trained teachers to determine if products are 1) technically reliable, 2) instructionally sound, and 3) easy to use. Those products which meet these criteria are described in *The Yellow Book* and are approved for identification with the "NEA Teacher Certified" trademark.

The NEA Educational Computer Service is jointly sponsored by The National Education Association, the National Foundation for the Improvement of Education, and Cordatum, Inc. The NEA is responsible for the review process, Cordatum (a high technology consulting firm) for technical and administrative assistance, and NFIE for liaison. The Service is governed by a Board consisting of representatives from these three organizations. The staff is headed by an Executive Director, responsible to the Board, and is drawn from all three organizations. The Service is intended to be financially self sustaining through revenues from publications and fees.

How To Use This Book

The Yellow Book is organized for easy identification of software in your areas of interest. Educational software is presented by educational level — preschool, elementary, secondary, and post-secondary. Within each level, subject categories are presented alphabetically, and within each subject category, the titles of the programs are presented alphabetically. To assist you in identifying specific software products, alphabetical indexes are provided by title, by level and subject, by hardware manufacturer, and by software publisher.

Within each review of educational software, you will find the following elements: (1) the system requirements needed to run the program, (2) the recommended target audience, a description of the content of the package, and (4) an overall commentary on the software.

In each review of applications software you will find the following elements: (1) its uses in an educational environment, (2) the experience level in computer and/or other knowledge required for successful use of the program, (3) a description of the content of the package, and (4) an overall commentary on the software.

TABLE OF CONTENTS

There are several ways to use the software products contained in *The Yellow Book*. Together and individually these programs represent a valuable resource for the owners of home computers. These owners may be individual adults, parents with school-age children, professional educators, community volunteers, or hobbyists. No matter which description best fits your reasons for using *The Yellow Book*, the book constitutes a resource you can use with confidence. We have detailed four categories of potential uses of *The Yellow Book:*

1. Independent Learning Resource
2. Supplemental Resources for Schoolwork
3. Adult Learning Resource
4. Community Resource

1. Independent Learning Resource

Completely separate from a school's curriculum, these software programs can be useful for a student's personal enrichment. There are stimulating programs on many different subjects and on many different levels. The description in the catalog will provide sufficient information for you to determine whether the program will meet your student's needs. If your student needs to develop skills which he or she does not presently have, you will find many programs in a variety of skill areas. i.e., English composition skills, math skills, or vocabulary in a foreign language. Your student can also develop new skills with the appropriate software. You may choose software that prepares your child for a new experience, such as math or reading readiness prior to entering school. You will also find software designed for users who have special needs, such as in bilingual or special education.

There are many uses for educational software at home.

2. Supplemental Resources for Schoolwork

You as a student or you as a parent wanting to help your child in school will also find much of the *NEA Teacher Certified* software very helpful. Most of the educational software in *The Yellow Book* is correlated with the standard school curriculum. Students can use the software to supplement what is taught in school in a manner that will improve school performance. (We do suggest that parents coordinate these supplemental learning programs with the child's teacher.) The organization of the book, described above, makes the identification of software for this purpose easy.

These software programs can be used to fill in gaps in what has been mastered at school. For example, a student may have a persistent weakness in some aspect of mathematics. *The Yellow Book* can be used to identify software that will help the student fill in this gap at home. There are programs at every level from preschool through postsecondary.

3. Adult Learning

The Yellow Book can be used by an adult who has completed schooling but wants to pursue new areas independently. You can identify software that is appropriate for your interest and that is designed at the appropriate level of experience and difficulty.

For example, you might like to learn computer programming, but have no previous experience with it. There are courses listed in the *Yellow Book* that you could use to develop this new skill.

You may have bought a computer but are not yet proficient in keyboard skills or in word processing. There are programs listed in the book that will help you to master these skills.

Perhaps you are about to travel to a foreign country and need to develop enough vocabulary to communicate basic needs. There are foreign language programs listed in the book that provide assistance in travel vocabulary, shopping vocabulary, and other areas helpful to the traveler.

Perhaps you want to manage a variety of information at home. There are data base management systems in the book that you can use at home.

You may be considering going back to school and need to refresh skills before enrolling. There are many drill and practice programs in a variety of subjects and academic skills that can help meet this need.

All these examples point out that the adult can find many uses for the programs listed and described in *The Yellow Book*.

4. Community Resource

You may be active in your community and find yourself in need of professional guidance in the purchase of software. Perhaps you need to identify appropriate educational and/or applications programs for the public library, the PTA, or a civic club. *The Yellow Book* can help you through the screening process that would otherwise take much longer and still might not provide identification of needed software.

If you want to identify and purchase software for your school or for some other worthy cause, you can be confident that the software selected from the *Yellow Book* will be appropriate for the need.

All this is to say that *The Yellow Book* is a rich resource of information about computer software products. All the products listed have passed a rigorous evaluation and can be used with confidence for a great variety of purposes.

The *Yellow Book* features all the "NEA Teacher Certified" courses on and about computers.

In addition to the Catalog, the Service also publishes a Summer Supplement and occasional Product Bulletins as especially interesting products complete the Service's assessment process.

A $30.00 subscription will ensure that you will receive all of the Service's publications. Each will offer products on which you can rely.

CATALOG SUBSCRIPTION

NS004 $30.00

The annual subscription to the Service includes: The Catalog shipped in the Winter, Product Bulletins in the Fall and Spring, and a supplement to the Catalog in the Summer. All items in the Catalog are indexed and cross-referenced. The Catalog lists only software that has been assessed and endorsed by the Service as "NEA Teacher Certified."

GUIDE TO THE SOFTWARE ASSESSMENT PROCEDURE

There are three documents in this series. Each document includes a checklist and a commentary on the checklist that is used by reviewers to assess a particular type of product. The series is also valuable to educational users and the general public who want to know precisely the criteria that are being used for "NEA Teacher Certified" software. This knowledge will enable them to select and use the certified software with confidence.

Reviewer Document #1:
Courseware

NS 001   each $5.00

This document is concerned with computer software designed for courses in which the computer is the primary medium of instruction.

Reviewer Document #2:
Applications Software

NS 02   each $3.50

This document is concerned with applications software tools for technical tasks such as budgeting, data base management, computer networking, and information storage. Applications software products are not intended for instructional use with students, but rather as aids for educators.

Reviewer Document #3:
Combination Products

NS 003   each $5.00

This document is concerned with products in which the computer is used but the actual instruction is conveyed through another medium, such as a User's or Student's Manual. These products thus "combine" instructional media (e.g., computers and print).

HOW TO ORDER:

Please fill in all the requested information. If mailing address and shipping address differ, please provide both. To facilitate the ordering process, the Service will honor purchase orders.

Make checks and money orders payable to NEA Educational Computer Service. If you prefer to charge your order, you may do so by filling in the necessary information or by phoning in your order. Call toll-free 800/632-6327 (VISA and MasterCard accepted).

Quantity discounts are available. Organizational accounts are welcomed. Information on both will be furnished upon request.

Return to: NEA EDUCATIONAL COMPUTER SERVICE — P.O. Box 70267 — Washington, D.C. 20088

Ship Order To:
Name
Organization
Street
City   State
Zip   Phone (   )

Bill Order To:
Name
Organization
Street
City   State
Zip   Phone (   )

Quantity	Item No.	Name of Item	Unit Price	Unit Shipping	Total
	NS004	Catalog Subscription	$30.00		

- **Purchase orders honored:** Add $1.00 per order
- **Maryland Residents Add 5% Sales Tax**

Total _____

Total Enclosed _____
(Check or money order)

Charge to my: (please check one)   ☐ MasterCard   ☐ VISA

Account Number   Card Expires: Mo._____ Yr._____

Signature

EDUCATIONAL SOFTWARE

NEA Teacher Certified: Existing Products

There are currently on the market several thousand software products listed as educational. It was considered imperative to review as many of these products as possible in order to make the best of them available in this first home edition of the *Yellow Book*.

The Service began operations in mid-1983 by researching, establishing, and publishing a set of standards for educational software in the series *Guide to the Software Assessment Procedure*.

Shortly after this, the Service started comparing 1500 titles to the guidelines. Publishers were invited to compare their products to the standards outlined in the *Guides* and to submit for assessment those products that, in the publisher's judgment, have the best chance to qualify for certification.

Since most of these products were developed prior to the publication of the *Guides,* some are lacking in one or another of the characteristics of the product profile elaborated in the *Guides*. However, in the opinion of the Teacher/Reviewers, the overall quality of each of the products listed below was sufficiently high to recommend their use. This publication contains 272 titles that have been certified by the Service as high quality products which will serve well those who use them.

PRESCHOOL

Math and Reading Readiness

ALPHABET ZOO

Spinnaker Software

System Requirements

Tested on:
Atari 800, 32K memory, disk drive, TV or monitor (color recommended), joystick

Also available (but not tested):
Apple II+, IIe
IBM PC
Commodore 64

Recommended Target Group
Reading Readiness, Preschool

Content
The program contains four games for practice in letter and sound recognition as well as spelling: (1) "ABC Time," (2) "The Letter Game," (3) "The Spelling Zoo," (4) "Alphabet Zoo."

Comment
Although the games can be programmed for different levels of difficulty, they are most useful with preschool children. Of the four games, "ABC Time" has the best educational value. The graphics are well done. List Price: $29.95

DINOSAURS

Advanced Ideas

System Requirements

Tested on:
Franklin ACE 1000, disk drive, TV or monitor (color recommended), Apple II+, 48K memory

Dinosaurs (continued)
Also available (but not tested):
Apple IIe

Recommended Target Group
Math and Reading Readiness; age 5, also ages 2-4 for first game

Content
The program includes five games: (1) direct matching of animals, one-to-one correspondence; (2) distinguishing dinosaurs according to their feeding behavior; (3) sorting and distributing animals according to their habitats; (4) matching a dinosaur to one of a set of dinosaurs and then counting them; (5) matching each dinosaur to its name for sight reading. The program provides skill development in visual recognition, matching, directionality, counting, classifying, and sorting.

Comment
Although the first game (matching) can be used by children ages 2-4, the other games are too advanced for all but five year olds. Teacher assistance will be required to introduce children to information about dinosaurs and to help them work through the program. The subject and the pacing are interesting for young children, and the program is easy to use. The manual is clearly written and explains all features of the program. The games in this package are designed to incorporate Montessori principles of early childhood education. They follow a progressive sequence with each game building on a skill used previously. List Price: $39.95.

JUGGLES' RAINBOW

The Learning Company

System Requirements

Tested on:
Apple IIe, 48K memory, disk drive, TV or monitor, (color recommended), DOS 3.3

Also available (but not tested):
Apple II, 48K memory, Applesoft

Math and Reading Readiness (continued)
Juggles' Rainbow (continued)

Recommended Target Group
Math and Reading Readiness, ages 3-6

Content
The instructional game provides teaching and practicing with right/left, above/below, and quartering. Color recognition and matching are also used.

Comment
The program can accomplish the goal of teaching its target audience effectively under parent or teacher direction. It uses simple verbal responses and directions and is appropriate for nonreaders. The color graphics and animation will make the program highly motivating for young children. The lessons are progressively sequenced and are within the attention span limits of children 3-6 years old. The teacher's manual very clearly follows the execution of the program. Special functions and options are explained in sufficient detail. List Price: $29.95

STICKYBEAR SHAPES

Xerox Education Publications

System Requirements
Tested on:
Apple II + , 48K memory, disk drive, TV or monitor, DOS 3.3

Also available (but not tested):
Apple II, 48K memory, Applesoft, Apple IIe

Recommended Target Group
Math and Reading Readiness, ages 3-6

Content
The package consists of three programs that reinforce shape recognition, left-right directionality, visual closure, and figure ground skills.

Comment
The three games in the program are recommended as an effective and motivational method to reinforce the recognition of five basic shapes. ''Pick It'' and ''Find It'' are designed effectively to motivate the child to identify the shapes within a larger picture. ''Name It'' involves the task of matching the label with the shape. Parent or teacher guidance is necessary for nonreaders in this game. Operational instructions included in the Parent's Guide are accurate. List Price: $39.95

ELEMENTARY

Bilingual Education

ARITHMETIC CLASSROOM SERIES

See review, Elementary, Mathematics, page 19.

Language Arts/Reading

COMPU-READ

Edu-Ware Division/Peachtree Software

System Requirements
Tested on:
Apple II, 48K memory, disk drive, TV or monitor, Applesoft, DOS 3.3

Also available (but not tested):
Apple II + , 48K memory
Apple IIe, 48K memory
Atari 800

Compu-Read (continued)

Recommended Target Group
English/Reading; ages 8 - adult, best for junior high age

Content
User can choose instruction or testing activities that present letters, words, sentences, or antonym/synonym exercises requiring timed responses. Program emphasizes improvement of memory and recognition speed.

Comment
This program, which is based on established tachistoscope methods, should contribute to improvement in reading comprehension and speed. The system operates as described in the manual. It should be noted that although the manual describes the purpose and use of the various programs in the system, the manual is written in language requiring teacher assistance for younger students. Terms such as ''defaulted parameters,'' ''reboot,'' and ''sub-menu'' might be troublesome for the younger student or the inexperienced computer user. Although an instruction frame preceding the various exercises would help users, younger users can benefit from the speed and recall drill on letters that are flashed at user-controlled, variable speeds and sizes. For older students, the various exercises can enhance concentration, recognition, vocabulary, and speed. For all, the program should contribute to improvement in reading comprehension and speed. List Price: $29.95

Language Arts/Reading (continued)

DRILL BUILDER SERIES

See review, Applications, Educational Formats/Multisubject, page 65.

LANGUAGE ARTS SKILL BUILDER SERIES

(six titles available separately)

DLM Teaching Resources

System Requirements

Tested on:
Apple II, 48K memory, disk drive, TV or monitor, Applesoft
Apple II+, 48K memory

Recommended Target Group

Language Arts/Reading and Language Arts/Writing; grades 4-5, remedial grades 5-9

Comment

Each of the six programs in the series provides drill and practice reinforcement in its designated area of concentration. The game format is particularly motivational for students provided that they have the necessary prerequisite skills in the area of reading, writing, or grammar that the program reinforces. These skills must be assessed by the teacher who uses the software. Younger students may be frustrated by the amount and movement of information on the screen, but older students (fourth grade and above) were fascinated by the high quality graphics and motivational game format. Teacher assistance will be required. One reviewer noted, "It is a pleasure to see that DLM computer software lives up to the high reputation DLM has for its other educational material." List Price Each: $44.00.

SPELLING WIZ

Content

This program reinforces instruction in spelling. A spelling wizard stands beside a pot that brews letters. A word missing one or two letters is at the top of the screen. Choices of letters are in a horizontal list. The child moves the wizard's wand to the missing letter and zaps it with the space bar. The completed word then appears at the top of the screen. The game is timed, and scores are accumulated per game.

VERB VIPER

Content

This program reinforces instruction in verb tenses and verb/subject agreement. The player feeds the correct tense of verbs emitted from caves to match the subject on the pad underneath. As the player's ability increases, so does the viper's neck.

WORD INVASION

Content

This program reinforces instruction in parts of speech. An octopus sits on a part of speech (verb, noun, pronoun, adjective, adverb, or preposition). Words start appearing in lists across

Language Arts Skill Builder Series (continued)

the top of the screen. An arrow at the tip of the octopus' feet can be moved from leg to leg until the correct word, representing the displayed part of speech, is zapped. Hits and misses are recorded.

WORD MASTER

Content

This program reinforces instruction in the identification of antonyms, synonyms, and homonyms. The player matches antonyms, synonyms, homonyms, or all three, to word stations. The word to be matched is in the center word scope with the skill at the bottom of the screen. Hits and misses are totaled after each game and tallied at the end of a turn.

WORD RADAR

Content

This program reinforces instruction in visual memory and discrimination by matching words. The graphics are designed to represent a radar screen. A word appears at the bottom of the screen. The child must match the word by opening covers over word choices. When the child finds a match, he/she zaps it. A new word then appears. This process continues until the student correctly matches all the words. The game is timed, and hits and misses are recorded.

WORDMAN

Content

This program reinforces instruction in basic phonetic patterns associated with short and long vowel sounds. A maze appears on the screen. A changing consonant moves around the exterior of the maze. When it comes to a group of letters, the user must decide if it makes a word. If it does, the letters are zapped and the word completed. If it doesn't, the user must let the letter go by. All the words on the outside of the maze must be completed before the user can move inside. The game is timed, and the maze disappears if not completed in the allotted time.

OPPOSITES

Hartley Courseware, Inc.

System Requirements

Tested on:
Apple IIe, 48K memory, disk drive, TV or monitor, DOS 3.3

Also available (but not tested):
Apple II+, 48K memory

Recommended Target Group

Language Arts/Reading, grades 3-6

Content

The program is designed to improve vocabulary by means of identifying words with opposite meanings. The lessons are ordered in increasing levels of difficulty.

Comment

This program is highly recommended for practice in vocabulary building. The reading level is judged as grades 3-4, which is lower than the skill level required. The student will not be

Language Arts/Reading (continued)

Opposites (continued)

bogged down with reading difficulties. A strong feature is that the teacher can modify or create new lessons and can monitor student progress. The documentation is clearly written and easy to follow. List Price: $29.95

PROGRESSIVE PHONICS SKILLS SERIES

(five titles listed separately)

Comp Ed

System Requirements

Tested on:
Apple II+, 48K memory, disk drive, color TV or monitor, DOS 3.3

Also available (but not tested):
Apple IIe
Commodore 64

Recommended Target Group

Language Arts/Reading, grades K-3

Content

This reading series contains five disks: (1) ''Beginning Consonants,'' (2) ''Ending Consonants,'' (3) ''Short Vowels,'' (4) ''Long Vowels,'' (5) ''Long/Short Vowel Discrimination.''

Comment

The series is recommended as one of the better instructional programs available for the early elementary grades. The drill and practice lessons are skill specific and are appropriate for the target audience. The documentation is adequate for the understanding of the purposes, features, and operation of the lessons.

The disk for ''Ending Consonants'' was not included in the package and has not been reviewed. Some other problems should be noted: (1) The screens and the acceptance of input are somewhat slow but acceptable. (2) The color bleed of text screens and the quality of ''inverse'' can be visually frustrating for some students. (3) Some of the screen instructions are clumsy and above the reading level of the users, e.g., ''Hit return when done typing your name.'' (4) The keyboard requirements of typing words may be difficult for some users.

BEGINNING CONSONANTS: List Price: $21.95
ENDING CONSONANTS: List Price: $21.95
LONG/SHORT VOWEL DISCRIMINATION: List Price: $21.95
LONG VOWELS: List Price: $21.95
SHORT VOWELS: List Price: $21.95

READER RABBIT AND THE FABULOUS WORD FACTORY

The Learning Company

System Requirements

Tested on:
Apple IIe, II+, 48K memory, disk drive, TV or monitor

Reader Rabbit and the Fabulous Word Factory (continued)

Also available (but not tested):
Apple II, 48K memory, Applesoft

Recommended Target Group

Language Arts/Reading, ages 5-7

Content

This program contains four games, which are designed to provide practice in the skills of: (1) identifying letters; (2) identifying words that differ by one letter; (3) locating letters in consonant-vowel-consonant combinations; (4) matching pictures with pictures, words, and parts of words. Each of the first three games practices a specific skill. The last game reinforces these skills and provides an opportunity to apply visual discrimination and memory skills in a computer game of Concentration.

Comment

This program is recommended both for home and school use, for students just beginning to read. It is highly motivational. Each game provides adequate practice examples on each skill. Students have the option to choose the game they want to play; so a weak skill can be reinforced. The narrative in the teacher's manual is short and to the point. It provides clear directions for executing the program. Nevertheless, it should be noted that an adult will have to instruct the young child before each game. List Price: $39.95.

READING SKILLS BUILDER— READINESS LEVEL

(four sets available separately or as series)

Morton-McManus Publications

System Requirements

Tested on:
Apple IIe, 48K memory, disk drive, TV or monitor, (color recommended)

Also available (but not tested):
Apple II, 48K memory, Applesoft
Apple II+, 48K memory
Atari 800

Recommended Target Group

Language Arts/Reading, Kindergarten and first grade

Comment

This combination product to supplement the teaching of sequential reading skills uses three methods of presentation: manipulative gameboards, worksheets, and computer games. Each method is interrelated and reinforces skills being taught through the other media — an integrated approach to instruction. The product uses GraFORTH, a graphics language that has the distinct advantage of presenting large lower case letters, which are helpful to young children learning to read. It has the disadvantage of not presenting perfect type for children to imitate, but rather a drawing style for the letters. The sequencing and instructional design are excellent, and children respond well both to the program and to the print materials. It should be noted that there is no student progress reporting feature, that teachers must keep their own records, and that individual assistance to students will be needed. List Price Series: $225.00; List Price Each: $60.00.

Language Arts/Reading (continued)
Reading Skills Builder (continued)

SET 1
Content

The skills taught with computer games and gameboards include: (1) "Visual Motor (Left/Right)," (2) "Visual Discrimination (Dissimilar Objects)," (3) "Visual Memory," (4) "Visual Discrimination (Direction in space)," (5) "Visual Discrimination (Dissimilar Shapes)," (6) "Visual Memory (Shapes)," (7) "Verbal Communication."

SET 2
Content

The skills taught with computer games and gameboards include: (1) "Spatial Relations (Up/Down, Left/Right)," (2) "Color Discrimination," (3) "Size Discrimination," (4) "Visual Discrimination (Sequential Order)," (5) "Visual Discrimination (Number Recognition)," (6) "Visual Discrimination (Dissimilar Letters)," (7) "Visual Discrimination (Similar Letters)," (8) "Visual Discrimination (Dissimilar Words)," (9) "Visual Discrimination (Similar Words)," (10) "Verbal Communication (Relational Thinking)."

SET 3
Content

The skills taught with computer games and gameboards include: (1) "Visual Discrimination (Upper Case-Keyboard)," (2) "Visual Discrimination (Lower Case-Keyboard)," (3) "Visual Discrimination (Sequential Relation)," (4) "Visual Memory (Words)," (5) "Verbal Communication (Categorizing)."

SET 4
Content

The skills taught with computer games and gameboards include: (1) "Auditory Discrimination (Letters)," (2) "Auditory Discrimination (Words Same/Different)," (3) "Auditory Discrimination (Beginning Sounds)," (4) "Auditory Discrimination (Rhyming Sounds)," (5) "Visual Discrimination (Concept Formation)," (6) "Skills Application (Word Meaning)," (7) "Verbal Communication (Classification)."

SPELLING BEE GAMES

Edu-Ware Division/Peachtree Software, Inc.

System Requirements

Tested on:
Apple IIe, 48K memory, disk drive, TV or monitor, DOS 3.3, game paddles

Spelling Bee Games (continued)

Also available (but not tested):
Apple II, 48K memory, Applesoft
Apple II + , 48K memory
Franklin ACE 1000
Atari 800XL

Recommended Target Group
Language Arts/Reading; grades 1-3, remedial grades 4-5

Content
The program contains four games consisting of activities designed to develop a beginning spelling and reading vocabulary. The four games utilize 22 lists of words of varying difficulty.

Comment
The package provides an excellent game activity for basic spelling review. The program allows the teacher or parent to select difficulty by selecting the lists of words to be used in the games. The documentation is well-written and easy to follow. The program loaded and ran smoothly. The game options requiring game paddles are easy to use. It should be noted that in most cases the program will not self-terminate without use of the Escape Key. List Price: $39.95

VOCABULARY SKILLS: CONTEXT CLUES

Milton Bradley Company

System Requirements

Tested on:
Apple II + , 48K memory, disk drive, TV or monitor, DOS 3.3, paddle

Also available (but not tested):
Apple IIe

Recommended Target Group
Language Arts/Reading; upper elementary, junior high

Content
The program provides instruction, drill and practice in five skill areas of vocabulary building: working with context, definition, contrast, educated guess, and example.

Comment
This program is recommended as a worthwhile addition to the classroom. It can be used in two ways: (1) student practice when time is available, and (2) a complete teaching unit featuring pretest, instruction, practice, posttest. It includes an excellent record management system. The documentation provides an overview of the program as well as details of the record management program that is available. The accompanying booklet contains reproducible worksheets and pre- and posttests to accompany the program on the disk. List Price: $49.95

Language Arts/Reading (continued)

VOCABULARY SKILLS: PREFIXES, SUFFIXES, AND ROOT WORDS

Milton Bradley Company

System Requirements
Tested on:
Apple IIe, 48K memory, disk drive, color TV or monitor, DOS 3.3

Also available (but not tested):
Apple II+, 48K memory

Recommended Target Group
Language Arts/Reading; upper elementary, secondary remedial

Content
This supplementary program covers five skills: (1) "Introductory Concepts," (2) "Prefix Tutor," (3) "Suffix Tutor — Common Suffixes," (4) "Suffix Tutor — Uncommon Suffixes," (5) "Root Word Tutor," (6) "Word Building." A student management section is also included.

Comment
This program is recommended as useful for specific groups. The programs are excellent in content and in developing the concept that words can be moved around to form new sentences. The documentation is comprehensive and complete. Using the student control section, the teacher must preselect the lessons and the level of mastery for each student. Students cannot do lessons the teacher has not preselected. The additional student and teacher record sheets do not appear necessary and could have been included in the computer program. List Price: $49.95

WHO, WHAT, WHERE, WHEN, WHY

Hartley Courseware, Inc.

System Requirements
Tested on:
Apple IIe, 48K memory, disk drive, TV or monitor, DOS 3.3

Also available (but not tested):
Apple II+, 48K memory

Recommended Target Group
Language Arts, grades 1-4

Content
This program contains 14 drill lessons on words and concepts in progressive levels of difficulty.

Comment
This program is recommended as worthwhile drill on an important skills area. The reading level of grades 1-2 is lower than the skill level. This design helps to eliminate the interference of reading problems with the skill focus. The program contains an excellent system for evaluating student progress, and is appropriate for classroom use. The instructional design is effective; it consists of a tutorial, followed by drill and practice ses-

Who, What, Where, When, Why (continued)

sions in graduated difficulty, and a system of evaluation. The student planning section is an excellent tool for the teacher to chart the progress of individual students and to analyze areas of weakness. The teacher can create new word lists or change existing ones. List Price: $35.95

WIZARD OF WORDS

Advanced Ideas

System Requirements
Tested on:
Apple II+, 48K memory, disk drive, TV or monitor

Also available (but not tested):
Apple II, 48K memory, Applesoft
Apple IIe

Recommended Target Group
Language Arts/Reading; ages 7-13 (gifted), 7-adult, persons with reading difficulties (LD)

Content
The program consists of five games that develop skills in vocabulary building, spelling, and thinking. A 38,000 word dictionary produces words and checks answers. An additional game enables students to create a personal word list. This feature makes the program useful for the diverse users in the recommended target group.

Comment
The program is highly recommended as excellent in design with superb animation. The games are effectively designed to strengthen language skills in different ways: (1) "anagrams," (2) "hangman," (3) "fill in a puzzle," (4) "guess a word" (learning how many letters in a guess are correct), and (5) "make little words from the letters in a long word." Note that instruction for start-up (p. 2) is incorrect: turn on computer *before* inserting disk. Otherwise, the documentation is comprehensive, with a detailed outline of each game and instructions for the beginner on how to use it. Also note that much disk turning and/or switching is needed to run these games. List Price: $39.95

WORD ATTACK!

Davidson and Associates

System Requirements
Tested on:
Apple IIe, 48K memory, disk drive, TV or monitor, printer (optional)

Also available (but not tested):
Apple II, 48K memory, Applesoft
Apple II+, 48 K memory
IBM PC

Language Arts/Reading (continued)

Word Attack! (continued)

Recommended Target Group
Language Arts/Reading, grades 4-12

Content
The program allows the student to choose the desired level of instruction for grades 4-12. It introduces new words with a word display exercise, and then reinforces learning with multiple choice, sentence completion, and game exercises. The program provides a list of words not successfully mastered and additional practice with these words.

Comment
The program is recommended both for instruction and for drill and practice in vocabulary building. It also allows for the creation of user word lists. A flexible, valuable program for classroom use, it contains an exceptionally good manual with easy-to-follow directions. List Price: $49.95

WORD SPINNER

The Learning Company

System Requirements
Tested on:
Apple IIe and Apple II + with 64K memory, disk drive, TV or monitor, Printer (optional)
IBM PC
Atari
Commodore 64

Also available (but not tested):
Apple II, 48K memory, Applesoft
Apple II + , 48K memory

Recommended Target Group
Language Arts/Reading, ages 6-10

Content
This drill and practice program in game format provides practice in the skills and concepts of exploring letter patterns, recognizing words, experimenting with similar looking words, and identifying correct spelling.

Comment
The program is recommended as effective drill and practice requiring students to concentrate. It is recommended as useful both in the classroom and for home study. An effective use of graphics is a definite strength. The program has an optional timing feature and sound capabilities. Prizes, a highly motivational feature, are awarded upon successful completion. The program is easy to run with few directions needed. The documentation is concise, clear, and easy to read. List Price: $34.99.

Language Arts/ Thinking Skills

ANALOGIES TUTORIAL

Hartley Courseware, Inc.

System Requirements
Tested on:
Apple IIe, disk drive, TV or monitor

Also available (but not tested):
Apple II, 48K memory, Applesoft
Apple II + , 48K memory
Franklin ACE 1000

Recommended Target Group
Language Arts/Thinking Skills, grades 5-8

Content
Using elementary vocabulary, the program presents to the user ten types of analogies, provides practice with cumulative examples, and monitors student progress. The ten types of analogies are: (1) "Synonyms," (2) "Antonyms," (3) "Object:Group," (4) "Group:Object," (5) "Part:Whole/ Whole:Part," (6) "Object:Description," (7) "Object:Use," (8) "Object:User," (9) "Cause:Effect," (10) "Grammar."

Comment
Repetition, reinforcement, and teacher adaptability make this program for teaching the basics of analogies most helpful to younger students. The lessons prepare students to apply the concepts to more difficult vocabulary and in more sophisticated circumstances. The level of vocabulary is simple enough for fifth grade students. The instructional design is well-conceived to teach the thinking skills involved in analogies. Teachers will want to add further exercises with more difficult vocabulary for older and more advanced students. The documentation is thorough, readable, and well-organized. List Price: $49.95

THE FOURTH (4TH) R — REASONING

MCE, Inc.

System Requirements
Tested on:
Apple IIe, 48K memory, disk drive, TV or monitor

Also available (but not tested):
Apple II, 48K memory, Applesoft
Apple II + , 48K memory

Recommended Target Group
Language Arts/Thinking Skills, grade 5 through junior high

Content
The program is an interactive introduction to logic, designed to improve thinking and reasoning skills. The program teaches the student to decide whether information has been obtained through observation, report, or reasoning, and to question its

Language Arts/Thinking Skills (continued)
The Fourth (4th) R - Reasoning (continued)

validity. Included in the program is an introduction to inductive and deductive logic. Students are presented with problems and puzzles to solve.

Comment
This program is recommended as an effective introduction to reasoning for the targeted age group. The teacher's manual is well-written and clear, and the program is easy to operate. Graphics are effective. An especially attractive feature is that the student can back up and reread a previous frame for review. It should be noted that the program could provide more help when a student cannot successfully solve a problem, and the program could provide more practice with concepts being developed. List Price: $44.95.

GERTRUDE'S PUZZLES

The Learning Company

System Requirements
Tested on:
Apple IIe, 48K memory, disk drive, TV or monitor, (color recommended), DOS 3.3

Also available (but not tested):
Apple II, 48K memory, Applesoft

Recommended Target Group
Language Arts/Thinking Skills, ages 10-13

Content
The program contains a series of puzzles, the solutions to which require the application of thinking skills, particularly deductive reasoning. Three puzzle types are used. In each type the student must follow a rule to organize different pieces by color and/or shape.

Comment
The program will be most effective with students who have good reasoning skills. Hard or easy puzzles may be selected, and samples are given to help students discover the pattern. Reinforcements are given for correct puzzle solutions in the form of treasures. Measurable objectives are not presented; however, the program follows a clear pattern of explanation, sample, and practice. The manual accurately represents the program. All special functions of the program are presented in a clear manner. All possible trouble spots are pointed out for the user. List Price: $44.95

GERTRUDE'S SECRETS

The Learning Company

System Requirements
Tested on:
Apple IIe, 48K memory, disk drive, TV or monitor, (color recommended), DOS 3.3

Gertrude's Secrets (continued)

Also available (but not tested):
Apple II, 48K memory, Applesoft

Recommended Target Group
Language Arts/Thinking Skills, ages 7-10

Content
The program is composed of a series of puzzles designed to teach categorizing and recognizing patterns. Students must find the pattern of color and/or shape to organize the game pieces properly. A sample is given for each puzzle to guide students to the rule.

Comment
The program is highly motivational in helping students to develop logical thinking through categorizing and patterning. Older students in the age range could utilize the "shape edit" function to create their own unique puzzle pieces. The program is technically sound, and the documentation provides all necessary information in a clear and readable form. Use of a joystick makes completion of the puzzles much easier. List Price: $44.95

MOPTOWN HOTEL

The Learning Company

System Requirements
Tested on:
Apple II +, 48K memory, disk drive, color TV or monitor, DOS 3.3

Also available (but not tested):
Apple II, 48K memory, Applesoft
Apple IIe

Recommended Target Group
Language Arts/Thinking Skills, ages 9 and up

Content
Seven attribute games, sequenced from easy to hard, involve 16 different characters (no two alike) to teach logic and language concepts. The game design requires children to differentiate among attributes of height, girth, color, and object (Gribbit or Bibbit creatures).

Comment
The program is recommended as worthwhile although time consuming. Color is essential for four of seven games. There is no provision for scoring success within each area. The program is primarily designed for differentiating attributes by means of assigned rules. Documentation is well-written in lay terms, and directions are, for the most part, easily understood. The program is excellent for simulation practice. The games are challenging and can be handled by the target audience after thorough explanation. List Price: $39.95

Language Arts/Thinking Skills (continued)

MOPTOWN PARADE

The Learning Company

System Requirements

Tested on:
Apple II + , 48K memory, disk drive, color TV or monitor, DOS 3.3

Also available (but not tested):
Apple II, 48K memory, Applesoft
Apple IIe

Recommended Target Group
Language Arts/Thinking Skills, ages 6-10

Content
Seven games, sequenced from easy to hard, involve 16 different characters (no two alike) to teach logic and language concepts. The attributes are tall/short, fat/thin, red/blue (the Bibbit or Gribbit creatures). The program incorporates the use of these attributes with regard to similarities, differences, opposites, patterns/sequence, and problem solving. It develops thinking skills that will help students make necessary discriminations in reading and in writing.

Comment
Moptown Parade is a junior version of *Moptown Hotel.* The program will be motivational for younger students once the necessary responses are explained thoroughly to nonreaders. The older end of the target age group could find the material too easy. The package is especially recommended as a supplementary program to be used in home or library. List Price: $39.95

PERCEPTION 3.0

Edu-Ware Division/Peachtree Software, Inc.

System Requirements

Tested on:
Apple II + , 48K memory, disk drive, TV or monitor, DOS 3.2 or 3.3, paddles

Also available (but not tested):
Apple II, 48K memory, Applesoft
Apple IIe

Recommended Target Group
Language Arts/Thinking Skills, ages 10 and up

Content
The course consists of seven programs in four areas: (1) "Visual Discrimination," (2) "Shape Memory," (3) "Size Comparison," (4) "Hand-Eye Coordination," the latter being subdivided into (a) "Star Trace," (b) "Centering a Fallen Line," (c) "Visual Pursuit," and (d) "Tilt Maze."

Perception 3.0 (continued)

Comment
The program is highly recommended for the development and refinement of perception skills. The software can be saved and restarted. Help options, prompts, and cues are present. The manual closely correlates with the program and instructions are clear. Learning objectives are stated in measurable terms, and data can be collected. Content is clear, logical, and well-presented. List Price: $29.95

ROCKY'S BOOTS

The Learning Company

System Requirements

Tested on:
Apple II + , 48K memory, disk drive, color TV or monitor, DOS 3.3

Also available (but not tested):
Apple II, 48K memory, Applesoft
Apple IIe

Recommended Target Group
Language Arts/Thinking Skills, ages 9 and up

Content
The program uses the simulation of building machines to teach the logic of what makes computers work, and how to reason: figuring out what belongs with what, why things work or do not work, and how to form logical solutions.

Comment
Reviewers recommend this program as a highly challenging problem solving simulation. It should also be noted that the program may be too advanced for some children at the low end of the age range. Also, a considerable amount of time may be required to master the basic components necessary prior to competing in the game mode. Another caution is that teachers should be aware that in the content the user is given the option of breaking an electrical connection with a knife. Nevertheless, the program is very effective in teaching and in reinforcing thinking skills from simple to complex. The documentation is well-written and easily understood. List Price: $49.95

Language Arts/Writing

BUILDING BETTER SENTENCES: COMBINING SENTENCE PARTS

Milton Bradley Company

System Requirements

Tested on:
Apple II+, 48K memory, disk drive, color TV or monitor, DOS 3.3

Also available (but not tested):
Apple II, 48K memory, Applesoft
Apple IIe

Recommended Target Group

Language Arts/Writing; upper elementary, secondary remedial

Content

The supplementary lessons include: (1) "Identifying Subjects and Predicates," (2) "Identifying Complements," (3) "Compounding Subjects," (4) "Compounding Predicates," (5) "Compounding Complements," (6) "Compounding Sentence Parts." A learning management section is also included.

Comment

This program is recommended as useful for the specified groups. The programs are excellent in content and in developing the concept that words can be moved around to form new sentences. The documentation is comprehensive and complete. Using the student control section, the teacher must preselect the lessons and the level of mastery for each student. Students cannot do lessons the teacher has not preselected. List Price: $49.95

BUILDING BETTER SENTENCES: CREATING COMPOUND & COMPLEX SENTENCES

Milton Bradley Company

System Requirements

Tested on:
Apple II+, 48K memory, disk drive, color TV or monitor, DOS 3.3

Also available (but not tested):
Apple II, 48K memory, Applesoft
Apple IIe

Recommended Target Group

Language Arts/Writing; upper elementary, secondary remedial, and special education

Content

The supplementary lessons cover the connection of compound and complex sentences, and emphasize four skills: (1) "Combining Simple Sentences Into Compound Sentences," (2) "Combining Simple Sentences Into Complex Sentences With Adverb Clauses," (3) "Combining Simple Sentences Into Complex Sentences With Adjective Clauses," (4) "Creating

Building Better Sentences (continued)

Compound and Complex Sentences." A learning management section is also included.

Comment

The lessons are designed well for all the target groups. The presentation is effective in communicating the concept that moving words around can form new sentences. The documentation is clear and comprehensive. Note that the teacher must preselect the lessons as well as the level of mastery for each student. Students are restricted to only those lessons. List Price: $49.95

CAPITALIZATION

Hartley Courseware, Inc.

System Requirements

Tested on:
Apple IIe, 48K memory, disk drive, TV or monitor, (color recommended), DOS 3.3

Also available (but not tested):
Apple II, 48K memory, Applesoft

Recommended Target Group

Language Arts/Writing, grades 2-6

Content

This program is designed to teach capital letter usage. The two major components are a practice disk for instruction and practice, and a test disk for testing and maintaining performance records.

Comment

The program is educationally sound and worthwhile in teaching capitalization. An exceptional added feature is the edit mode, which allows for teacher revision of subject matter. The documentation is well-written and sufficiently details all portions of the program. All portions of the program run with no difficulties. List Price: $49.95

MAGIC SPELLS

The Learning Company

System Requirements

Tested on:
Apple II+, 48K memory, disk drive, TV or monitor, (color recommended)
IBM PC
Atari

Also available (but not tested):
Apple II, 48K memory, Applesoft
Apple IIe

Recommended Target Group

Language Arts/Writing, ages 6-10

Language Arts/Writing (continued)
Magic Spells (continued)

Content
The program consists of two games that provide two different approaches to practicing spelling. ''Flash Spells'' requires the student to compete against the computer by correctly spelling words that are flashed on the screen for a set time. ''Scramble Spells'' requires the student to unscramble anagrams into correctly spelled words. An edit function allows the teacher to create new lists for both games.

Comment
The package is recommended as a smoothly running program that is useful for a teacher in helping groups of students learn to spell or unscramble lists of words being taught. Graphics and sound are used well, and the machine responses are fun for children. Although the program does not provide primary instruction in spelling, it does provide effective practice and the edit function enables the teacher to customize the content. List Price: $34.95.

NOUNS/PRONOUNS

Hartley Courseware, Inc.

System Requirements
Tested on:
Apple IIe, 48K memory, disk drive, TV or monitor, DOS 3.3

Also available (but not tested):
Apple II + , 48K memory

Recommended Target Group
Language Arts/Writing, grades 3-6

Content
This drill program provides practice with noun identification, plurals, possessives, and pronoun identification and antecedents.

Comment
Documentation is clear and comprehensive. Directions are given for modifying existing lessons or creating new ones. The instructional design presents students with tutorial, drill, immediate correction of mistakes, and a record of student progress. A student planning section allows the teacher to analyze progress and prescribe a further course of study. The program does not automatically branch to harder or easier work as the student succeeds or struggles with the material; this decision is left to the teacher. The program is recommended as excellent for independent drill because the computer monitors student progress for teacher evaluation. The reading level required is grades 3-4. List Price: $32.95

PUNCTUATION SKILLS: COMMAS

Milton Bradley Company

System Requirements
Tested on:
Apple II + , 48K memory, disk drive, TV or monitor, game paddle (needed for reward game)

Also available (but not tested):
Apple II, 48K memory, Applesoft
Apple IIe

Recommended Target Group
Language Arts/Writing, grades 5-8

Content
This program supplements and reinforces uses of the comma. It contains lessons for five specific skills plus two cumulative review drills — introductory elements; items in a series; interrupting elements; independent clauses; dates, addresses, letters, and titles; the Review Drills and the *Alien Raiders* game. All lessons are organized into an instruction-practice-mastery quiz sequence.

Comment
The program is clever and well-paced. The system of rewards and supports is creative, as is the idea of ''shooting'' the commas by cannon (for which the game paddle is needed). The student takes a written pretest, and results are recorded on paper and on the computer. Then the student receives appropriate instruction, practice, and quizzes from the teacher, worksheets, and computer. The final test is written. The teacher's manual is thorough and easily read. It describes and explains the program and how to operate it using narration, screen simulations, and flow charts. The worksheets are easily used and corrected. The integration of teacher instruction, written tests and practice, and computer instruction and drill is well-designed. List Price: $49.95

PUNCTUATION SKILLS: END MARKS, SEMICOLON, AND COLON

Milton Bradley Company

System Requirements
Tested on:
Apple II + , 48K memory, disk drive, TV or monitor, game paddle (for reward game)

Also available (but not tested):
Apple II, 48K memory, Applesoft
Apple IIe

Recommended Target Group
Language Arts/Writing, upper elementary and junior high grades

Content
This program reinforces the instruction of basic punctuation skills. Five specific skills and one review drill are covered on the

Language Arts/Writing (continued)
Magic Spells (continued)

disk: (1) periods, (2) exclamation marks, (3) question marks, (4) semicolons with parenthetical expressions and items in a series, and (5) colons. Following the review drill, students' final scores are converted to seconds of playing time on a video game, *Alien Raiders,* which serves as a motivator to do well on the drill.

Comment
Rewards and supports are creative and motivational, especially the space travel approach. The program combines the use of written pretests and posttests, written drill sheets, computer instruction and practice, and teacher instruction. Teacher and student track progress as student moves from instruction through practice to mastery level. The teacher's manual is thorough and accurate. It describes and explains the program and its operation by using narration, screen simulations, and flow charts. The worksheets and tests are well-done, easily used, and quickly corrected. The integration of teacher instruction, written tests and practice, and computer instruction and drill is well-considered and well-executed. List Price: $49.95

STORY MACHINE

Spinnaker Software

System Requirements
Tested on:
Commodore 64, cartridge, TV or monitor (color recommended)

Also available (but not tested):
Atari 400/800/Xl's
Apple II + /IIe
IBM PC

Recommended Target Group
Language Arts/Writing, ages 5-10

Content
The program in game format teaches children to write sentences, paragraphs, and simple stories. It uses a supplied list of 40 words, including nouns, verbs, prepositions, and other parts of speech.

Comment
The program is recommended as a creative method for teaching the designated writing components. The program has four learning levels, sound, and color graphics. The user may replay, save, call up the dictionary, or exit the program at any time. Objectives are presented in the explanation of how to play the options. Teacher assistance may be required for younger learners. List Price: $34.95

THAT'S MY STORY

Learning Well

System Requirements
Tested on:
Apple IIe, II +, 48K memory, disk drive, TV or monitor, printer (optional)

Also available (but not tested):
Apple II, 48K memory, Applesoft

Recommended Target Group
Language Arts/Writing; upper elementary grades, although program can be modified for some lower elementary and junior high grades.

Content
This program provides a structure that motivates the creative writing process. It uses "story starters" and "what if" situations to stimulate thinking and to provide the impetus for students to create stories by completing one that is provided or by inventing their own. By using simple word processing techniques, the student can go back and edit or change the story at any time. The student also has the option of printing the story.

Comment
The program is highly recommended as an effective means of promoting the creative writing process for children. Through the utilities section, the teacher can monitor a student's work, add another story starter, or change program specifications for the stories. This enables the teacher to modify the program for older students. Students in lower elementary grades who have no keyboard skills may be overly frustrated in trying to use the program. Some teacher assistance will be needed for most lower elementary students. List Price: $59.95.

VERBS

Hartley Courseware, Inc.

System Requirements
Tested on:
Apple IIe, 48K memory, disk drive, TV or monitor, DOS 3.3

Also available (but not tested):
Apple II +, 48K memory

Recommended Target Group
Language Arts/Writing, grades 2-8

Content
The program is a multilevel drill on verbs, which includes an explanation of the skill to be learned, drill in the form of multiple choice and fill in the blank, and immediate feedback on all answers. There is a student planning section in which the student's results are automatically stored for teacher review.

Comment
This program is highly recommended as an educationally sound drill on skills that are frequently difficult for children to learn. It is a useful addition to a school's software library. An

Language Arts/Writing (continued)

Verbs (continued)

appealing feature is teacher options, including design changes as well as modification and creation of new lessons. Documentation is well-written and easy to understand. The reading level throughout is judged to be elementary enough that reading problems should not appear as students work with the verb skills. List Price: $32.95

Mathematics

ADDITION MAGICIAN

The Learning Company

System Requirements

Tested on:
Apple II + , 48K memory, disk drive, TV or monitor, (color recommended), joystick (optional)
IBM PC
Commodore 64

Also available (but not tested):
Apple II, 48K memory, Applesoft
Apple IIe

Recommended Target Group
Mathematics, ages 6-10

Content
This program provides practice in basic addition. Students are required to identify addends for predetermined sums by drawing boxes around numbers arranged in a grid ("magic square"). A student can play against the clock or against another player.

Comment
The program is recommended as a highly motivational math program using a problem solving approach which stimulates flexible thinking. Sound effects, point tallies, and prizes are effectively used. It should be noted that younger students will need teacher assistance because of the vocabulary level. Younger students may also have difficulty using the required four keys to draw the boxes around the numbers in the Apple version. Joysticks are used in the other versions. List Price: $34.99.

ALIENCOUNTER & FACE FLASH

Milliken Publishing Company

System Requirements

Tested on:
Apple II + , 48K memory, disk drive, TV or monitor, printer (optional)

Aliencounter & Face Flash (continued)

Also available (but not tested):
Apple IIe
Atari, 32K memory, diskette

Recommended Target Group
Mathematics (*Aliencounter*), K-1; Mathematics (*Face Flash*), K-3

Content
Aliencounter is a game for beginners. It involves numeral recognition and counting skill from 0 to 10. For a perfect encounter with ten numbers, students are rewarded with fireworks. *Face Flash* is a game involving counting, base 10 numeration, and visual memory. The student is shown a number of faces and is asked how many there are. The student has a choice of 0-5, 0-9, 0-19, 0-49. Groups of 10 faces each are shown in rectangles for easy counting. Package contains 32 reproducibles, stickers, and *Extending MathFun* booklet with enrichment activities. The disk also contains a manager program that records students' scores, for which the optional printer is useful.

Comment
The program is recommended for its reinforcement and interest value for young children. It can be set for the ability of the child. It does not put the child under any time pressure to enter the answer. It should be noted that there is no teacher's manual. The needed information can be found, however, in the enrichment booklet and miscellaneous sheets in the package. List Price: $32.95.

THE ARITHMETIC CLASSROOM SERIES

(nine titles available separately)

Sterling Swift

System Requirements

Tested on:
Apple II + , 48K memory, disk drive, TV or monitor, DOS 3.3

Also available (but not tested):
Apple II, 48K memory, Applesoft
Apple IIe

Comment
For all nine programs, the educational design and delivery are consistently well done. Lesson objectives and sequence are clearly and accurately outlined in the teacher's manual. All sections begin by showing in detail how to solve two sample problems; then several drill problems are presented. An incorrect response results in a review of the teaching directions for the problem. A quiz and automatic check-off are provided to reward and record lesson mastery. Each lesson can be studied several times without fear of repetition. This program is technically sound. The documentation provides a clear description of the instructional design of the courseware. Note that teacher support may be needed in the lower grades. Also note that *the programs are available in a Spanish language edition*.

Mathematics (continued)
The Arithmetic Classroom Series (continued)

Addition
Recommended Target Group
Mathematics; grades 2-4, remedial 5-7
Content
This drill and practice program contains six lessons in increasing levels of difficulty: (1) ''Basic Addition Facts: Sums To Nine''; (2) ''Basic Addition Facts: Sums To Eighteen''; (3) ''The Addition Algorithm: Instances That Do Not Require Regrouping''; (4) ''The Addition Algorithm: Instances That Require Regrouping From Ones To Tens''; (5) ''The Addition Algorithm: Regrouping From Ones To Tens and Tens To Hundreds''; (6) ''The Addition Algorithm: Two or More Multi-digit Numbers. List Price: $49.95.

Subtraction
Recommended Target Group
Mathematics; grades 2-5, remedial 6-8
Content
This drill and practice program contains five lessons in increasing levels of difficulty: (1) ''Basic Subtraction Facts''; (2) ''The Subtraction Algorithm: Instances That Do Not Require Regrouping''; (3) ''The Subtraction Algorithm: Regrouping From Tens To Ones''; (4) ''The Subtraction Algorithm: One Regrouping Move''; (5) ''The Subtraction Algorithm: More Than One Regrouping Move.'' List Price: $49.95

Multiplication
Recommended Target Group
Mathematics; grades 3-6, remedial 7-9
Content
This drill and practice program contains six lessons in increasing levels of difficulty: (1) ''Basic Multiplication Facts: Both Factors > 5''; (2) ''Basic Multiplication Facts: At Least One Factor < 5''; (3) ''Product of a One-Digit Number and a Two- or Three-Digit Number Where No Regrouping is Required''; (4) ''Product of a One-Digit Number and a Two- or Three-Digit Number Where Regrouping Is Required''; (5) ''Product of a Pair of Two-Digit Numbers Where No Regrouping Is Required''; (6) ''Product of a Pair of Two-Digit Numbers Where Regrouping Is Required.'' List Price: $49.95

Division
Recommended Target Group
Mathematics; grades 3-6, remedial 7-9
Content
This drill and practice program contains five lessons in increasing levels of difficulty: (1) ''Basic Division Facts''; (2) ''One-Digit Divisors, No Regrouping''; (3) ''One-Digit Divisors With Regrouping''; (4) ''Two-Digit Divisors, No Regrouping''; (5) ''Two-Digit Divisors With Regrouping.'' List Price: $49.95

The Arithmetic Classroom Series (continued)

Fractions—Basic Concepts
Recommended Target Group
Mathematics; grades 5-6, remedial 7-9
Content
This drill and practice program contains five lessons in increasing levels of difficulty: (1) ''Basic Fraction Concepts''; (2) ''Fraction Equivalence''; (3) ''Comparing Fractions''; (4) ''Changing Improper Fractions To Mixed Numbers''; (5) ''Changing Mixed Numbers To Improper Fractions.'' List Price: $49.95

Fractions—Addition and Subtraction
Recommended Target Group
Mathematics; grades 5-6, remedial 7-10
Content
This drill and practice program contains four lessons in increasing levels of difficulty: (1) ''Addition of Fractions and Mixed Numbers With Common Denominators''; (2) ''Subtraction of Fractions and Mixed Numbers With Common Denominators''; (3) ''Addition of Fractions and Mixed Numbers With Different Denominators''; (4) ''Subtraction of Fractions and Mixed Numbers With Different Denominators.'' List Price: $49.95

Fractions—Multiplication and Division
Recommended Target Group
Mathematics; grades 6-7, remedial 7-12
Content
This drill and practice program contains four lessons in increasing levels of difficulty: (1) ''Multiplication of Fractional Numbers''; (2) ''Multiplication of Mixed Numbers''; (3) ''Dividing Fractional Numbers''; (4) ''Division of Mixed Numbers.'' List Price: $49.95

Decimals
Recommended Target Group
Mathematics; grades 5-7, remedial 7-12
Content
This drill and practice program contains five lessons in increasing levels of difficulty: (1) ''Basic Decimal Concepts''; (2) ''Comparing and Rounding Decimals''; (3) ''Adding and Subtracting Decimals''; (4) ''Multiplying Decimals''; (5) ''Dividing Decimals.'' List Price: $49.95

Games
Recommended Target Group
Mathematics; grades 2-4 for game #1, grades 4-6 for game #2, grades 5-7 for game #3, remedial grades 5-9 for all games
Content
Three game formats review basic skills in operations with whole numbers and fractions. Each game reviews a different type and difficulty of material. The easier (lower level) game provides hints if the learner misses a question. List Price: $29.95

Mathematics (continued)

BASIC NUMBER FACTS: PRACTICE

Control Data Corporation

System Requirements

Tested on:
Apple II+, 48K memory, disk drive, TV or monitor, DOS 3.3

Also available (but not tested):
Atari 800, 48K memory, DOS 2
Texas Instruments 99/4A, 32K memory expansion, PLATO Interpreter Cartridge

Recommended Target Group
General Mathematics, grades 6-8 remedial

Content
In game format, the program provides remedial practice on the basic mathematical operations of addition, subtraction, multiplication, and division. The design emphasizes increasing speed in using number facts as the student chooses game and pace, and monitors progress.

Comment
Reviewers recommend this program as highly motivational remediation in its game format with very clear and well-written documentation for the computer beginner. Teachers should be aware, however, that the reading level in the computer component is more difficult than the math material being presented. The "Fry Readability Scale" test revealed a sixth grade reading level.
Educational Version: List Price: $60.00. Consumer Package: List Price: $49.95

BATTLING BUGS & CONCENTRATION

Milliken Publishing Company

System Requirements

Tested on:
Apple IIe, disk drive, TV or monitor, DOS 3.3

Also available (but not tested):
Apple II, 48K memory, Applesoft
Apple II+, 48K memory
Atari, 32K memory, disk drive

Recommended Target Group
Mathematics, grades 4-8

Content
The complete package includes two games that introduce and reinforce math concepts. *Battling Bugs* introduces the concept of addition of integers and requires approximately five minutes to complete. *Concentration* reinforces the concept of equivalent fractions and requires approximately fifteen minutes to complete.

Comment
Both games provide effective supplementary experience for students of varying abilities in grades 4-8. Instructions for both games are clear and to the point. Although no manual is included, necessary information is packaged loosely in a folder

Battling Bugs & Concentration (continued)

inside the game carton. The game format combines the instructional techniques of drill and practice and problem solving. Devices and tactics that stimulate and maintain student interest include graphics, color, scoring, sound, personalization, timing, and animation. List Price: $32.95

BUMBLE GAMES

The Learning Company

System Requirements

Tested on:
Apple IIe, 48K memory, disk drive, TV or monitor, (color recommended), DOS 3.3

Also available (but not tested):
Apple II, 48K memory, Applesoft

Recommended Target Group
Mathematics, ages 4-10

Content
This program consists of six games in progressive order of difficulty. They provide drill and practice in teaching ordered pairs and elementary logic through the use of numerical arrays and the number line.

Comment
This program is recommended as effective drill and practice. The documentation is easily read and understood. The program would be difficult, without teacher direction, for the younger members of the target group or for the remedial reading student because of the vocabulary level. List Price: $39.95

BUMBLE PLOT

The Learning Company

System Requirements

Tested on:
Apple IIe, 48K memory, disk drive, TV or monitor, (color recommended), DOS 3.3

Also available (but not tested):
Apple II, 48K memory, Applesoft

Recommended Target Group
Mathematics, grades 5-8

Content
In a progressive sequence of five games, *Bumble Plot* moves students in a logical pattern from guided placement of positive/negative numbers to plotting points on a coordinate grid. Students can extend the lesson by using the coordinate geometry skills to create their own images.

Mathematics (continued)
Bumble Plot (continued)

Comment

Although the publisher recommends this program for ages 8-13, the content of negative numbers is more advanced than age 8. The games are highly motivational, especially as graphic and verbal corrections and reinforcement are used throughout to enhance the program's effectiveness. Each section of the program offers the option of getting instructions. A skills listing is provided to help teachers determine the appropriateness of the program for their students. Special functions and options are explained clearly, and the glossary of terminology related to coordinate geometry is a helpful inclusion. List Price: $39.95

CLOCK

Hartley Courseware, Inc.

System Requirements

Tested on:
Apple II+, 48K memory, disk drive, TV or monitor, DOS 3.3, printer (optional)

Also available (but not tested):
Apple II, 48K memory, Applesoft
Franklin ACE 1000

Recommended Target Group
Mathematics, grades 2-5

Content
The program is designed to help students learn to tell time with an analog clock. Lessons also permit the student to convert from digital to analog and vice versa.

Comment
This presentation is well-designed for drill and practice in telling time. Record keeping feature can be useful for teachers, especially for the lower grade levels. The program would also serve as good remediation at the higher grade levels. Vocabulary level may require some assistance from the teacher with the lower grades. Data can be printed for permanent record of achievement. The program provides sufficient repetition for the student to succeed in learning to tell time in minutes, quarter hours, half hours, and full hours. List Price: $39.95

CRASH

Acorn Computers Corporation

System Requirements

Tested on:
Acorn, disk drive, TV or monitor

Crash (continued)

Recommended Target Group
Mathematics, Programming Languages, Thinking Skills, grades 2-6

Content
The student's objective is to write a program that will enable a vehicle to complete an obstacle course. A vehicle, represented by an arrow, is stationed at the bottom center of a grid of squares. Drawn on this grid is an obstacle course through which the arrow must travel without crashing. It must reach the target at the top of the grid to complete the game. The student must use mathematical, thinking, and programming skills to play the game.

Comment
The user can operate the program easily. The program makes good use of the computer and is accurate and reliable. Operating and technical instructions are clear. There are photographs of sample screens. Sample lesson plans, follow-up lessons, and worksheets are included. The program achieves its objectives and has more than a one-time use. This program provides for and encourages risk taking and logical thinking, and it deserves an overall high rating. Reviewers note that the program needs a clearer description of the location of the target. The grid could also be improved with clearer definition and the use of color. List Price: $39.95.

DECIMAL SKILLS

Milton Bradley Company

System Requirements

Tested on:
Apple II+, 48K memory, disk drive, TV or monitor, DOS 3.3

Also available (but not tested):
Apple II, 48K memory, Applesoft

Recommended Target Group
Mathematics, upper elementary and junior high

Content
This practice and review program begins with four readiness subskills: (1) "Place Value," (2) "Names and Numbers," (3) "Comparing," (4) "Ordering." Then four major skills with decimals are treated: (1) addition, (2) subtraction, (3) multiplication, (4) division.

Comment
The program is recommended as having a well-planned and well-executed instructional design. Documentation is clear and easy to follow. The record keeping section is helpful. It should be noted that sound in the readiness section could be distracting. It should also be noted that no whole numbers are incorporated in the multiplication and division sections. List Price: $49.95

Mathematics (continued)

DECIMALS: PRACTICE

Control Data Corporation

System Requirements

Tested on:
Apple II + / IIe, 48K memory, disk drive, TV or monitor, DOS up through 3.3

Also available (but not tested):
Atari 800, 48K memory, DOS up through 2
Texas Instruments 99/4A, 32K memory expansion, PLATO Interpreter Cartridge

Recommended Target Group
Mathematics, upper elementary grades

Content
This fast-paced, fun program in game format stresses identifying decimal fractions using number line segments. It changes number line segments, provides for optional negative numbers and requires satisfactory completion of each level for a student to advance.

Comment
Reviewers recommend this program as highly motivational practice in decimals with definite educational value. In addition, its documentation is clear and easy to read.
Educational Version: List Price: $60.00. **Consumer Package:** List Price: $49.95.

DIVISION SKILLS

Milton Bradley Company

System Requirements

Tested on:
Apple II +, 48K memory, disk drive, TV or monitor, DOS 3.3

Also available (but not tested):
Apple II, 48K memory, Applesoft

Recommended Target Group
Mathematics, grades 4-9

Content
The program provides instruction, practice, and mastery testing on basic skills required to perform division functions. It contains lessons on: one-digit divisors, two-digit divisors, whole number remainders, fractional remainders, and decimal remainders.

Comment
Overall, the instructional design was judged to be excellent. The only exception is that students must enter an ''R'' between the whole number and fraction in quotients expressed as mixed numbers. This may cause confusion with the remainder concept. Instructional techniques include drill and practice, tutorial, gaming, and testing. Motivational devices include graphics, scoring, sound, personalization, animation, and variation of computer responses. Student records are stored on disk, but no print option is available. Users should note that software cannot be terminated except at the end of the lesson.

Division Skills (continued)
Upon completion of one phase the option to progress is not available; teacher interaction is required. Cues, prompts, and ''help'' option are present. List Price: $49.95

DRILL BUILDER SERIES

See review, Applications, Educational Formats/Multisubject, page 28.

EXPANDED NOTATION

Hartley Courseware, Inc.

System Requirements

Tested on:
Apple II +, 48K memory, disk drive, TV or monitor

Also available (but not tested):
Apple II, 48K memory, Applesoft
Apple IIe
Franklin ACE 1000

Recommended Target Group
Mathematics, grades 2-5

Content
The program contains 20 lessons on place value and expanded form in a tutorial and drill format. Missed questions are reviewed at the end of the lesson. The program will hold up to 50 student records.

Comment
The instructional design of a tutorial followed by appropriate drill questions is well done. An appealing feature is the option for the teacher to modify or delete existing lessons or create new ones. Teacher support will be needed in the lower grades. Unfortunately, teacher reports generated by the program are not very valuable. List Price: $29.95

FRACTIONS

Edu-Ware Division, Peachtree Software, Inc.

System Requirements

Tested on:
Apple II +, 48K memory, disk drive, color TV or monitor

Also available (but not tested):
Apple II, 48K memory, Applesoft
Apple IIe

Recommended Target Group
Mathematics, upper elementary, secondary remedial

Mathematics (continued)
Fractions (continued)

Content

This review and reinforcement package contains five instructional units on fractions: (1) "Definitions and Parts of the Fraction," (2) "Denominators," (3) "Addition," (4) "Subtraction," (5) "Multiplication," (6) "Division."

Comment

The program is recommended as excellent practice with fractions. Features include printable student results and forward and backward movement of screen displays. Speed is user-controlled, and sound is optional. Documentation is clear and thorough. The design provides a pre- and posttest feature that will select the instructional units for the student. The learner management feature allows the teacher much control of student activity. Note that only one student at a time can be handled by the Learning Manager. List Price Apple: $49.00. List Price Atari: $39.95.

FRACTIONS: PRACTICE

Control Data Corporation

System Requirements

Tested on:
Apple II+/IIe, 48K memory, disk drive, TV or monitor, DOS up through 3.3

Also available (but not tested):
Atari 800, 48K memory, disk drive, DOS up through 2
Texas Instruments 99/4A, 32K memory expansion, disk drive, PLATO Interpreter Cartridge

Recommended Target Group

Mathematics, upper elementary through eighth grade

Content

This fraction math practice program in game format is designed to improve fractional differentiation and identification skills. It uses fractions, mixed numbers, decimals, and expressions. The game provides instructions, negative number options, and controlled progress based on successful completion of one level at a time.

Comment

Reviewers recommend this program as highly motivational practice in fractions. The teacher should note two reservations, however, when using the program: (1) the program includes many different fraction skills in one game; (2) the students can switch back and forth between the different types of fractions outside the teacher's control.

Educational Package: List Price: $60.00
Consumer Package: List Price: $49.95

FRENZY & FLIP FLOP

Milliken Publishing Company

System Requirements

Tested on:
Apple II+, 48K memory, disk drive, TV or monitor, printer (optional for Manager Program)

Also available (but not tested):
Atari, 16K, Cassette
Atari, 32K, Diskette

Recommended Target Group

Mathematics, grades 2-5

Content

Frenzy provides drill and practice in subtraction or division with a choice of easy or hard. *Flip Flop* asks the student to decide whether turning or flipping the design would result in a match with the second figure.

Comment

The package is recommended as useful enrichment in subtraction, division, and visual discrimination, especially for the upper grades in the range. The documentation is clear and scores are automatically recorded on the Manager program—a helpful feature. It should be noted that the rationale for putting subtraction and division in the same program is not clear. Also note that the program provides no teaching of missed facts; it does not continue until a question is answered correctly. List Price: $32.95

GOLF CLASSIC & COMPUBAR

Milliken Publishing Company

System Requirements

Tested on:
Apple IIe, 48K memory, disk drive, TV or monitor, DOS 3.3, printer (optional)

Also available (but not tested):
Apple II, 48K memory, Applesoft
Apple II+, 48K memory
Atari, 32K memory, diskette

Recommended Target Group

Mathematics, grades 4-10

Content

The package contains two games to drill students on math skills. *Golf Classic,* for 1-4 players, provides practice in angle and length estimation and geometric skills. *Compubar* provides practice in reading graphs and constructing arithmetic expressions. Also included are 32 reproducible sheets for student and teacher use and a booklet with suggestions for additional activities.

Comment

Reviewers recommend these educational games as highly motivating with competition. They offer valuable practice in early geometry and trigonometry, as well as the planning stage for problem solving. List Price: $32.95

Mathematics (continued)

GULP!! & ARROW GRAPHICS

Milliken Publishing Company

System Requirements

Tested on:
Apple II+, 48K memory, Applesoft, disk drive, TV or monitor, DOS 3.3

Also available (but not tested):
Apple IIe
Atari, 32K memory, diskette

Recommended Target Group

Mathematics, grades 3-6

Content

Gulp!! contains 20 basic facts problems in addition and multiplication. *Arrow Graphics* requires students to reprogram the path of a bouncing arrow in direction and number of steps. The game provides practice in problem solving, construction of geometric figures, and spatial visualization.

Comment

In *Gulp!!* wrong answers speed up the big fish chasing the little fish. Correct answers keep the little fish in the lead. Time is an essential element. In *Arrow Graphics* directionality and graphics are presented well. List Price: $32.95

HEY TAXI!

Milton Bradley Company

System Requirements

Tested on:
Apple IIe, 48K memory, disk drive, color TV or monitor

Also available (but not tested):
Apple II, 48K memory, Applesoft
Apple II+, 48K memory

Recommended Target Group

Mathematics, grades 2-5 and 6-7 (remedial)

Content

This drill and practice program in game format teaches or reinforces basic facts in addition, subtraction, multiplication, and division. The object of the game is to earn more in fares than to pay in expenses, as the user drives a taxi through the city in competition with another taxi company.

Comment

The program is recommended as highly motivational. Useful features include student choice of operation, difficulty, and speed. Although there is no record keeping of students' progress, the teacher can ascertain learning by points scored for the game. A first-time user can run the game easily; the manual is concise and easy to follow. Hand and eye coordination skills are also emphasized. List Price: $39.95.

INTRODUCTION TO COUNTING

Edu-Ware Division/Peachtree Software, Inc.

System Requirements

Tested on:
Apple II+, 48K memory, disk drive, color TV or monitor, DOS 3.3, printer (optional for record keeping)

Also available (but not tested):
Apple IIe
Atari

Recommended Target Group

Mathematics; ages 4-6, remedial 6-8

Content

This program in game format presents the concepts of counting in the contexts of eight separate units: (1) ''Blocks,'' (2) ''Circles,'' (3) ''Shape,'' (4) ''Height,'' (5) ''Weight,'' (6) ''Length,'' (7) ''Addition,'' (8) ''Subtraction.''

Comment

The program is recommended as most useful for the younger age group (4-6). Teacher assistance is required. The drill and practice is accompanied by a scoreboard for recording results. The documentation is clear and easily understood. One error is noted on the *Apple Disk Learning Manager Menu*. Option 6 is ''Configuration Speech Board.'' There is no such item found on the disk menu when booted, but this omission does not interfere with operation or effectiveness of the program. List Price: $39.95

THE JAR GAME AND CHAOS

Milliken Publishing Company

System Requirements

Tested on:
Apple II+, 48K memory, disk drive, color TV or monitor, printer (for Manager)

Also available (but not tested):
Apple IIe
Atari, 32K memory, disk drive

Recommended Target Group

Mathematics; grades 2-6; K-2 if I, J, K, M keys are used to move ''gold pieces''

Content

''The Jar Game'' is an enrichment program in which students are asked to choose the jar in which a buzzing fly will have the best chance of landing on a gold piece. The game introduces elementary concepts of probability. ''Chaos'' is an enrichment program in which students try to capture alien satellites that match the shape and/or color of the satellite in the center square. The game provides enrichment in directional and visual discrimination.

Comment

These two programs are recommended as enrichment for young students. The games are supplementary and not primary means of instruction. List Price: $32.95

Mathematics (continued)

MATH BLASTER!

Davidson and Associates

System Requirements

Tested on:
Apple II+, 48K memory, disk drive, TV or monitor, Math Blaster Program Disk, Math Blaster Data Disk, printer (optional), joystick (optional)

Also available (but not tested):
Apple II, 48K memory, Applesoft
Apple IIe
IBM PC
Commodore 64

Recommended Target Group
Mathematics, grades K-6 and above

Content
The program contains tutorial and drill and practice lessons in addition, subtraction, multiplication, division, fractions, and decimals. Each subject has five levels of difficulty. The teacher can modify the program by entering math facts being learned by the students.

Comment
The program is recommended as highly motivational drill and practice in basic math facts, especially in the arcade game format. The manual is well-organized and easy to follow. A teacher inexperienced with computers will be able to use the program without difficulty. It should be noted that the program lacks a teacher management and student report feature. List Price: $49.95

MATH CONCEPTS I & II

Hartley Courseware, Inc.

System Requirements

Tested on:
Apple II+, 48K memory, disk drive, TV or monitor, DOS 3.3, printer (recommended)

Also available (but not tested):
Apple II, 48K memory, Applesoft
Apple IIe

Recommended Target Group
Mathematics, grades 2-6

Content
Two disks contain 24 drill and practice lessons about basic math concepts. Lessons are arranged in increasing levels of difficulty. Lessons begin with a tutorial explaining the objectives, which students can review at any time with a single keystroke. The program provides hints and/or a chance to redo incorrect responses. The teacher can modify an existing lesson or create a new one. The program holds up to 50 files of student records.

Comment
Reviewers recommend this program as especially flexible and effective tutorial and drill for students studying basic math concepts. Teacher support will be needed in the lower grades. An unusually attractive feature of this program is that the teacher can modify or create programs. List Price: $39.95

MIXED NUMBERS

Milton Bradley Company

System Requirements

Tested on:
Apple II+, 48K memory, disk drive, TV or monitor, DOS 3.3

Also available (but not tested):
Apple II, 48K memory, Applesoft

Recommended Target Group
Mathematics, upper elementary and junior high

Content
First, three readiness subskills are covered in a speed drill format: (1) "Converting Mixed Numbers to Improper Fractions," (2) "Converting Improper Fractions to Mixed Numbers," (3) "Comparing Mixed Numbers." Then four major skills with mixed numbers are presented: (1) addition, (2) subtraction, (3) multiplication, (4) division.

Comment
The program is recommended as well-designed and executed practice. The teacher's manual is easy to follow, and the work sheets are good. Note that although the title is "Mixed Numbers," much of the content involves fractions as well. List Price: $49.95

NUMBER STUMPER

The Learning Company

System Requirements

Tested on:
Apple II+, 48K memory, disk drive, TV or monitor, (color recommended)

Also available (but not tested):
Apple II, 48K memory, Applesoft
Apple IIe

Recommended Target Group
Mathematics, ages 8-10, 6-7 with teacher assistance

Content
This drill program in dice game format provides four games in increasing levels of difficulty. Students practice counting numbers to 12, adding and subtracting numbers to 12, doing arithmetic mentally, and recognizing multiple solutions to problems.

Comment
The program is recommended as an effective supplemental program for basic mathematics. The fourth game is particularly useful in developing thinking skills. Strong motivational devices include rewarding success with "prizes," good graphics, and optional sound. It should be noted that much teacher supervision will be needed for younger children, particularly since the player is not given sufficient help in the program. This fact makes the program less useful for children 6-7. The program does not keep any records beyond a tally of correct answers and provides no response to incorrect answers. List Price: $34.99.

Mathematics (continued)

PERCENTS

Milton Bradley Company

System Requirements

Tested on:
Apple II + , 48K memory, disk drive, TV or monitor, DOS 3.3

Also available (but not tested):
Apple II, 48K memory, Applesoft
Apple IIe

Recommended Target Group
Mathematics, upper elementary and junior high

Content
This supplementary drill and practice program is for the study of percents through five skills: (1) finding a percent of a number, (2) finding a base number, (3) finding a percent, (4) solving percent problems, and (5) solving two-step percent problems.

Comment
Reviewers especially recommend the feature of this program that allows the student the choice of solving problems either by the fraction or the decimal method. The program is well-conceived and well-executed. It should be noted that answers are sometimes typed in a right-to-left sequence and other times in a left-to-right sequence. Answers should be typed in slowly to assure that the program records them properly. List Price: $49.95

PRESCRIPTIVE MATH DRILL

Hartley Courseware, Inc.

System Requirements

Tested on:
Apple II + , 48K memory, disk drive, TV or monitor, printer (recommended)

Also available (but not tested):
Apple II, 48K memory, Applesoft
Apple IIe

Recommended Target Group
Mathematics, grades 1-4

Content
The program contains 99 lessons that provide an individualized review and enhancement of horizontal addition, subtraction, multiplication, and division of whole numbers from 1 to 99. Each lesson stresses a number from 1 to 99. The program will hold up to 100 student records.

Comment
Reviewers recommend this program as a sound individualized review of basic whole number operations. The horizontal only format for math skills is useful for students needing practice with that format although some teachers may find it too limiting for general use. An attractive feature is the flexibility for the teacher to set both the skill level at which each student begins work and the competence each student must attain before advancing to the next level. List Price: $79.95

PROGRESSIVE MATH SKILLS SERIES

(six titles available separately)

Comp Ed

System Requirements

Tested on:
Apple II + , 48K memory, disk drive, color TV or monitor, DOS 3.3

Also available (but not tested):
Apple IIe
Commodore 64

Recommended Target Group
Mathematics; grades K-1, remedial 2-3

Content
The series contains six disks: (1) "Addition 0-5," (2) "Subtraction 0-5," (3) "Addition & Subtraction 0-5," (4) "Addition 6-10," (5) "Subtraction 6-10," (6) "Addition & Subtraction 1-10." (The numbers indicate the digits used.)

Comment
These drill and practice lessons are recommended as a well-designed series for the designated age group. Each lesson is skill specific. The management section allows the teacher to monitor students' progress through the lessons and vary the lesson speed. The reproducible student workbook provides additional skill practice.

Some cautions should be noted: (1) The programs operate slowly. (2) The reading vocabulary in some instances is above the level of the content and may require teacher assistance. (3) The limited text on the graphic screen has bleed-through of colors. (4) A student cannot correct a typing error, and a means of exiting the programs has not been provided. (5) The programs operate as specified in the manual except that the graphing of scores is not available on these disks.
ADDITION: List Price: $21.95
SUBTRACTION: List Price: $21.95
ADDITION & SUBTRACTION: List Price: $21.95
ADDITION 6-10: List Price: $21.95
SUBTRACTION 6-10: List Price: $21.95
ADDITION & SUBTRACTION 1-10: List Price: $21.95

PUT TOGETHER, TAKE AWAY

Milton Bradley Company

System Requirements

Tested on:
Apple IIe, disk drive, TV or monitor

Also available (but not tested):
Apple II, 48K memory, Applesoft

Recommended Target Group
Mathematics, lower elementary, upper elementary (remedial)
Content
The program provides instruction, drill and practice in the basic math facts of addition and subtraction, up through three digits, with carrying and borrowing.

Mathematics (continued)
Put Together, Take Away (continued)

Comment
The program is recommended as effective in teaching the basic facts of addition and subtraction for younger students, and as remedial instruction for older elementary students. The element of timed tests challenges the student who can choose the skill and level of difficulty. In the instruction mode, the student is led through the problem step by step. Next, the practice mode allows for individual work, with help if needed. As a final step, the mastery quiz presents problems and allows one answer to be scored to determine the level of mastery achieved. List Price: $39.95.

SUPERMATH II

Learning Technologies

System Requirements
Tested on:
Apple IIe, 48K memory, disk drive, TV or monitor, printer (recommended), Class Records Disk, Class Data Disk

Also available (but not tested):
Apple II + , 48K memory

Recommended Target Group
Mathematics, grades 2-6

Content
The program offers drill and practice in the four areas of basic arithmetic: addition, subtraction, multiplication, division.

Comment
The program itself is a very well-constructed elementary school drill and practice tool in arithmetic. The program can be used alone or in conjunction with the *Class Records* program (see review, page 41). The documentation is so well written that even the teacher who is inexperienced with computers will have no difficulty using the program. The program offers students and teachers a considerable number of choices. There are provisions for the teacher to enter questions, individually designed to meet individual needs. List Price: $39.95

TIME MASTER

Micro Power & Light

System Requirements
Tested on:
Apple II + , 48K memory, disk drive, TV or monitor

Also available (but not tested):
Apple II, 48K memory, Applesoft
Apple IIe
Corvus (compatible)

Recommended Target Group
Mathematics; grades 1-2, remedial grade 3

Time Master (continued)

Content
This drill and practice program helps children learn to tell time in three ways: (1) by asking the child to enter the time, first hours then minutes; (2) by asking the child to position the hands to show a specified time; and (3) by asking the child to start the clock at a specified time.

Comment
Reviewers recommend this program as more realistic practice than most other means. It is flexible in that the number of times to set the hands can be varied. The clock is large (half screen) and easy to work with. There is no manual, but the program is easy to operate without one. List Price: $29.95

WHOLE NUMBERS: PRACTICE

Control Data Corporation

System Requirements
Tested on:
Apple II + , 48K memory, disk drive, TV or monitor, DOS up through 3.3

Also available (but not tested):
Atari 800, 48K memory, disk drive, DOS up through 2
Texas Instruments 99/4A, 32K memory expansion, disk drive, PLATO Interpreter Cartridge

Recommended Target Group
Mathematics; grades 3-6, grades 7-8 remedial

Content
The program is an interactive game for practice in accuracy and speed with whole number facts. It allows three tries per problem, decreases time permitted for successive problems, rewards high score, and provides cumulative points for correct answers. It also includes some supplemental pencil and paper activities.

Comment
The program is recommended as highly motivational practice with addition, subtraction, multiplication, and division. It is very interactive and easy to use. The documentation is well written, clear, and concise.
Educational Package: List Price: $60.00.
Consumer Package: List Price: $49.95.

Music/Art

COLORASAURUS

The Learning Company

System Requirements
Tested on:
Atari 800 XL, 48K memory, disk drive, color TV or monitor, joystick

Recommended Target Group
Art, ages 3-6, especially Kindergarten

Music/Art (continued)
Colorasaurus (continued)

Content
This program provides beginning instruction for a young computer user to learn the basic colors and what happens when colors are mixed. The user matches Colorasaurus with a background color or colors a dinosaur.

Comment
The program is recommended as motivational and effective with very young children. Considerable teacher or parent assistance will be needed to read the manual and follow the directions. The design is self-paced, and the user may proceed from simple to more complex concepts. The menu may be recalled. Sound is at the option of the user. Help keys are provided when needed, and color cues are a help. List Price: $29.95.

PICTURE WRITER

Scarborough Systems

System Requirements
Tested on:
Apple II + , 64K memory, disk drive, color TV or monitor, joystick or Koala Pad, graphics printer and grappler interface (optional)

Also available (but not tested):
Apple II, 64K memory, Applesoft

Recommended Target Group
Art, grades 5-12

Content
This package is a drawing tool, with tutorial, for use in teaching art. Eight colors are available as well as a library of premade shapes. The user can create pictures or even games and combine them with music. A list of sixteen options is presented on the screen: restarting, coloring, framing, drawing ovals, changing the size of the cursor, deleting the last step, redrawing the picture, editing, saving and getting a picture.

Comment
This program is recommended as a fast and easy way for children to produce pictures and develop their visual creativity. The documentation is easy to read, easy to follow, and complete. It should be noted that reviewers found the Koala Pad to require more practice than a joystick, and that younger children, ages 12 and below, will require much teacher assistance. Nevertheless, the tutorial provided sufficient opportunity to acquaint the user with the program. The picture symbols on the right margin of the screen are most helpful, as are the counter and the warning sound when Picture Writer's limits are reached. List Price: $39.95.

SONGWRITER

Scarborough Systems

System Requirements
Tested on:
Apple IIe, 48K memory, disk drive, TV or monitor, (color recommended)
Atari, 48K memory

Also available (but not tested):
Apple II, 48K memory, Applesoft
Apple IIe
Commodore 64, 48K memory
IBM PC

Recommended Target Group
Music, ages 9 and above

Content
This program enables users to write and save their own songs. They learn some basic principles about composing music.

Comment
This program is recommended as an effective tool with which students can create a pleasing musical piece and then save it for future use or study. It is particularly recommended for use in schools that do not have music classes for students. The program may not be useful with students who have studied music or a musical instrument in depth. The manual is well written, easy to understand, and comprehensive. The program can be used by a computer beginner. List Price: $39.95.

Social Science

GAME OF THE STATES

Milton Bradley Company

System Requirements
Tested on:
Apple II + , 48K memory, disk drive, TV or monitor, DOS 3.3

Also available (but not tested):
Apple II, 48K memory, Applesoft
Apple IIe, 48K memory

Recommended Target Group
Social Science, Geography; grades 5-8

Content
This program contains five games to provide drill and practice for students learning to identify states by shape and location, as well as capital cities, state abbreviations, and major cities.

Comment
This program is recommended for drill and practice in the identification of states and cities. It is effective in working with that goal even though the program is not more highly motivating than rote learning. The program does keep the scores of student responses on disk for the teacher to recall at a later date. All technical features work as specified. Documentation is ade-

Social Science (continued)
Game of the States (continued)

quate with sample pictures of the screen, a running narrative, and special instructions. States are identified only in the context of neighboring states; there is no presentation of all states in the United States together in scale. List Price: $39.95

THE MEDALIST SERIES

(four programs available separately)

See review, Secondary, Social Science, page 49.

Technology/ Computer Science

KIDS ON KEYS

Spinnaker Software

System Requirements
Tested on:
Atari 800, 48K memory, disk drive, TV or monitor, (color recommended), joystick

Also available (but not tested):
Atari 400, 48K memory, cartridge
Commodore 64, cartridge or diskette

Recommended Target Group
Technology/Computer Science, ages 7-9
Content
This program is designed to familiarize young students with the computer keyboard. Students utilize three games that advance from simple letter and number location to identifying and typing the names of pictured objects. The program allows for teacher-created objects to be added to it.
Comment
This program is recommended as a worthwhile activity for keyboard recognition. Only one portion of the program would be appropriate for nonreaders. (Publisher recommends the program for ages 3-9.) The instructional design does not provide much guidance for incorrect answers. Nor does it include provisions for measuring student progress. The documentation gives clear and understandable directions for using the program. It is intended for teacher or parent use. Use of the Option Key to generate a new set of objects is not mentioned in the manual. All portions of the program load and run smoothly. List Price: $29.95

Technology/ Programming Languages

COMMODORE LOGO

Commodore Business Machines, Inc.

System Requirements
Commodore 64, VIC-1541 disk drive, TV or monitor (color recommended), LOGO Language Disk, Utilities Disk, ''Tutorial''

Recommended Target Group
Technology/Programming Languages; ages 7-10, with beginning understanding of basic geometry
Content
This package is a complete course in LOGO for the Commodore 64. As a tutorial, it introduces the student and teacher to the nature of LOGO, then progresses through its use in ''Graphics,'' ''Computation: Handling Numbers,'' ''Words and Lists,'' ''Sprites,'' and ''Music.'' In addition, an appendix is included for ''Error Messages,'' ''Edit Mode,'' ''Graphics Chapter Project,'' ''Strategies for the Words and Lists Projects,'' ''The Commodore LOGO Utilities Disk,'' and other items. The manual is a complete guide to the course.
Comment
This package is highly recommended to teach LOGO to the teacher by means of the manual and the computer program although the manual is too advanced for the students to use successfully. Nevertheless, with teacher direction the course can be very successful with students in the recommended age range. It is recommended that a simplified workbook be used as well, such as the ones noted in the manual. The program was found to run flawlessly. The manual is well-organized and divided into easy-to-understand sections. The presentation is exciting and interesting. It is being used successfully in math and language arts classes but can be used with other subjects as well. A blank disk is needed to save work. List Price: $79.95

CRASH

See review, Elementary, Methematics, page 22.

KRELL'S LOGO

Krell Software Corporation

System Requirements
Tested on:
Apple II+, 48K memory, disk drive, TV or monitor, DOS 3.3

Also available (but not tested):
Apple II, 48K memory, Applesoft

Technology/Programming Languages
(continued)
Krell's Logo (continued)

Recommended Target Group
Technology/Programming Languages, grades K-6 and above
Content
LOGO is a programming language for teachers to use with students to develop various cognitive skills. The package contains a language disk with back-up, a utility disk, and "Alice in LOGOland" disk, which illustrates some uses of LOGO.
Comment
This package is recommended for the teacher who is already fully familiar with the LOGO language before working with students. A technical manual describes how to start the system and use its commands, a booklet on using "Alice in LOGOland," and a poster of commands and procedures. It is recommended that a book on LOGO by one of the following authors be purchased for use with this package: Watt, Tipps and Bull, or Abelson. These books contain much instruction with the turtle. This package alone is not intended to be used as a tutorial. Rather, it provides practice with the turtle. List Price: $89.95 *Learning With LOGO,* Daniel Watt List Price: 19.95

KRELL'S TURTLE PAK

Krell Software Corporation

System Requirements
Tested on:
Apple II +, 48K memory, disk drive, TV or monitor, DOS 3.3, Daniel Watt's *Learning With LOGO*
Also available (but not tested):
Apple II, 48K memory, Applesoft
Recommended Target Group
Technology/Programming Languages, grades K-6 and above
Content
LOGO is a programming language for teachers to use with students to develop various cognitive skills. The *Turtle Pak* contains either 20 or 40 M.I.T. authorized LOGO disks for Apple; 2 "Alice in LOGOland" disks and primers; 2 utility disks with M.I.T.'s programs including "Dynatrack," "Shape and Music Editors," and "Sprite Driver Software"; 4 comprehensive wall charts; 2 LOGO & *Educational Computing Journals;* 1 *Learning With LOGO* by Daniel Watt; and 1 M.I.T. "Technical Manual: LOGO for Apple II."
Comment
The addition of Watt's *Learning With LOGO* and the package containing either 20 or 40 LOGO disks makes this product much more useful for the classroom. The full range of LOGO philosophy and uses can thus be explored with students. Students can learn about their environment and geometry by controlling the turtle. Critical thinking and creativity are used in the process. Vocabulary for commands is simple for programming concepts that are to be experienced. 20 Pak: List Price: $499.95. 40 Pak: List Price: $899.95.

THE TERRAPIN LOGO LANGUAGE

Terrapin, Inc.

System Requirements
Tested on:
Apple II +, 64K memory, disk drive, color TV or monitor
Recommended Target Group
Technology/Programming Languages; elementary grades, but useful for any age group
Content
The program instructs the student or the teacher in programming with the LOGO computer language. The tutorial format instructs the student in graphics, use of the Terrapin Turtle, music, words and lists, and computation.
Comment
This program is very highly recommended for anyone wanting to learn the fundamentals of computer programming in the LOGO language. The language resides in the extra 16K of memory. Commands offer a variety of possibilities. The tutorial is sufficient for the teacher to learn the language and use the technical manual for easy reference. The program language is designed to permit children to take control of the computer in order to solve problems. The graphics make it very appealing to youngsters. The procedural format is especially helpful in developing problem solving skills. The programming can be used for any subject area. The publisher notes that a blank disk is necessary if work is to be saved. List Price: $149.95

Technology/Word Processing

BANK STREET WRITER

Broderbund Software

System Requirements
Tested on:
Apple IIe, disk drive, TV or monitor, DOS 3.3, printer
Also available (but not tested):
Apple II, 48K memory, Applesoft
Apple II +, 48K memory
Atari 400/800/XL's
Commodore 64
Recommended Target Group
Business Education/Word Processing, grades 6-adult
Content
This word processing program is divided into three modes: (1) In the "Write" mode the user types in a document. (2) In the "Edit" mode the user makes changes in the document. (3) In the "Transfer" mode the user performs such operations as storing on a disk, deleting or printing a document, and initialing disks.

Technology/Word Processing
(continued)
Bank Street Writer (continued)

Comment

This program is highly recommended for a wide range of uses and users. Most high school students and junior high students should be able to use the program with little or no difficulty. The program is designed to do most of the common functions of a higher level word processing program without being cumbersome to use. It can be used by a computer beginner with keyboarding skill. The program is easy to learn and prompts the user every step of the way. There are only a few simple commands that need to be remembered. A tutorial program is available on the flip side of the disk. List Price: $69.95

LET'S EXPLORE WORD PROCESSING

Milton Bradley Company

System Requirements

Tested on:
Apple IIe, disk drive, TV or monitor, (color recommended), printer (optional)

Also available (but not tested):
Apple II + , 48K memory

Let's Explore Word Processing (continued)

Recommended Target Group

Technology/Word Processing, grades 3-6.

Content

The program presents four lessons in game format for student to learn the fundamental skills of word processing. The firs game provides practice in learning the keyboard as the studen searches for required letters. The second game requires the student to type in specific parts of speech (a valuable language art addition). The third game provides practice in using the cursor. The fourth game teaches editing skills (insert, erase, an transfer text). A fifth section of the program allows a student t use these skills in writing a story up to 120 lines long. Th printer function can be used for printouts.

Comment

This program is recommended as an effective introductor package for word processing skills. The pacing of the progran makes it appropriate for students at the third grade level an above. The program is self-directed and easy to follow. There storage capacity on the reverse side of the disk for a student work. The author has shown awareness of the sequence of ski development necessary for word processing. The games cha lenge the students, utilize language skills, and familiarize th student with correct terminology. List Price: $39.95.

SECONDARY

Bilingual

ARITHMETIC CLASSROOM SERIES

See review, Elementary, Mathematics, page 19.

ELEMENTARY MATHEMATICS

See review, Mathematics, General Math, page 41.

Business Education/ Accounting

PERSONAL ACCOUNTING

See review, Applications, Spreadsheets/Management Tool page 72.

Cordatum Inc.

4720 MONTGOMERY LANE • BETHESDA, MARYLAND 20814-5383 • (301) 652-5424

DISCOUNT PRICE LIST

For all NEA Teacher Certified Products

teacher certified
NEA™

ADDITIONAL DISCOUNT COUPON INSIDE

PUBLISHER'S CODE FOR ORDER NUMBER

Prefix to Number	Hardware Manufacturer
AC	Acorn Computers Corporation
AY	Arthur Young
BS	Broderbund Software
CA	(Computer) Advanced Ideas
CB	Commodore Business Machines, Inc.
CD	Control Data Corporation
CE	Comp Ed
CL	Computer Learning Systems, Inc.
CP	COMPress Division/ Wadsworth, Inc.
CS	Center for Science in the Public Interest
DA	Davidson & Associates
DC	D.C. Heath and Company
DL	DLM Teaching Resources
DS	Datasoft, Inc.
ET	Electronic Tabulating Corporation (etc)
EW	Edu-Ware Division/ Peachtree Software, Inc.
HC	Hartley Courseware, Inc.
HT	Hi Tech
ID	Info-Disc Corporation
KA	Kapstrom, Inc.
KS	Krell Software Corporation
LC	The Learning Company

Prefix to Number	Hardware Manufacturer
LT	Learning Technologies
LW	Learning Well
MB	Milton Bradley Company
MC	MCE, Inc.
ML	Micro Power and Light
MM	Morton-McManus Publications
MP	Milliken Publishing Company
MU	Muse Software
OC	Owlcat Division/ Digital Research
OS	Ohaus Scale Corporation
PE	Pearlsoft Division/ Relational Systems International Corporation
PG	Peterson's Guides, Inc.
RM	Rocky Mountain Education Systems
SC	Scarborough Systems
SP	Spinnaker Software
SS	Sterling Swift
SW	The Soft Warehouse
TH	Thoroughbred/ SMC Software Systems
TI	Terrapin, Inc.
3M	3M Corporation/Optical Recording Corporation
VD	Videodiscovery
XE	Xerox Education Publications

Prefix to Number	Hardware Manufacturer
ZAM	Ask Micro
ZAT	Ashton-Tate
ZBP	BPI Systems
ZDR	Digital Research
ZFG	Fox and Geller
ZIU	Information Unlimited Software
ZLD	Lotus Development Corporation
ZLS	Lexisoft, Inc.
ZMB	Micro Business Applications
ZMC	Micro Business Software
ZMI	Micro International Corporation
ZMP	Micropro International Corporation
ZMS	Microsoft, Inc.
ZMU	Mark of the Unicorn
ZNW	Northwest Analytical
ZOA	Oasis Systems
ZPL	Pearlsoft Division/ Relational Systems International Corporation
ZPS	Perfect Software
ZPT	Peachtree Software, Inc.
ZSC	Star Computer Systems
ZSO	Sorcim
ZVC	Visicorp

ACORN

Order #/Discount Price/Shipping

I. EDUCATIONAL SOFTWARE

Elementary
  MATHEMATICS
    Crash (page 22)

AC001AC	$37.95	$2.50

  TECHNOLOGY
    Crash (page 22)

AC001AC	$37.95	$2.50

Secondary
  ENGLISH/COMPREHENSIVE
    Krell's College Board SAT Exam Preparation (page 53)

KS401AC	$254.95	$4.50

  MATHEMATICS/COMPREHENSIVE
    Krell's College Board SAT Exam Preparation (page 53)

KS401AC	$254.95	$4.50

  MISCELLANEOUS
    Krell's College Board SAT Exam Preparation Series (page 53)

KS401AC	$254.95	$4.50

ALTOS

Order #/Discount Price/Shipping

I. EDUCATIONAL SOFTWARE

Secondary
  TECHNOLOGY/DATA BASE MANAGEMENT SYSTEMS (DBMS)
    Personal Pearl (page 62)

ZPL006AL	$172.60	$4.50

  TECHNOLOGY/PROGRAMMING LANGUAGES
    MBASIC-80 (page 68)

ZMS008AL	$249.00	$4.50

Postsecondary
  ACCOUNTING
    Accounting Plus Series (page 69)
      4 in series

Accounts Payable	ZAM035AL	$386.00	$4.50
Accounts Receivable	ZAM1035AL	$386.00	$4.50
General Ledger	ZAM2035AL	$386.00	$4.50
Payroll	ZAM3035AL	$386.00	$4.50

  STATISTICS
    Statpak (page 73)

ZNW027AL	$349.00	$4.50

  TECHNOLOGY/DATA BASE MANAGEMENT SYSTEMS (DBMS)
    Perfect Filer (page 61)

ZPS003AL	$249.00	$4.50

    Personal Pearl (page 62)

ZPL006AL	$172.60	$4.50

  TECHNOLOGY/PROGRAMMING LANGUAGES
    CBASIC (page 67)

ZDR009AL	$115.00	$4.50

    MBASIC-80 (page 68)

ZMS008AL	$249.00	$4.50

  TECHNOLOGY/WORD PROCESSING
    Peach Text 5000 (page 77)

ZPT018AL	$254.50	$4.50

II. APPLICATIONS SOFTWARE

  DATA BASE MANAGEMENT SYSTEMS (DBMS)
    dbase II (page 60)

ZAT005AL	$455.15	$4.50

Altos (continued)
Data Base Management Systems (continued)

Order #/Discount Price/Shipping

Personal Pearl (page 62)

ZPL006AL	$172.60	$4.50

PROGRAMMING LANGUAGES
  CBASIC (page 67)

ZDR009AL	$115.00	$4.50

  MBASIC-80 (page 68)

ZMS008AL	$249.00	$4.50

SPREADSHEETS/MANAGEMENT TOOLS
  Accounting Plus Series (page 69)
    4 in series

Accounts Payable	ZAM035AL	$386.00	$4.50
Accounts Receivable	ZAM1035AL	$386.00	$4.50
General Ledger	ZAM2035AL	$386.00	$4.50
Payroll	ZAM3035AL	$386.00	$4.50

  Perfect Calc (page 72)

ZPS030AL	$175.00	$4.50

  Realworld Series (page 73)
    4 in series

Accounts Payable	ZMC029AL	$431.00	$4.50
Accounts Receivable	ZMC1029AL	$431.00	$4.50
General Ledger	ZMC2029AL	$431.00	$4.50
Payroll	ZMC3029AL	$431.00	$4.50

  Star System I—General Ledger (page 73)

ZSC028AL	$305.00	$4.50

  Statpak (page 73)

ZNW027AL	$349.00	$4.50

  Supercalc (page 73)

ZSO026AL	$195.00	$4.50

SYSTEMS SUPPORT
  Quickcode (page 75)

ZFG012AL	$207.10	$4.50

WORD PROCESSING SYSTEMS & UTILITIES
  Final Word (page 76)

ZMU019AL	$228.00	$4.50

  Peach Text 5000 (page 77)

ZPT018AL	$254.50	$4.50

  Perfect Writer (page 77)

ZPS017AL	$194.00	$4.50

  Spellbinder (page 77)

ZLS016AL	$275.00	$4.50

APPLE

Note: The original model of the Apple II used a standard language known as Integer BASIC. When upgraded with a floppy disk controller and drive, the Apple II ran under version 3.2 of the Apple Disk Operating System (DOS 3.2). The floppy disk format for DOS 3.2 used 13 sectors per track of recorded data.

The Apple II+ and the Apple IIe were both upgraded to run under DOS 3.3 which uses a 16 sector per track format. Applesoft BASIC is also available with these models. Therefore:
  1. Software written for the Apple II will run on Apple II+ and Apple IIe.
  2. Software written originally for the Apple II+ or the Apple IIe (under DOS 3.3) will not run on the Apple II.
  3. Software written under Applesoft with DOS 3.3 – which is only possible on the Apple II+ or the Apple IIe – will not run on an Apple machine without Applesoft.

Apple (continued)

4. In order to run CP/M software on any Apple, a printed circuit board with a 2-80 processor (such as the Microsoft Softcard listed here) must be physically inserted into your Apple computer.
5. Most II or II+ software must be run with the CAP LOCK in the DOWN position.
6. Not all IIe software will load on the IIc.
7. Ap II with a 16K memory card installed (available for under $40) will allow many programs that have "Applesoft language" catalogued to load Applesoft into the 16K card, and then run the program. Try the software first to see if it loads.

Please bear these facts in mind when ordering software for your Apple computer.

Order #/Discount Price/Shipping

I. EDUCATIONAL SOFTWARE

Preschool

MATH & READING READINESS

Alphabet Zoo (page 7)			
	SP006AP	$28.50	$1.50
Dinosaurs (page 7)			
	CA005AP	$37.95	$2.50
Juggles' Rainbow (page 7)			
	LC001AP	$28.50	$1.50
Stickybear Shapes (page 8)			
	XE001AP	$37.95	$2.50

Elementary

BILINGUAL EDUCATION

Arithmetic Classroom Series (page 19)

9 in series

Addition	SS001AP	$44.95	$2.50
Decimals	SS008AP	$44.95	$2.50
Division	SS004AP	$44.95	$2.50
Fractions—Add/Sub.	SS006AP	$44.95	$2.50
Fractions—			
Basic Concepts	SS005AP	$44.95	$2.50
Fractions—Multi./Div.	SS007AP	$44.95	$2.50
Games	SS009AP	$28.50	$1.50
Multiplication	SS003AP	$44.95	$2.50
Subtraction	SS002AP	$44.95	$2.50

LANGUAGE ARTS/READING

Compu-Read (page 8)			
	EW001AP	$28.50	$1.50
Drill Builder Series (page 65)			
6 in series			
Alien Action	DL001AP	$39.75	$2.50
Alligator Alley	DL003AP	$39.75	$2.50
Idea Invasion	DL005AP	$39.75	$2.50
Master Match	DL006AP	$39.75	$2.50
Meteor Mission	DL002AP	$39.75	$2.50
Wiz Works	DL004AP	$39.75	$2.50
Language Arts Skill Builder Series (page 9)			
6 in series			
Spelling Wiz	DL010AP	$39.75	$2.50
Verb Viper	DL007AP	$39.75	$2.50
Word Invasion	DL009AP	$39.75	$2.50
Wordman	DL008AP	$39.75	$2.50
Word Master	DL012AP	$39.75	$2.50
Word Radar	DL011AP	$39.75	$2.50
Opposites (page 9)			
	HC001AP	$28.50	$1.50

Language Arts/Reading (continued)

Order #/Discount Price/Shipping

Progressive Phonics Skills Series (page 10)

5 in series

Beginning Consonants	CE007AP	$20.95	$1.50
Ending Consonants	CE008AP	$20.95	$1.50
Long/Short Vowel			
Discrimination	CE011AP	$20.95	$1.50
Long Vowels	CE010AP	$20.95	$1.50
Short Vowels	CE009AP	$20.95	$1.50
Reader Rabbit & the Fabulous Word Factory (page 10)			
	LC009AP	$37.95	$2.50
Reading Skills Builder—Readiness Level (page 10)			
4 in series	MM001AP	$191.25/series	$7.00
Set 1	MM002AP	$50.95	$2.50
Set 2	MM003AP	$50.95	$2.50
Set 3	MM004AP	$50.95	$2.50
Set 4	MM005AP	$50.95	$2.50
Spelling Bee Games (page 11)			
	EN011AP	$37.95	$2.50
Vocabulary Skills: Context Clues (page 11)			
	MB008AP	$44.95	$2.50
Vocabulary Skills: Prefixes, Suffixes & Root Words (page 12)			
	MB009AP	$44.95	$2.50
Who, What, Where, When, Why (page 12)			
	HC006AP	$34.25	$2.50
Wizard of Words (page 12)			
	CA004AP	$37.95	$2.50
Word Attack! (page 12)			
	DA003AP	$44.95	$2.50
Word Spinner (page 13)			
	LC010AP	$37.95	$2.50

LANGUAGE ARTS/THINKING SKILLS

Analogies-Tutorial (page 13)			
	HC011AP	$44.95	$2.50
Fourth (4th) R—Reasoning (page 13)			
	MC023AP	$40.50	$2.50
Backup disk	MC024AP	$17.50	$1.50
Gertrude's Puzzles (page 14)			
	LC005AP	$40.50	$2.50
Gertrude's Secrets (page 14)			
	LC004AP	$40.50	$2.50
Moptown Hotel (page 14)			
	LC008AP	$37.95	$2.50
Moptown Parade (page 15)			
	LC007AP	$37.95	$2.50
Perception 3.0 (page 15)			
	EW009AP	$28.50	$1.50
Rocky's Boots (page 15)			
	LC006AP	$44.95	$2.50

LANGUAGE ARTS/WRITING

Building Better Sentences: Combining Sentence Parts (page 16)			
	MB011AP	$44.95	$2.50
Building Better Sentences: Creating Compound & Complex Sentences (page 16)			
	MB010AP	$44.95	$2.50
Capitalization (page 16)			
	HC012AP	$44.95	$2.50
Magic Spells (page 16)			
	LC013AP	$33.25	$2.50
Nouns/Pronouns (page 17)			
	HC004AP	$31.25	$1.50
Punctuation Skills: Commas (page 17)			
	MB006AP	$44.95	$2.50
Punctuation Skills: End Marks, Semicolon & Colon (page 17)			
	MB007AP	$44.95	$2.50
Story Machine (page 18)			
	SP001AP	$33.25	$1.50
That's My Story (page 18)			
	LW001AP	$50.95	$4.50

Apple (continued)
Language Arts/Writing (continued)

		Order #/Discount Price/Shipping	
Verbs (page 18)			
Level 1	HC005AP	$31.25	$1.50
Level 2	HC105AP	$31.25	$1.50
Level 3	HC205AP	$31.25	$1.50
MATHEMATICS			
Addition Magician (page 19)			
	LC011AP	$33.25	$2.50
Aliencounter & Face Flash (page 19)			
	MP005AP	$31.25	$1.50
Arithmetic Classroom Series (page 19)			
9 in series			
Addition	SS001AP	$44.95	$2.50
Decimals	SS008AP	$44.95	$2.50
Division	SS004AP	$44.95	$2.50
Fractions—Add/Sub.	SS006AP	$44.95	$2.50
Fractions—Basic			
Concepts	SS005AP	$44.95	$2.50
Fractions—Multi./Div.	SS007AP	$44.95	$2.50
Games	SS009AP	$28.50	$1.50
Multiplication	SS003AP	$44.95	$2.50
Subtraction	SS002AP	$44.95	$2.50
Basic Number Facts: Practice (page 21)			
School	CD014AP	$50.95	$4.50
Consumer	CD1014AP	$44.95	$2.50
Battling Bugs & Concentration (page 21)			
	MP004AP	$31.25	$1.50
Bumble Games (page 21)			
	LC002AP	$37.95	$2.50
Bumble Plot (page 21)			
	LC003AP	$37.95	$2.50
Clock (page 22)			
	HC008AP	$37.95	$2.50
Decimal Skills (page 22)			
	MB004AP	$44.95	$2.50
Decimals: Practice (page 23)			
School	CD001AP	$50.95	$4.50
Consumer	CD1001AP	$44.95	$2.50
Division Skills (page 23)			
	MB002AP	$44.95	$2.50
Drill Builder Series (page 65)			
6 in series			
Alien Action	DL001AP	$39.75	$2.50
Alligator Alley	DL003AP	$39.75	$2.50
Idea Invasion	DL005AP	$39.75	$2.50
Master Match	DL006AP	$39.75	$2.50
Meteor Mission	DL002AP	$39.75	$2.50
Wiz Works	DL004AP	$39.75	$2.50
Elementary Mathematics (page 41)			
Set 1, Whole Nos.	SS012AP	$420.75	$6.00
Set 2, Fractions/			
Decimals	SS013AP	$420.75	$6.00
Expanded Notations (page 23)			
	HC002AP	$28.50	$1.50
Fractions (page 23)			
	EW003AP	$44.25	$2.50
Fractions: Practice (page 24)			
School	CD002AP	$50.95	$4.50
Consumer	CD1002AP	$44.95	$2.50
Frenzy & Flip Flop (page 24)			
	MP002AP	$31.25	$1.50
Golf Classic & Compubar (page 24)			
	MP003AP	$31.25	$1.50
Gulp!! & Arrow Graphics (page 25)			
	MP006AP	$31.25	$1.50
Hey Taxi! (page 25)			
	MB017AP	$37.95	$2.50
Introduction to Counting (page 25)			
	EW002AP	$37.95	$2.50
Jar Game & Chaos (page 25)			
	MP001AP	$31.25	$1.50
Math Blaster (page 26)			
	DA001AP	$44.95	$2.50

		Order #/Discount Price/Shipping	
Math Concepts I & II (page 26)			
	HC007AP	$37.95	$2.50
Mixed Numbers (page 26)			
	MB001AP	$44.95	$2.50
Number Stumper (page 26)			
	LC012AP	$33.25	$2.50
Percents (page 27)			
	MB003AP	$44.95	$2.50
Prescriptive Math Drill (page 27)			
	HC013AP	$67.95	$4.50
Progressive Math Skills Series (page 27)			
6 in series			
Add. 0-5	CE001AP	$20.95	$1.50
Sub. 0-5	CE002AP	$20.95	$1.50
Add./Sub. 0-5	CE003AP	$20.95	$1.50
Add. 6-10	CE004AP	$20.95	$1.50
Sub. 6-10	CE005AP	$20.95	$1.50
Add./Sub. 6-10	CE006AP	$20.95	$1.50
Put Together, Take Away (page 27)			
	MB015AP	$37.95	$2.50
Supermath II (page 28)			
	LT002AP	$37.95	$2.50
Time Master (page 28)			
	ML001AP	$28.50	$1.50
Whole Numbers: Practice (page 28)			
School	CD003AP	$50.95	$4.50
Consumer	CD1003AP	$44.95	$2.50
MUSIC/ART			
Picture Writer (page 29)			
	SC002AP	$37.95	$2.50
Songwriter (page 29)			
	SC004AP	$37.95	$2.50
SOCIAL SCIENCE			
Game of the States (page 29)			
	MB012AP	$37.95	$2.50
Medalist/Black Americans (page 49)			
	HC014AP	$37.95	$2.50
Medalist/Continents (page 49)			
	HC010AP	$37.95	$2.50
Medalist/States (page 49)			
	HC009AP	$37.95	$2.50
Medalist/Women in History (page 49)			
	HC015AP	$37.95	$2.50
TECHNOLOGY/PROGRAMMING LANGUAGES			
Krell's LOGO (page 30)			
	KS002AP	$76.50	$4.50
Watt's Learning w/LOGO Book (page 30)			
	KS005AP	$19.95	$1.50
Krell's Turtle Pak (page 31)			
20 Pak	KS003AP	$424.95	$6.00
40 Pak	KS004AP	$764.95	$6.00
Terrapin LOGO Language (page 31)			
	TI001AP	$127.50	$4.50
TECHNOLOGY/WORD PROCESSING			
Bank Street Writer (page 31)			
	BS001AP	$59.50	$4.50
Let's Explore Word Processing (page 32)			
	MB016AP	$37.95	$2.50

Secondary
BILINGUAL

Arithmetic Classroom Series (page 19)			
9 in series			
Addition	SS001AP	$44.95	$2.50
Decimals	SS008AP	$44.95	$2.50
Division	SS004AP	$44.95	$2.50
Fractions—Add/Sub.	SS006AP	$44.95	$2.50
Fractions—Basic			
Concepts	SS005AP	$44.95	$2.50
Fractions—Multi./Div.	SS007AP	$44.95	$2.50
Games	SS009AP	$28.50	$1.50

Bilingual (continued)

	Order #	Discount Price	Shipping
Multiplication	SS003AP	$44.95	$2.50
Subtraction	SS002AP	$44.95	$2.50

BUSINESS EDUCATION/ACCOUNTING
Star System I—General Ledger (page 73)

	Order #	Discount Price	Shipping
	ZSC028AP	$305.00	$4.50

BUSINESS EDUCATION/WORD PROCESSING
Bank Street Writer (page 31)

	Order #	Discount Price	Shipping
	BS001AP	$59.50	$4.50

Master Type (page 33)

	Order #	Discount Price	Shipping
	SC001AP	$37.95	$2.50

Peach Text 5000 (page 77)

	Order #	Discount Price	Shipping
	ZPT018AP	$254.50	$4.50

ENGLISH AS A SECOND LANGUAGE (ESL)
Analyzing an Ad (page 43)

	Order #	Discount Price	Shipping
	MC021AP	$40.50	$2.50
Backup disk	MC002AP	$17.50	$1.50

Job Survival Series (page 44)

	Order #	Discount Price	Shipping
3 in series			
Series Price	MC013AP	$101.95	$7.00
Backup disks	MC014AP	$40.50	$2.50
First Day on the Job	MC017AP	$40.50	$2.50
Backup disk	MC020AP	$17.50	$1.50
Personal Habits for Job Success	MC016AP	$40.50	$2.50
Backup disk	MC019AP	$17.50	$1.50
Work Habits for Job Success	MC015AP	$40.50	$2.50
Backup disk	MC018AP	$17.50	$1.50

ENGLISH/COMPREHENSIVE
Krell's College Board SAT Exam Preparation (page 53)

	Order #	Discount Price	Shipping
	KS001AP	$254.95	$4.50

PSAT/SAT Analogies (page 53)

	Order #	Discount Price	Shipping
	EW016AP	$44.25	$2.50

PSAT/SAT Word Attack Skills (page 54)

	Order #	Discount Price	Shipping
PSAT	EW012AP	$44.25	$2.50
SAT	EW013AP	$44.25	$2.50

ENGLISH/GRAMMAR AND COMPOSITION
Building Better Sentences: Combining Sentence Parts (page 16)

	Order #	Discount Price	Shipping
	MB011AP	$44.95	$2.50

Building Better Sentences: Creating Compound & Complex Sentences (page 16)

	Order #	Discount Price	Shipping
	MB010AP	$44.95	$2.50

Introduction to Poetry (page 34)

	Order #	Discount Price	Shipping
	EW105AP	$28.50	$2.50

Punctuation Skills: Commas (page 17)

	Order #	Discount Price	Shipping
	MB006AP	$44.95	$2.50

Punctuation Skills: End Marks, Semicolon & Colon (page 17)

	Order #	Discount Price	Shipping
	MB007AP	$44.95	$2.50

That's My Story (page 18)

	Order #	Discount Price	Shipping
	LW001AP	$50.95	$4.50

Verbs (page 18)

	Order #	Discount Price	Shipping
Level 1	HC005AP	$31.25	$1.50
Level 2	HC105AP	$31.25	$1.50
Level 3	HC205AP	$31.25	$1.50

Writing Skills Series (page 35)

	Order #	Discount Price	Shipping
5 in series			
Vol. 1	EW017AP	$37.95	$2.50
Vol. 2	EW018AP	$37.95	$2.50
Vol. 3	EW019AP	$37.95	$2.50
Vol. 4	EW020AP	$37.95	$2.50
Vol. 5	EW021AP	$37.95	$2.50

ENGLISH/READING
Compu-Read (page 8)

	Order #	Discount Price	Shipping
	EW001AP	$28.50	$1.50

Speed Reader II (page 35)

	Order #	Discount Price	Shipping
	DA002AP	$59.50	$4.50

Vocabulary Skills: Context Clues (page 11)

	Order #	Discount Price	Shipping
	MB008AP	$44.95	$2.50

Vocabulary Skills: Prefixes, Suffixes & Root Words (page 12)

	Order #	Discount Price	Shipping
	MB009AP	$44.95	$2.50

	Order #	Discount Price	Shipping
Wizard of Words (page 12)			
	CA004AP	$37.95	$2.50
Word Attack! (page 12)			
	DA003AP	$44.95	$2.50

ENGLISH/THINKING SKILLS
Analogies-Tutorial (page 13)

	Order #	Discount Price	Shipping
	HC011AP	$44.95	$2.50
Fourth (4th) R—Reasoning (page 13)	MC023AP	$40.50	$2.50
Backup disk	MC024AP	$17.50	$1.50
Gertrude's Puzzles (page 14)	LC005AP	$40.50	$2.50
In Search of the Most Amazing Thing (page 36)	SP004AP	$37.95	$2.50
Moptown Hotel (page 14)	LC008AP	$37.95	$2.50
Perception 3.0 (page 15)	EW009AP	$28.50	$1.50
Reasoning: The Logical Process (page 55)	MC025AP	$40.50	$2.50
Backup disk	MC026AP	$17.50	$1.50
Rocky's Boots (page 15)	LC006AP	$44.95	$2.50
Snooper Troops—Case #1 (page 37)	SP002AP	$40.50	$2.50

FOREIGN LANGUAGE/FRENCH
French Language Vocabulary Series
Classroom Words (page 37)

	Order #	Discount Price	Shipping
School	CD013AP	$50.95	$4.50
Consumer	CD1013AP	$44.95	$2.50
Vocabulary Builder (page 37)			
School	CD012AP	$50.95	$4.50
Consumer	CD1012AP	$44.95	$2.50

Le Francais Par Ordinateur Series (page 38)

	Order #	Discount Price	Shipping
3 in series			
Le Demenagement	DC002AP	$68.95	$4.50
Paris en Metro	DC001AP	$68.95	$4.50
Un Repas Francais	DC003AP	$68.95	$4.50

FOREIGN LANGUAGE/GERMAN
German Language Vocabulary Series
Classroom Words (page 38)

	Order #	Discount Price	Shipping
School	CD010AP	$50.95	$4.50
Consumer	CD1010AP	$44.95	$2.50
Travel Vocabulary (page 38)			
School	CD011AP	$50.95	$4.50
Consumer	CD1011AP	$44.95	$2.50
Vocabulary Builder (page 38)			
School	CD009AP	$50.95	$4.50
Consumer	CD1009AP	$44.95	$2.50
Vocabulary for Shopping (page 38)			
School	CD016AP	$50.95	$4.50
Consumer	CD1016AP	$44.95	$2.50

FOREIGN LANGUAGE/SPANISH
Spanish Language Vocabulary Series
Classroom Words (page 39)

	Order #	Discount Price	Shipping
School	CD006AP	$50.95	$4.50
Consumer	CD1006AP	$44.95	$2.50
Travel Vocabulary (page 39)			
School	CD008AP	$50.95	$4.50
Consumer	CD1008AP	$44.95	$2.50
Vocabulary Builder (page 39)			
School	CD005AP	$50.95	$4.50
Consumer	CD1005AP	$44.95	$2.50
Vocabulary for Shopping (page 39)			
School	CD007AP	$50.95	$4.50
Consumer	CD1007AP	$44.95	$2.50

LOGIC
Reasoning: The Logical Process (page 55)

	Order #	Discount Price	Shipping
	MC025AP	$40.50	$2.50
Backup disk	MC026AP	$17.50	$1.50

Order #/Discount Price/Shipping

Order #/Discount Price/Shipping

MATHEMATICS/ALGEBRA

Algebra Series (page 39)

5 in series			
Vol. 1	EW004AP	$37.95	$2.50
Vol. 2	EW005AP	$37.95	$2.50
Vol. 3	EW006AP	$37.95	$2.50
Vol. 4	EW007AP	$37.95	$2.50
Vols. 5&6	EW008AP	$37.95	$2.50

Elementary Algebra Series (page 39)

9 in series			
Comprehensive Testing Package	CD036AP	$37.95	$2.50
Equations & Inequalities	CD026AP	$44.95	$2.50
Testing Pkg.	CD027AP	$37.95	$2.50
Exponents, Roots, & Radicals	CD020AP	$44.95	$2.50
Testing Pkg.	CD021AP	$37.95	$2.50
Factoring	CD024AP	$44.95	$2.50
Testing Pkg.	CD025AP	$37.95	$2.50
Graphic Lines	CD032AP	$44.95	$2.50
Testing Pkg.	CD033AP	$37.95	$2.50
Polynomials	CD022AP	$44.95	$2.50
Testing Pkg.	CD023AP	$37.95	$2.50
Quadratic Equations	CD028AP	$44.95	$2.50
Testing Pkg.	CD029AP	$37.95	$2.50
Rational Expressions	CD030AP	$44.95	$2.50
Testing Pkg.	CD031AP	$37.95	$2.50
Set of 10 Activity Guides	CD037AP	$18.95	$1.50
Signed Numbers/ Operations	CD018AP	$44.95	$2.50
Testing Pkg.	CD019AP	$37.95	$2.50
Systems of Equations	CD034AP	$44.95	$2.50
Testing Pkg.	CD035AP	$37.95	$2.50

Factoring Machine (page 40)

	ML002AP	$33.25	$1.50

Ratios and Proportions (page 41)

	MB005AP	$44.95	$2.50

MATHEMATICS/COMPREHENSIVE

Krell's College Board SAT Exam Preparation (page 53)

	KS001AP	$254.95	$4.50

MATHEMATICS/GENERAL MATHEMATICS

Arithmetic Classroom Series (page 19)

9 in series			
Addition	SS001AP	$44.95	$2.50
Decimals	SS008AP	$44.95	$2.50
Division	SS004AP	$44.95	$2.50
Fractions—Add/Sub.	SS006AP	$44.95	$2.50
Fractions—Basic Concepts	SS005AP	$44.95	$2.50
Fractions—Multi./Div.	SS007AP	$44.95	$2.50
Games	SS009AP	$28.50	$1.50
Multiplication	SS003AP	$44.95	$2.50
Subtraction	SS002AP	$44.95	$2.50

Basic Number Facts: Practice (page 21)

School	CD014AP	$50.95	$4.50
Consumer	CD1014AP	$44.95	$2.50

Battling Bugs & Concentration (page 21)

	MP004AP	$31.25	$1.50

Decimal Skills (page 22)

	MB004AP	$44.95	$2.50

Division Skills (page 23)

	MB002AP	$44.95	$2.50

Elementary Mathematics (page 41)

Set 2, Fractions/ Decimals	SS013AP	$420.75	$6.00
Set 1, Whole Nos.	SS012AP	$420.75	$6.00

Fractions (page 23)

	EW003AP	$44.25	$2.50

Fractions: Practice (page 24)

School	CD002AP	$50.95	$4.50
Consumer	CD1002AP	$44.95	$2.50

Function Game (page 41)

	MU001AP	$37.95	$2.50

Introduction to Counting (page 25)

	EW002AP	$37.95	$2.50

Math Blaster (page 26)

	DA001AP	$44.95	$2.50

Mixed Numbers (page 26)

	MB001AP	$44.95	$2.50

Percents (page 27)

	MB003AP	$44.95	$2.50

Whole Numbers: Practice (page 28)

School	CD003AP	$50.95	$4.50
Consumer	CD1003AP	$44.95	$2.50

MATHEMATICS/GEOMETRY

Bumble Plot (page 21)

	LC003AP	$37.95	$2.50

Golf Classic & Compubar (page 24)

	MP003AP	$31.25	$1.50

Rendezvous (page 42)

	EW010AP	$37.95	$2.50

MATHEMATICS/STATISTICS

Going Together (page 43)

	ML005AP	$28.50	$1.50

Normal Deviations (page 43)

	ML004AP	$28.50	$1.50

Off Line (page 43)

	ML003AP	$28.50	$1.50

MUSIC/ART

Picture Writer (page 29)

	SC002AP	$37.95	$2.50

Songwriter (page 29)

	SC004AP	$37.95	$2.50

PERSONAL SKILLS DEVELOPMENT

Analyzing an Ad (page 43)

	MC021AP	$40.50	$2.50
Backup disk	MC022AP	$17.50	$1.50

Job Survival Series (page 44)

3 in series			
Series Price	MC013AP	$101.95	$7.00
Backup disks	MC014AP	$40.50	$2.50
First Day on the Job	MC017AP	$40.50	$2.50
Backup disk	MC020AP	$17.50	$1.50
Personal Habits for Job Success	MC016AP	$40.50	$2.50
Backup disk	MC019AP	$17.50	$1.50
Work Habits for Job Success	MC015AP	$40.50	$2.50
Backup disk	MC018AP	$17.50	$1.50

Learning Improvement Series (page 44)

4 in series			
Series Price	MC005AP	$140.25	$7.00
Backup disks	MC009AP	$50.95	$2.50
Effective Study Skills	MC029AP	$40.50	$2.50
Backup disk	MC030AP	$17.50	$1.50
Following Written Instructions	MC007AP	$40.50	$2.50
Backup disk	MC011AP	$17.50	$1.50
Improving Your Memory	MC006AP	$40.50	$2.50
Backup disk	MC010AP	$17.50	$1.50
Strategies for Test Taking	MC008AP	$40.50	$2.50
Backup disk	MC012AP	$17.50	$1.50

Managing Your Time (page 45)

	MC001AP	$40.50	$2.50
Backup Disk	MC002AP	$17.50	$1.50

Order #/Discount Price/Shipping

SCIENCE/PHYSICS
Apple Physics (page 48)

	ML007AP	$33.25	$1.50

Data Logging & Graphics Display System (page 64)

	OS001AP	$131.75	$4.50

Eco-Paradise (page 47)

	CS001AP	$37.95	$2.50

Introduction to General Chemistry (page 47)

	CP001AP	$399.50	$4.50

Nutri-Bytes (page 46)

	CS002AP	$37.95	$2.50

Physics: Elementary Mechanics (page 41)

School	CD015AP	$59.50	$4.50
Consumer	CD1015AP	$50.95	$4.50

Rendezvous (page 42)

	EW010AP	$37.95	$2.50

SOCIAL SCIENCE
Eco-Paradise (page 47)

	CS001AP	$37.95	$2.50

Game of the States (page 29)

	MB012AP	$37.95	$2.50

Medalist/Black Americans (page 49)

	HC014AP	$37.95	$2.50

Medalist/Continents (page 49)

	HC010AP	$37.95	$2.50

Medalist/States (page 49)

	HC009AP	$37.95	$2.50

Medalist/Women in History (page 49)

	HC015AP	$37.95	$2.50

SPECIAL EDUCATION
Analyzing an Ad (page 43)

	MC021AP	$40.50	$2.50
Backup disk	MC022AP	$17.50	$1.50

Financing a Car (page 49)

	MC027AP	$40.50	$2.50
Backup disk	MC028AP	$17.50	$1.50

Job Survival Series (page 44)
3 in series

Series Price	MC013AP	$101.95	$7.00
Backup disk	MC014AP	$40.50	$2.50
First Day on the Job	MC017AP	$40.50	$2.50
Backup disk	MC020AP	$17.50	$1.50
Personal Habits for Job Success	MC016AP	$40.50	$2.50
Backup disk	MC019AP	$17.50	$1.50
Work Habits for Job Success	MC015AP	$40.50	$2.50
Backup disk	MC018AP	$17.50	$1.50

TECHNOLOGY/COMPUTER SCIENCE
A Computer Is: (page 50)

	ML006AP	$33.25	$1.50

Computer Concepts Series (page 50)

4 in series	CD017AP	$153.00/series	$7.00

Computer Curriculum Guide (page 64)

	CC001AP	$335.75	$7.00

Computer Literacy (page 51)

School	CD004AP	$59.50	$4.50
Consumer	CD1004AP	$50.95	$4.50

TECHNOLOGY/PROGRAMMING LANGUAGES
Discover BASIC (page 51)

	SS010AP	$63.75	$4.50
Workbook	SS011AP	$5.00	-0-

Hands on BASIC (page 51)

	EW014AP	$67.25	$4.50

Krell's LOGO (page 30)

	KS002AP	$76.50	$4.50

Watt's Learning w/LOGO Book (page 30)

	KS005AP	$19.95	$1.50

Order #/Discount Price/Shipping

Krell's Turtle Pak (page 31)

20 Pak	KS003AP	$424.95	$6.00
40 Pak	KS004AP	$764.95	$6.00

Let's Explore BASIC (page 32)

	MB014AP	$37.95	$2.50

MBASIC-80 (page 52)

	ZMS008AP	$249.00	$4.50

Terrapin LOGO Language (page 31)

	TI001AP	$127.50	$4.50

MISCELLANEOUS
Go to the Head of the Class (page 52)

	MB013AP	$37.95	$2.50

Krell's College Board SAT Exam Preparation (page 53)

	KS001AP	$254.95	$4.50

PSAT/SAT Analogies (page 53)

	EW016AP	$44.25	$2.50

PSAT/SAT Word Attack Skills (page 54)

PSAT	EW012AP	$44.25	$2.50
SAT	EW013AP	$44.25	$2.50

Postsecondary
ACCOUNTING
Accounting Plus Series (page 69)
4 in series

Accounts Payable	ZAM035AP	$386.00	$4.50
Accounts Receivable	ZAM1035AP	$386.00	$4.50
General Ledger	ZAM2035AP	$386.00	$4.50
Payroll	ZAM3035AP	$386.00	$4.50

Perfect Calc (page 72)

	ZPS030AP	$175.00	$4.50

SCIENCE/PHYSICS
Apple Physics (page 48)

	ML007AP	$33.25	$1.50

Data Logging & Graphics Display System (page 64)

	OS001AP	$131.75	$4.50

Molecular Animator (page 55)

	CP002AP	$72.25	$4.50

Physics: Elementary Mechanics (page 48)

School	CD015AP	$59.50	$4.50
Consumer	CD1015AP	$50.95	$4.50

STATISTICS
Going Together (page 43)

	ML005AP	$28.50	$1.50

Normal Deviations (page 43)

	ML004AP	$28.50	$1.50

Off Line (page 43)

	ML003AP	$28.50	$1.50

Statpak (page 73)

	ZNW027AP	$349.00	$4.50

TECHNOLOGY/DATA BASE MANAGEMENT SYSTEMS (DBMS)
Perfect Filer (page 61)

	ZPS003AP	$249.00	$4.50

TECHNOLOGY/PROGRAMMING LANGUAGES
CBASIC (page 67)

	ZDR009AP	$115.00	$4.50

Discover BASIC (page 51)

	SS010AP	$63.75	$4.50
Workbook	SS011AP	$5.00	-0-

Hands on BASIC (page 51)

	EW014AP	$67.25	$4.50

Let's Explore BASIC (page 52)

	MB014AP	$37.95	$2.50

MBASIC-80 (page 68)

	ZMS008AP	$249.00	$4.50

TECHNOLOGY/WORD PROCESSING
Peach Text 5000 (page 77)

	ZPT018AP	$254.50	$4.50

Perfect Writer (page 77)

	ZPS017AP	$194.00	$4.50

Order #/Discount Price/Shipping

Order #/Discount Price/Shipping

MISCELLANEOUS

Introduction to Poetry (page 34)			
	EW015AP	$28.50	$2.50
Le Francais Par Ordinateur Series (page 38)			
3 in series			
Le Demenagement	DC002AP	$68.95	$4.50
Paris en Metro	DC001AP	$68.95	$4.50
Un Repas Francais	DC003AP	$68.95	$4.50
French Language Vocabulary Series			
Classroom Words (page 37)			
School	CD013AP	$50.95	$4.50
Consumer	CD1013AP	$44.95	$2.50
Vocabulary Builder (page 37)			
School	CD012AP	$50.95	$4.50
Consumer	CD1012AP	$44.95	$2.50
German Language Vocabulary Series			
Classroom Words (page 38)			
School	CD010AP	$50.95	$4.50
Consumer	CD1010AP	$44.95	$2.50
Travel Vocabulary (page 38)			
School	CD011AP	$50.95	$4.50
Consumer	CD1011AP	$44.95	$2.50
Vocabulary Builder (page 38)			
School	CD009AP	$50.95	$4.50
Consumer	CD1009AP	$44.95	$2.50
Vocabulary for Shopping (page 38)			
School	CD016AP	$50.95	$4.50
Consumer	CD1016AP	$44.95	$2.50
Spanish Language Vocabulary Series			
Classroom Words (page 39)			
School	CD006AP	$50.95	$4.50
Consumer	CD1006AP	$44.95	$2.50
Travel Vocabulary (page 39)			
School	CD008AP	$50.95	$4.50
Consumer	CD1008AP	$44.95	$2.50
Vocabulary Builder (page 39)			
School	CD005AP	$50.95	$4.50
Consumer	CD1005AP	$44.95	$2.50
Vocabulary for Shopping (page 39)			
School	CD007AP	$50.95	$4.50
Consumer	CD1007AP	$44.95	$2.50
Snooper Troops—Case #1 (page 37)			
	SP002AP	$40.50	$2.50
Writing Skills Series (page 35)			
5 in series			
Vol. 1	EW017AP	$37.95	$2.50
Vol. 2	EW018AP	$37.95	$2.50
Vol. 3	EW019AP	$37.95	$2.50
Vol. 4	EW020AP	$37.95	$2.50
Vol. 5	EW021AP	$37.95	$2.50

I. APPLICATIONS SOFTWARE

DATA BASE MANAGEMENT SYSTEMS (DBMS)

Class Records (page 59)			
	LT001AP	$76.50	$4.50
Complete IEP Manager Storage System (page 60)			
	RM001AP	$373.25	$4.50
dBase II (page 60)			
	ZAT005AP	$455.15	$4.50
Immunization Data Manager—IDM (page 61)			
	RM002AP	$106.25	$4.50
Infostar System (page 61)			
	ZMP007AP	$347.50	$4.50
Perfect Filer (page 61)			
	ZPS003AP	$249.00	$4.50
Personal Pearl (page 62)			
	ZPL006AP	$172.60	$4.50
College Selection Guide (page 59)			
	PG001AP	$123.25	$4.50

Phi Beta Filer (page 62)			
	SC003AP	$44.95	$2.50
Visifile (page 63)			
	ZVC002AP	$230.00	$4.50

EDUCATIONAL FORMATS/MULTISUBJECT

Classmate (page 63)			
	DA004AP	$44.95	$2.50
Create Intermediate (page 64)			
	HC003AP	$25.50	$1.50
Data Logging & Graphics Display System (page 64)			
	OS001AP	$131.75	$4.50
Delta Drawing (page 65)			
	SP003AP	$42.45	$2.50
Drill Builder Series (page 65)			
6 in series			
Alien Action	DL001AP	$39.75	$2.50
Alligator Alley	DL003AP	$39.75	$2.50
Idea Invasion	DL005AP	$39.75	$2.50
Master Match	DL006AP	$39.75	$2.50
Meteor Mission	DL002AP	$39.75	$2.50
Wiz Works	DL004AP	$39.75	$2.50
Game Show (page 66)			
	CA001AP	$37.95	$2.50
Go to the Head of the Class (page 52)			
	MB013AP	$37.95	$2.50
Master Match (page 66)			
	CA003AP	$37.95	$2.50
Tic Tac Show (page 66)			
	CA002AP	$37.95	$2.50
Word Match (page 67)			
	HT002AP	$23.75	$1.50
Word Scramble (page 67)			
	HT001AP	$23.75	$1.50
Word Search (page 67)			
	HT003AP	$33.25	$2.50

PROGRAMMING LANGUAGES

CBASIC (page 67)			
	ZDR009AP	$115.00	$4.50
Discover BASIC (page 51)			
	SS010AP	$63.75	$4.50
Workbook	SS011AP	$5.00	-0-
Hands on BASIC (page 51)			
	EW014AP	$67.25	$4.50
Krell's LOGO (page 30)			
	KS002AP	$76.50	$4.50
Watt's Learning w/LOGO book (page 30)			
	KS005AP	$19.95	$1.50
Krell's Turtle Pak (page 31)			
20 Pak	KS003AP	$424.95	$6.00
40 Pak	KS004AP	$764.95	$6.00
Let's Explore BASIC (page 52)			
	MB014AP	$37.95	$2.50
MBASIC-80 (page 68)			
	ZMS008AP	$249.00	$4.50
Terrapin LOGO Language (page 31)			
	TI001AP	$127.45	$4.50

SPREADSHEETS/MANAGEMENT TOOLS

Accounting Plus Series (page 69)			
4 in series			
Accounts Payable	ZAM035AP	$386.00	$4.50
Accounts Receivable	ZAM1035AP	$386.00	$4.50
General Ledger	ZAM2035AP	$386.00	$4.50
Payroll	ZAM3035AP	$386.00	$4.50
Grade AAA Grade Book (page 70)			
	SW001AP	$55.25	$4.50
Learning Multiplan (page 70)			
	AY002AP	$332.50	$4.50

Apple (continued)
Spreadsheets/Management Tools (continued)

	Order #	Discount Price	Shipping
Extra Manual & Backup disk	AY005AP	$63.75	$2.50
Learning Visicalc (page 71)	AY003AP	$250.75	$4.50
Extra Manual & Backup disk	AY006AP	$44.95	$2.50
MBA Series (page 71)			
3 in series			
Accounts Receivable	ZMB032AP	$385.00	$4.50
General Ledger	ZMB1032AP	$385.00	$4.50
Payroll	ZMB2032AP	$385.00	$4.50
Multiplan (page 71)	ZMS031AP	$195.00	$4.50
Peach Pak (page 72)	ZPT037AP	$255.00	$4.50
Perfect Calc (page 72)	ZPS030AP	$175.00	$4.50
Realworld Series (page 73)			
4 in series			
Accounts Payable	ZAC029AP	$431.00	$4.50
Accounts Receivable	ZAC1029AP	$431.00	$4.50
General Ledger	ZAC2029AP	$431.00	$4.50
Payroll	ZAC3039AP	$431.00	$4.50
Star System I—General Ledger (page 73)	ZSC028AP	$305.00	$4.50
Statpak (page 73)	ZNW027AP	$349.00	$4.50
Supercalc I (page 73)	ZSO026AP	$136.50	$4.50
Supercalc II (page 74)	ZSO038AP	$206.50	$4.50
Supercalc III (page 74)	ZSO039AP	$276.50	$4.50
Visicalc (page 74)	ZVC001AP	$190.00	$4.50
SYSTEMS SUPPORT			
Quickcode (page 75)	ZFG012AP	$207.10	$4.50
Softcard (page 75)	ZMS011AP	$265.00	$4.50
WORD PROCESSING SYSTEMS & UTILITIES			
Bank Street Writer (page 31)	BS001AP	$59.45	$4.50
Final Word (page 76)	ZMU019AP	$228.00	$4.50
Mailmerge (page 76)	ZMP021AP	$159.00	$4.50
Peach Text 5000 (page 77)	ZPT018AP	$254.50	$4.50
Perfect Writer (page 77)	ZPS017AP	$194.00	$4.50
Spellbinder (page 77)	ZLS016AP	$275.00	$4.50
Spellstar (page 78)	ZMI022AP	$159.00	$4.50
Word Plus (page 78)	ZOA015AP	$105.00	$4.50
Wordstar (page 78)	ZMP020AP	$298.00	$4.50
Wordstar Professional (page 79)	ZMP023AP	$590.75	$4.50

ATARI

I. EDUCATIONAL SOFTWARE

Atari (continued)

Preschool

	Order #	Discount Price	Shipping
MATH & READING READINESS			
Alphabet Zoo (page 7)	SP206AT	$28.50	$1.5
Elementary			
BUSINESS EDUCATION/WORD PROCESSING			
Bank Street Writer (page 31)	BS101AT	$59.50	$4.5
Master Type (page 33)	SC101AT	$37.95	$2.5
LANGUAGE ARTS/READING			
Compu-Read (page 8)	EW101AT	$28.50	$1.5
Reading Skills Builder—Readiness Level (page 10)			
4 in series	MM001AT	$191.25/series	$7.0
Set 1	MM002AT	$50.95	$2.5
Set 2	MM003AT	$50.95	$2.5
Set 3	MM004AT	$50.95	$2.5
Set 4	MM005AT	$50.95	$2.5
Spelling Bee Games (page 11)	EW111AT	$37.95	$2.5
Word Spinner (page 13)	LC010AT	$33.25	$2.5
LANGUAGE ARTS/THINKING			
Moptown Hotel (page 14)	LC008AT	$37.95	$2.5
Moptown Parade (page 15)	LC007AT	$37.95	$2.5
LANGUAGE ARTS/WRITING			
Magic Spells (page 16)	LC013AT	$33.25	$2.5
Story Machine (page 18)	SP201AT	$33.25	$1.5
MATHEMATICS			
Aliencounter & Face Flash (page 19)	MP105AT	$31.25	$1.5
Basic Number Facts: Practice (page 21)			
School	CD114AT	$50.95	$4.5
Consumer	CD1114AT	$44.95	$2.5
Battling Bugs & Concentration (page 21)	MP104AT	$31.25	$1.5
Bumble Games (page 21)	LC002AT	$37.95	$2.5
Decimals: Practice (page 23)			
School	CD101AT	$50.95	$4.5
Consumer	CD1101AT	$44.95	$2.5
Fractions (page 23)	EW103AT	$37.95	$2.5
Fractions: Practice (page 24)			
School	CD102AT	$50.95	$4.5
Consumer	CD1102AT	$44.95	$2.5
Frenzy & Flip Flop (page 24)	MP102AT	$31.25	$1.5
Golf Classic & Compubar (page 24)	MP103AT	$31.25	$1.5
Gulp!! & Arrow Graphics (page 25)	MP106AT	$31.25	$1.5
Introduction to Counting (page 25)	EW102AT	$37.95	$2.5
Jar Game and Chaos (page 25)	MP101AT	$31.25	$1.5
Whole Numbers: Practice (page 28)			
School	CD103AT	$50.95	$4.5
Consumer	CD1103AT	$44.95	$2.5
MUSIC/ART			
Colorasaurus (page 28)	LC014AT	$28.50	$1.5
Songwriter (page 29)	SC004AT	$37.95	$2.5

Atari (continued)

TECHNOLOGY/COMPUTER SCIENCE
Kids on Keys (page 30)

	SP205AT	$28.50	$1.50

TECHNOLOGY/WORD PROCESSING
Bank Street Writer (page 31)

	BS101AT	$59.50	$4.50

Secondary

ENGLISH/COMPREHENSIVE
Krell's College Board SAT Exam Preparation (page 53)

	KS301AT	$254.95	$4.50

Letter Wizard (page 76)

	DS001AT	$44.95	$2.50

ENGLISH/READING
Compu-Read (page 8)

	EW101AT	$28.50	$1.50

ENGLISH/THINKING SKILLS
In Search of the Most Amazing Thing (page 36)

	SP204AT	$37.95	$2.50

Snooper Troops—Case #1 (page 37)

	SP202AT	$40.50	$2.50

FOREIGN LANGUAGE/FRENCH
French Language Vocabulary Series
Vocabulary Builder (page 37)

School	CD112AT	$50.95	$4.50
Consumer	CD1112AT	$44.95	$2.50

FOREIGN LANGUAGE/GERMAN
German Language Vocabulary Series
Vocabulary Builder (page 38)

School	CD109AT	$50.95	$4.50
Consumer	CD1109AT	$44.95	$2.50

FOREIGN LANGUAGE/SPANISH
Spanish Language Vocabulary Series
Vocabulary Builder (page 39)

School	CD105AT	$50.95	$4.50
Consumer	CD1105AT	$44.95	$2.50

MATHEMATICS/COMPREHENSIVE
Krell's College Board SAT Exam Preparation (page 53)

	KS301AT	$254.95	$4.50

MATHEMATICS/GEOMETRY
Golf Classic & Compubar (page 24)

	MP103AT	$31.25	$1.50

MUSIC/ART
Songwriter (page 29)

	SC004AT	$37.95	$2.50

SCIENCE/PHYSICS
Physics: Elementary Mechanics (page 48)

School	CD115AT	$59.50	$4.50
Consumer	CD1115AT	$50.95	$4.50

Rendezvous (page 42)

	EW110AT	$37.95	$2.50

TECHNOLOGY/COMPUTER SCIENCE
Computer Literacy (page 51)

School	CD104AT	$59.50	$4.50
Consumer	CD1104AT	$50.95	$4.50

MISCELLANEOUS
Krell's College Board SAT Exam Preparation (page 53)

	KS301AT	$254.95	$4.50

Postsecondary

SCIENCE/PHYSICS
Physics: Elementary Mechanics (page 48)

School	CD115AT	$59.50	$4.50
Consumer	CD1115AT	$50.95	$4.50

MISCELLANEOUS
French Language Vocabulary Series
Vocabulary Builder (page 37)

School	CD112AT	$50.95	$4.50
Consumer	CD1112AT	$44.95	$2.50

Miscellaneous (continued)

German Language Vocabulary Series
Vocabulary Builder (page 38)

School	CD109AT	$50.95	$4.50
Consumer	CD1109AT	$44.95	$2.50

Spanish Language Vocabulary Series
Vocabulary Builder (page 39)

School	CD105AT	$50.95	$4.50
Consumer	CD1105AT	$44.95	$2.50

Snooper Troops—Case #1 (page 37)

	SP202AT	$40.50	$2.50

II. APPLICATIONS SOFTWARE

COMMUNICATIONS
Tele Talk (page 59)

	DS003AT	$44.95	$2.50

WORD PROCESSING & UTILITIES
Letter Wizard (page 76)

	DS001AT	$44.95	$2.50

Spell Wizard (page 78)

	DS002AT	$44.95	$2.50

COMMODORE

I. EDUCATIONAL SOFTWARE

Preschool

MATH & READING READINESS
Alphabet Zoo (page 7)

	SP306CB	$28.50	$1.50

Juggles' Rainbow (page 7)

	LC001CB	$28.50	$1.50

Elementary

LANGUAGE ARTS/READING
Progressive Phonics Skills Series (page 10)
5 in series

Beginning Consonants	CE007CB	$20.95	$1.50
Ending Consonants	CE008CB	$20.95	$1.50
Long Vowels	CE010CB	$20.95	$1.50
Long/Short Vowel Discrimination	CE011CB	$20.95	$1.50
Short Vowels	CE009CB	$20.95	$1.50

Word Attack! (page 12)

	DA003CB	$44.95	$2.50

Word Spinner (page 13)

	LC010CB	$33.25	$2.50

LANGUAGE ARTS/WRITING
Story Machine (page 18)

	SP301CB	$33.25	$1.50

MATHEMATICS
Addition Magician (page 19)

	LC011CB	$33.25	$2.50

Math Blaster (page 26)

	DA201CB	$44.95	$2.50

Progressive Math Skills Series (page 10)
6 in series

Add. 0-5	CE001CB	$20.95	$1.50
Sub. 0-5	CE002CB	$20.95	$1.50
Add./Sub. 0-5	CE003CB	$20.95	$1.50
Add. 6-10	CE004CB	$20.95	$1.50
Sub. 6-10	CE005CB	$20.95	$1.50
Add./Sub. 6-10	CE006CB	$20.95	$1.50

MUSIC/ART
Songwriter (page 29)

	SC004CB	$37.95	$2.50

TECHNOLOGY/COMPUTER SCIENCE
Kids on Keys (page 30)

	SP305CB	$28.50	$1.50

Commodore (continued)

TECHNOLOGY/PROGRAMMING LANGUAGES
Commodore LOGO (page 30)

	Order #	Discount Price	Shipping
Commodore LOGO (page 30)	CB001CB	$67.95	$4.50

TECHNOLOGY/WORD PROCESSING
Bank Street Writer (page 31)

	BS201CB	$59.50	$4.50

Secondary

BUSINESS EDUCATION/WORD PROCESSING
Bank Street Writer (page 31)

	BS201CB	$59.50	$4.50
Master Type (page 33)	SC201CB	$37.95	$2.50

ENGLISH/COMPREHENSIVE
Krell's College Board SAT Exam Preparation (page 53)

	KS201CB	$254.95	$4.50

ENGLISH/READING
Speed Reader II (page 35)

	DA202CB	$59.50	$4.50
Word Attack! (page 12)	DA203CB	$44.95	$2.50

ENGLISH/THINKING SKILLS
Snooper Troops—Case #1 (page 37)

	SP302CB	$40.50	$2.50

MATHEMATICS/COMPREHENSIVE
Krell's College Board SAT Exam Preparation (page 53)

	KS201CB	$254.95	$4.50

MISCELLANEOUS
Krell's College Board SAT Exam Preparation (page 53)

	KS201CB	$254.95	$4.50

Postsecondary

MISCELLANEOUS
Snooper Troops—Case #1 (page 37)

	SP302CB	$40.50	$2.50

II. APPLICATIONS SOFTWARE

AUTHORING LANGUAGES
Pilot (page 58)

	CB002CB	$42.50	$2.50

INSTRUCTIONAL FORMATS/MULTISUBJECT
Delta Drawing (page 65)

	SP303CB	$42.45	$2.50
Game Show (page 66)	CA201CB	$33.95	$2.50
Tic Tac Show (page 66)	CA202CB	$33.95	$2.50

WORD PROCESSING SYSTEMS & UTILITIES
Bank Street Writer (page 31)

	BS201CB	$59.45	$4.50

CROMEMCO

I. EDUCATIONAL SOFTWARE

Secondary

TECHNOLOGY/PROGRAMMING LANGUAGES
MBASIC-80 (page 68)

	ZMS008CR	$249.00	$4.50

Postsecondary

ACCOUNTING
Perfect Calc (page 72)

	ZPS030CR	$175.00	$4.50

STATISTICS
Statpak (page 73)

	ZNN027CR	$349.00	$4.50

Cromemco (continued)

TECHNOLOGY/PROGRAMMING LANGUAGES
CBASIC (page 67)

	ZDR009CR	$115.00	$4.5
MBASIC-80 (page 68)	ZMS008CR	$249.00	$4.5

TECHNOLOGY/WORD PROCESSING
Perfect Writer (page 77)

	ZPS017CR	$194.00	$4.5

II. APPLICATIONS SOFTWARE

DATA BASE MANAGEMENT SYSTEMS (DBMS)
dBase II (page 60)

	ZAT005CR	$455.15	$4.5
Perfect Filer (page 61)	ZPS003CR	$249.00	$4.5
Personal Pearl (page 62)	ZPL006CR	$172.60	$4.5

SPREADSHEETS/MANAGEMENT TOOLS
Star System I—General Ledger (page 73)

	ZSC028CR	$305.00	$4.5
Statpak (page 73)	ZNW027CR	$349.00	$4.5
Supercalc I (page 73)	ZSO026CR	$136.50	$4.5
Supercalc II (page 74)	ZSO038CR	$206.50	$4.5
Supercalc III (page 74)	ZSO039CR	$276.50	$4.5

SYSTEMS SUPPORT
Quickcode (page 75)

	ZFG012CR	$207.10	$4.5

TECHNOLOGY/PROGRAMMING LANGUAGES
CBASIC (page 67)

	ZDR009CR	$115.00	$4.5
MBASIC-80 (page 68)	ZMS008CR	$249.00	$4.5

WORD PROCESSING SYSTEMS & UTILITIES
Final Word (page 76)

	ZMU019CR	$228.00	$4.5
Spellbinder (page 77)	ZLS016CR	$275.00	$4.5
Spellstar (page 78)	ZMI022CR	$159.00	$4.5
Wordstar (page 78)	ZMP020CR	$298.00	$4.5

EPSON

I. EDUCATIONAL SOFTWARE

Secondary

BUSINESS EDUCATION/WORD PROCESSING
Peach Text 5000 (page 77)

	ZPT018EP	$254.50	$4.5

TECHNOLOGY/PROGRAMMING LANGUAGES
MBASIC-80 (page 68)

	ZMS008EP	$249.00	$4.5

Postsecondary

ACCOUNTING
Accounting Plus Series (page 69)
4 in series

Accounts Payable	ZAM035EP	$386.00	$4.5
Accounts Receivable	ZAM1035P	$386.00	$4.5
General Ledger	ZAM2035EP	$386.00	$4.5
Payroll	ZAM3035EP	$386.00	$4.5

Perfect Calc (page 72)

	ZPS030EP	$175.00	$4.5

Epson (continued)

STATISTICS
Statpak (page 73)

	Order #	Discount Price	Shipping
	ZNW027EP	$349.00	$4.50

TECHNOLOGY/DATA BASE MANAGEMENT SYSTEMS (DBMS)
Perfect Filer (page 61)

	ZPS003EP	$249.00	$4.50

TECHNOLOGY/PROGRAMMING LANGUAGES
CBASIC (page 67)

	ZDR009EP	$115.00	$4.50

MBASIC-80 (page 68)

	ZMS008EP	$249.00	$4.50

TECHNOLOGY/WORD PROCESSING
Peach Text 5000 (page 77)

	ZPT018EP	$254.50	$4.50

Perfect Writer (page 77)

	ZPS017EP	$194.00	$4.50

II. APPLICATIONS SOFTWARE

DATA BASE MANAGEMENT SYSTEMS (DBMS)
dBase II (page 60)

	ZAT005EP	$455.15	$4.50

Infostar System (page 61)

	ZMP007EP	$347.50	$4.50

Perfect Filer (page 61)

	ZPS003EP	$249.00	$4.50

PROGRAMMING LANGUAGES
CBASIC (page 67)

	ZDR009EP	$115.00	$4.50

MBASIC-80 (page 68)

	ZMS008EP	$249.00	$4.50

SPREADSHEETS/MANAGEMENT TOOLS
Accounting Plus Series (page 69)
   4 in series

	Order #	Discount Price	Shipping
Accounts Payable	ZAM035EP	$386.00	$4.50
Accounts Receivable	ZAM1035EP	$386.00	$4.50
General Ledger	ZAM2035EP	$386.00	$4.50
Payroll	ZAM3035EP	$386.00	$4.50

Financial Planner (page 70)

	ZAT034EP	$425.00	$4.50

MBA Series (page 71)
   3 in series

Accounts Receivable	ZMB032EP	$385.00	$4.50
General Ledger	ZMB1032EP	$385.00	$4.50
Payroll	ZMB2032EP	$385.00	$4.50

Multiplan (page 71)

	ZMS031EP	$195.00	$4.50

Perfect Calc (page 72)

	ZPS030EP	$175.00	$4.50

Statpak (page 73)

	ZNW027EP	$349.00	$4.50

Supercalc I (page 73)

	ZSO026EP	$136.50	$4.50

Supercalc II (page 74)

	ZSO038EP	$206.50	$4.50

Supercalc III (page 74)

	ZSO039EP	$276.50	$4.50

Visicalc (page 74)

	ZVC001EP	$190.00	$4.50

SYSTEMS SUPPORT
Quickcode (page 75)

	ZFG012EP	$207.10	$4.50

WORD PROCESSING SYSTEMS & UTILITIES
Final Word (page 76)

	ZMU019EP	$228.00	$4.50

Mailmerge (page 76)

	ZMP021EP	$159.00	$4.50

Peach Text 5000 (page 77)

	ZPT018EP	$254.50	$4.50

Perfect Writer (page 77)

	ZPS017EP	$194.00	$4.50

Word Processing Systems & Utilities (continued)

	Order #	Discount Price	Shipping
Spellbinder (page 77)	ZLS016EP	$275.00	$4.50
Spellstar (page 78)	ZMP022EP	$159.00	$4.50
Wordstar (page 78)	ZMP020EP	$298.00	$4.50
Wordstar Professional (page 79)	ZMP023EP	$590.75	$4.50

FRANKLIN

I. EDUCATIONAL SOFTWARE

Preschool
  MATH & READING READINESS
    Dinosaurs (page 7)

	CA005FR	$37.95	$2.50

Elementary
  LANGUAGE ARTS/THINKING SKILLS
    Analogies-Tutorial (page 13)

	HC111FR	$44.95	$2.50

Drill Builder Series (page 65)
  6 in series

Alien Action	DL001FR	$39.75	$2.50
Alligator Alley	DL003FR	$39.75	$2.50
Idea Invasion	DL005FR	$39.75	$2.50
Master Match	DL006FR	$39.75	$2.50
Meteor Mission	DL002FR	$39.75	$2.50
Wiz Works	DL004FR	$39.75	$2.50

MATHEMATICS
Clock (page 22)

	HC108FR	$37.95	$2.50

Drill Builder Series (page 65)
  6 in series

Alien Action	DL001FR	$39.75	$2.50
Alligator Alley	DL003FR	$39.75	$2.50
Idea Invasion	DL005FR	$39.75	$2.50
Master Match	DL006FR	$39.75	$2.50
Meteor Mission	DL002FR	$39.75	$2.50
Wiz Works	DL004FR	$39.75	$2.50
Expanded Notations (page 23)	HC102FR	$28.50	$1.50

SOCIAL SCIENCE
Medalist/Black Americans (page 49)

	HC014FR	$37.95	$2.50

Medalist/Continents (page 49)

	HC010FR	$37.95	$2.50

Medalist/States (page 49)

	HC009FR	$37.95	$2.50

Medalist/Women in History (page 49)

	HC015FR	$37.95	$2.50

Secondary
  ENGLISH/THINKING SKILLS
    Analogies-Tutorial (page 13)

	HC111FR	$44.95	$2.50

SOCIAL SCIENCE
Medalist/Black Americans (page 49)

	HC014FR	$37.95	$2.50

Medalist/Continents (page 49)

	HC010FR	$37.95	$2.50

Medalist/States (page 49)

	HC009FR	$37.95	$2.50

Medalist/Women in History (page 49)

	HC015FR	$37.95	$2.50

Franklin (continued)

II. APPLICATIONS SOFTWARE
EDUCATIONAL FORMATS/MULTISUBJECT
Classmate (page 63)

DA004FR	$44.95	$2.50

Drill Builder Series (page 65)
6 in series

Alien Action	DL001FR	$39.75	$2.50
Alligator Alley	DL003FR	$39.75	$2.50
Idea Invasion	DL005FR	$39.75	$2.50
Master Match	DL006FR	$39.75	$2.50
Meteor Mission	DL002FR	$39.75	$2.50
Wiz Works	DL004FR	$39.75	$2.50

HEATH/ZENITH

I. EDUCATIONAL SOFTWARE
Secondary
TECHNOLOGY/PROGRAMMING LANGUAGES
MBASIC-80 (page 68)

ZMS008HZ	$249.00	$4.50

Postsecondary
ACCOUNTING
Perfect Calc (page 72)

ZPS030HZ	$175.00	$4.50

STATISTICS
Statpak (page 73)

ZNW027HZ	$349.00	$4.50

TECHNOLOGY/DATA BASE MANAGEMENT SYSTEMS (DBMS)
Perfect Filer (page 61)

ZPS003HZ	$249.00	$4.50

TECHNOLOGY/PROGRAMMING LANGUAGES
CBASIC (page 67)

ZDR009HZ	$115.00	$4.50

MBASIC-80 (page 71)

ZMS008HZ	$249.00	$4.50

TECHNOLOGY/WORD PROCESSING
Peach Text 5000 (page 77)

ZPT018HZ	$254.50	$4.50

Perfect Writer (page 77)

ZPS017HZ	$194.00	$4.50

II. APPLICATIONS SOFTWARE
DATA BASE MANAGEMENT SYSTEMS (DBMS)
dbase II (page 60)

ZAT005HZ	$455.15	$4.50

PROGRAMMING LANGUAGES
CBASIC (page 67)

ZDR009HZ	$115.00	$4.50

MBASIC-80 (page 68)

ZMS008HZ	$249.00	$4.50

SPREADSHEETS/MANAGEMENT TOOLS
Perfect Calc (page 72)

ZPS030HZ	$175.00	$4.50

Supercalc I (page 73)

ZSO026HZ	$136.50	$4.50

Supercalc II (page 74)

ZSO038HZ	$206.50	$4.50

Supercalc III (page 74)

ZSO039HZ	$276.50	$4.50

WORD PROCESSING SYSTEMS & UTILITIES
Final Word (page 76)

ZMU019HZ	$228.00	$4.50

Mailmerge (page 76)

ZMP021HZ	$159.00	$4.50

Word Processing Systems & Utilities (continued)

Spellbinder (page 77)

ZLS016HZ	$275.00	$4.5

Wordstar (page 78)

ZMP020HZ	$298.00	$4.5

HEWLETT-PACKARD

I. EDUCATIONAL SOFTWARE
Secondary
TECHNOLOGY/DATA BASE MANAGEMENT SYSTEMS (DBMS)
Personal Pearl (page 62)

ZPL006HP	$172.60	$4.

TECHNOLOGY/PROGRAMMING LANGUAGES
MBASIC-80 (page 80)

ZMS008HP	$249.00	$4.

Postsecondary
ACCOUNTING
Perfect Calc (page 72)

ZPS030HP	$175.00	$4.

STATISTICS
Statpak (page 73)

ZNW027HP	$349.00	$4.

TECHNOLOGY/DATA BASE MANAGEMENT SYSTEMS (DBMS)
Perfect Filer (page 61)

ZPS003HP	$249.00	$4.

Personal Pearl (page 62)

ZPL006HP	$172.60	$4.

TECHNOLOGY/PROGRAMMING LANGUAGES
CBASIC (page 67)

ZDR009HP	$115.00	$4.

MBASIC-80 (page 68)

ZMS008HP	$249.00	$4.

TECHNOLOGY/WORD PROCESSING
Perfect Writer (page 77)

ZPS017HP	$194.00	$4.

II. APPLICATIONS SOFTWARE
DATA BASE MANAGEMENT SYSTEMS (DBMS)
dbase II (page 60)

ZAT005HP	$455.15	$4.

Personal Pearl (page 62)

ZPL006HP	$172.60	$4.

PROGRAMMING LANGUAGES
CBASIC (page 67)

ZDR009HP	$115.00	$4.

MBASIC-80 (page 68)

ZMS008HP	$249.00	$4.

SPREADSHEETS/MANAGEMENT TOOLS
Realworld Series (page 73)
4 in series

Accounts Payable	ZAC029HP	$431.00	$4.
Accounts Receivable	ZAC1029HP	$431.00	$4.
General Ledger	ZAC2029HP	$431.00	$4.
Payroll	ZAC3039HP	$431.00	$4.

Star System I—General Ledger (page 73)

ZSC028HP	$305.00	$4.

Statpak (page 73)

ZNW027HP	$349.00	$4.

SYSTEMS SUPPORT
Quickcode (page 75)

ZFG012HP	$207.10	$4.

WORD PROCESSING SYSTEMS & UTILITIES
Final Word (page 76)

ZMU019HP	$228.00	$4.

Mailmerge (page 76)

ZMP021HP	$159.00	$4.

IBM

I. EDUCATIONAL SOFTWARE

Preschool

MATH & READING READINESS
Alphabet Zoo (page 7)

	SP106IB	$28.50	$1.50

Elementary

LANGUAGE ARTS/READING
Drill Builder Series (page 65)
  6 in series

Alien Action	DL001IB	$39.75	$2.50
Alligator Alley	DL003IB	$39.75	$2.50
Idea Invasion	DL005IB	$39.75	$2.50
Master Match	DL006IB	$39.75	$2.50
Meteor Mission	DL002IB	$39.75	$2.50
Wiz Works	DL004IB	$39.75	$2.50

Language Arts Skill Builder Series (page 9)
  6 in series

Spelling Wiz	DL010IB	$39.75	$2.50
Verb Viper	DL007IB	$39.75	$2.50
Word Invasion	DL009IB	$39.75	$2.50
Wordman	DL008IB	$39.75	$2.50
Word Master	DL012IB	$39.75	$2.50
Word Radar	DL011IB	$39.75	$2.50

Word Attack! (page 12)

	DA103IB	$44.95	$2.50

Word Spinner (page 13)

	LC010IB	$33.25	$2.50

LANGUAGE ARTS/THINKING
Moptown Hotel (page 14)

	LC008IB	$37.95	$2.50

Moptown Parade (page 15)

	LC007IB	$37.95	$2.50

LANGUAGE ARTS/WRITING
Magic Spells (page 16)

	LC013IB	$33.25	$2.50

Story Machine (page 18)

	SP101IB	$33.25	$1.50

MATHEMATICS
Addition Magician (page 19)

	LC011IB	$37.95	$2.50

Drill Builder Series (page 65)
  6 in series

Alien Action	DL001IB	$39.75	$2.50
Alligator Alley	DL003IB	$39.75	$2.50
Idea Invasion	DL005IB	$39.75	$2.50
Master Match	DL006IB	$39.75	$2.50
Meteor Mission	DL002IB	$39.75	$2.50
Wiz Works	DL004IB	$39.75	$2.50

Math Blaster (page 26)

	DA101IB	$44.95	$2.50

MUSIC/ART
Songwriter (page 29)

	SC004IB	$37.95	$2.50

Secondary

BUSINESS EDUCATION/ACCOUNTING
Personal Accounting (page 72)

	ZBP033IB	$136.90	$4.50

BUSINESS EDUCATION/WORD PROCESSING
Easywriter II (page 76)

	ZIU024IB	$259.00	$4.50

Master Type (page 33)

	SC301IB	$44.95	$2.50

ENGLISH/COMPREHENSIVE
Krell's College Board SAT Exam Preparation Series (page 53)

	KS101IB	$254.95	$4.50

Owlcat SAT Preparatory Course (page 53)

	OC001IB	$212.45	$4.50

ENGLISH/GRAMMAR-COMPOSITION
Writing is Thinking (page 34)

	KA001IB	$140.25	$4.50
Teacher Manual	KA002IB	$23.75	$2.50

ENGLISH/READING
Speed Reader II (page 35)

	DA102IB	$59.50	$4.50

Word Attack! (page 35)

	DA103IB	$44.95	$2.50

ENGLISH/THINKING SKILLS
In Search of the Most Amazing Thing (page 36)

	SP104IB	$37.95	$2.50

Snooper Troops—Case #1 (page 37)

	SP402IB	$40.50	$2.50

MATHEMATICS/ALGEBRA
Algebra Series (page 39)
  5 in series

Vol. 1	EW004IB	$37.95	$2.50
Vol. 2	EW005IB	$37.95	$2.50
Vol. 3	EW006IB	$37.95	$2.50
Vol. 4	EW007IB	$37.95	$2.50
Vols. 5&6	EW008IB	$37.95	$2.50

MATHEMATICS/COMPREHENSIVE
Krell's College Board SAT Exam Preparation Series (page 53)

	KS101IB	$254.95	$4.50

SCIENCE
Biology Series (page 45)
  4 in series
  Exploring That
    Amazing Food

Factory	TH004IB	$44.95	$2.50

  Fascinating Story

of Cell Growth	TH003IB	$44.95	$2.50
How Plants Grow	TH001IB	$44.95	$2.50
Photosynthesis	TH002IB	$44.95	$2.50

Chemistry Series (page 46)
  2 in series
  Hows & Whys of

Migrating Molecules	TH006IB	$44.95	$2.50
Molecules & Atoms	TH005IB	$44.95	$2.50

Eco-Paradise (page 47)

	CS001IB	$37.95	$2.50

Nutri-Bytes (page 46)

	CS002IB	$37.95	$2.50

Postsecondary

ACCOUNTING
Accounting Plus Series (page 69)
  4 in series

Accounts Payable	ZAM035IB	$386.00	$4.50
Accounts Receivable	ZAM1035IB	$386.00	$4.50
General Ledger	ZAM2035IB	$386.00	$4.50
Payroll	ZAM3035IB	$386.00	$4.50

Financial Management Series (page 69)

	ZIU036IB	$1,755.00/series	$7.00

Perfect Calc (page 72)

	ZPS030IB	$175.00	$4.50

Personal Accounting (page 72)

	ZBP033IB	$136.90	$4.50

STATISTICS
Statpak (page 73)

	ZNW027IB	$349.00	$4.50

TECHNOLOGY/DATA BASE MANAGEMENT SYSTEMS (DBMS)
Perfect Filer (page 61)

	ZMS003IB	$249.00	$4.50

IBM (continued)

TECHNOLOGY/PROGRAMMING LANGUAGES
Microsoft "C" (page 56)

	ZMS010IB	$351.00	$4.50

M Pascal Compiler (page 74)

| | ZMS014IB | $250.00 | $4.50 |

TECHNOLOGY/WORD PROCESSING
Easywriter II (page 76)

| | ZIU024IB | $259.00 | $4.50 |

Multitool Word (page 77)

| | ZMS025IB | $277.00 | $4.50 |

Perfect Writer (page 77)

| | ZPS017IB | $194.00 | $4.50 |

II. APPLICATIONS SOFTWARE
DATA BASE MANAGEMENT SYSTEMS (DBMS)
dbase II (page 60)

| | ZAT005IB | $455.15 | $4.50 |

Easyfiler (page 61)

| | ZIU004IB | $289.00 | $4.50 |

Perfect Filer (page 61)

| | ZPS003IB | $249.00 | $4.50 |

Personal Pearl (page 62)

| | ZPL006IB | $172.60 | $4.50 |

Pupil Information Profiler (page 62)

| | ET001IB | $2,082.50 | $4.50 |

Visifile (page 63)

| | ZVC002IB | $230.00 | $4.50 |

EDUCATIONAL FORMATS/MULTISUBJECT
Classmate (page 63)

| | DA104IB | $44.95 | $2.50 |

Delta Drawing (page 65)

| | SP103IB | $42.45 | $2.50 |

Drill Builder Series (page 65)
6 in series

Alien Action	DL001IB	$39.75	$2.50
Alligator Alley	DL003IB	$39.75	$2.50
Idea Invasion	DL005IB	$39.75	$2.50
Master Match	DL006IB	$39.75	$2.50
Meteor Mission	DL002IB	$39.75	$2.50
Wiz Works	DL004IB	$39.75	$2.50

Game Show (page 66)

| | CA101IB | $33.95 | $2.50 |

Tic Tac Show (page 66)

| | CA102IB | $33.95 | $2.50 |

PROGRAMMING LANGUAGES
Microsoft "C" (page 56)

| | ZMS010IB | $351.00 | $4.50 |

SPREADSHEETS/MANAGEMENT TOOLS
Accounting Pearl (page 68)

| | PE001IB | $577.50 | $6.00 |

Accounting Plus Series (page 69)
4 in series

Accounts Payable	ZAM035IB	$386.00	$4.50
Accounts Receivable	ZAM1035IB	$386.00	$4.50
General Ledger	ZAM2035IB	$386.00	$4.50
Payroll	ZAM3035IB	$386.00	$4.50

Financial Management Series (page 69)

| 3 in series | ZIU036IB | $1,755.00/series | $6.00 |

Learning Lotus 1, 2, 3 (page 70)

| | AY001IB | $335.75 | $4.50 |

Extra Manual &
Backup disk

| | AY004IB | $63.75 | $2.50 |

Learning Multiplan (page 70)

| | AY002IB | $332.50 | $4.50 |

Extra Manual &
Backup disk

| | AY005IB | $63.75 | $2.50 |

Spreadsheets/Management Tools (continued)

Learning Visicalc (page 71)

| | AY003IB | $250.75 | $4.50 |

Extra Manual &
Backup disk

| | AY006IB | $44.95 | $2.50 |

Lotus 1, 2, 3 (page 71)

| | ZLD040IB | $346.50 | $4.50 |

MBA Series (page 71)
3 in series

Accounts Receivable	ZMB032IB	$385.00	$4.50
General Ledger	ZMB1032IB	$385.00	$4.50
Payroll	ZMB2032IB	$385.00	$4.50

Multiplan (page 71)

| | ZMS031IB | $195.00 | $4.50 |

Peach Pak (page 72)

| | ZPT037IB | $255.00 | $4.50 |

Perfect Calc (page 72)

| | ZPS030IB | $175.00 | $4.50 |

Personal Accounting (page 72)

| | ZBP033IB | $136.90 | $4.50 |

Realworld Series (page 73)
4 in series

Accounts Payable	ZAC029IB	$431.00	$4.50
Accounts Receivable	ZAC1029IB	$431.00	$4.50
General Ledger	ZAC2029IB	$431.00	$4.50
Payroll	ZAC3039IB	$431.00	$4.50

Statpak (page 73)

| | ZNW027IB | $349.00 | $4.50 |

Supercalc I (page 73)

| | ZSO026IB | $136.50 | $4.50 |

Supercalc II (page 74)

| | ZSO038IB | $206.50 | $4.50 |

Supercalc III (page 74)

| | ZSO039IB | $276.50 | $4.50 |

Visicalc (page 74)

| | ZVC001IB | $190.00 | $4.50 |

SYSTEMS SUPPORT
Mouse (page 74)

| | ZMS013IB | $136.90 | $4.50 |

M Pascal Compiler (page 74)

| | ZMS014IB | $250.00 | $4.50 |

Quickcode (page 75)

| | ZFG012IB | $207.10 | $4.50 |

WORD PROCESSING SYSTEMS & UTILITIES
Easywriter II (page 76)

| | ZIU024IB | $259.00 | $4.50 |

Final Word (page 76)

| | ZMU019IB | $228.00 | $4.50 |

Mailmerge (page 76)

| | ZMP021IB | $159.00 | $4.50 |

Multitool Word (page 77)

| | ZMS025IB | $277.00 | $4.50 |

Peach Text 5000 (page 77)

| | ZPT018IB | $254.50 | $4.50 |

Perfect Writer (page 77)

| | ZPS017IB | $194.00 | $4.50 |

Spellbinder (page 77)

| | ZLS016IB | $275.00 | $4.50 |

Spellstar (page 78)

| | ZMI022IB | $159.00 | $4.50 |

Word Plus (page 78)

| | ZOA015IB | $105.00 | $4.50 |

Wordstar (page 78)

| | ZMP020IB | $298.00 | $4.50 |

Wordstar Professional (page 79)

| | ZMP023IB | $590.75 | $4.50 |

NORTHSTAR

I. EDUCATIONAL SOFTWARE

Secondary

TECHNOLOGY/DATA BASE MANAGEMENT SYSTEMS (DBMS)
Personal Pearl (page 62)

	Order #	Discount Price	Shipping
	ZPL006NS	$172.60	$4.50

TECHNOLOGY/PROGRAMMING LANGUAGES
MBASIC-80 (page 68)

	ZMS008NS	$249.00	$4.50

Postsecondary

ACCOUNTING
Perfect Calc (page 72)

	ZPS030NS	$175.00	$4.50

STATISTICS
Statpak (page 73)

	ZNW027NS	$349.00	$4.50

TECHNOLOGY/DATA BASE MANAGEMENT SYSTEMS (DBMS)
Perfect Filer (page 61)

	ZPS003NS	$249.00	$4.50

Personal Pearl (page 62)

	ZPS003NS	$249.00	$4.50

TECHNOLOGY/PROGRAMMING LANGUAGES
CBASIC (page 67)

	ZDR009NS	$115.00	$4.50

MBASIC-80 (page 68)

	ZMS008NS	$249.00	$4.50

TECHNOLOGY/WORD PROCESSING
Perfect Writer (page 77)

	ZPS017NS	$194.00	$4.50

II. APPLICATIONS SOFTWARE

DATA BASE MANAGEMENT SYSTEMS (DBMS)
dbase II (page 60)

	ZAT005NS	$455.15	$4.50

Infostar System (page 61)

	ZMP007NS	$347.50	$4.50

Perfect Filer (page 61)

	ZPS003NS	$249.00	$4.50

Personal Pearl (page 62)

	ZPL006NS	$172.60	$4.50

PROGRAMMING LANGUAGES
CBASIC (page 67)

	ZDR009NS	$115.00	$4.50

MBASIC-80 (page 68)

	ZMS008NS	$249.00	$4.50

SPREADSHEETS/MANAGEMENT TOOLS
Peach Pak (page 72)

	ZPT037NS	$255.00	$4.50

Perfect Calc (page 72)

	ZPS030NS	$175.00	$4.50

Realworld Series (page 73)

4 in series			
Accounts Payable	ZAC029NS	$431.00	$4.50
Accounts Receivable	ZAC1029NS	$431.00	$4.50
General Ledger	ZAC2029NS	$431.00	$4.50
Payroll	ZAC3029NS	$431.00	$4.50

Star System I—General Ledger (page 73)

	ZSC028NS	$305.00	$4.50

Statpak (page 73)

	ZNW027NS	$349.00	$4.50

Supercalc I (page 73)

	ZSO026NS	$136.50	$4.50

Supercalc II (page 74)

	ZSO038NS	$206.50	$4.50

Supercalc III (page 74)

	ZSO039NS	$276.50	$4.50

SYSTEMS SUPPORT
Quickcode (page 75)

	ZFG012NS	$207.10	$4.50

WORD PROCESSING SYSTEMS & UTILITIES
Final Word (page 77)

	ZMU019NS	$228.00	$4.50

Mailmerge (page 76)

	ZMP021NS	$159.00	$4.50

Perfect Writer (page 77)

	ZPS017NS	$194.00	$4.50

Spellbinder (page 77)

	ZLS016NS	$275.00	$4.50

Spellstar (page 78)

	ZMI022NS	$159.00	$4.50

Word Plus (page 78)

	ZOA015NS	$105.00	$4.50

Wordstar (page 78)

	ZMP020NS	$298.00	$4.50

Wordstar Professional (page 79)

	ZMP023NS	$590.75	$4.50

OSBORNE

I. EDUCATIONAL SOFTWARE

Secondary

BUSINESS EDUCATION/WORD PROCESSING
Peach Text 5000 (page 77)

	ZPT018OS	$254.50	$4.50

TECHNOLOGY/PROGRAMMING LANGUAGES
MBASIC-80 (page 68)

	ZMS008OS	$249.00	$4.50

Postsecondary

ACCOUNTING
Perfect Calc (page 72))

	ZPS030OS	$175.00	$4.50

STATISTICS
Statpak (page 73)

	ZNW027OS	$349.00	$4.50

TECHNOLOGY/DATA BASE MANAGEMENT SYSTEMS (DBMS)
Perfect Filer (page 61)

	ZPS003OS	$249.00	$4.50

TECHNOLOGY/PROGRAMMING LANGUAGES
CBASIC (page 67)

	ZDR009OS	$115.00	$4.50

MBASIC-80 (page 68)

	ZMS008OS	$249.00	$4.50

TECHNOLOGY/WORD PROCESSING
Peach Text 5000 (page 77)

	ZPT018OS	$254.50	$4.50

Perfect Writer (page 77)

	ZPS017OS	$194.00	$4.50

II. APPLICATIONS SOFTWARE

DATA BASE MANAGEMENT SYSTEMS (DBMS)
Infostar System (page 61)

	ZMP007OS	$347.50	$4.50

PROGRAMMING LANGUAGES
CBASIC (page 67)

	ZDR009OS	$115.00	$4.50

MBASIC-80 (page 68)

	ZMS008OS	$249.00	$4.50

SPREADSHEETS/MANAGEMENT TOOLS
MBA Series (page 71)

3 in series			
Accounts Receivable	ZMB032OS	$385.00	$4.50
General Ledger	ZMB1032OS	$385.00	$4.50
Payroll	ZMB2032OS	$385.00	$4.50

Osborne (continued)
Spreadsheets/Management Tools (continued)

	Order #/Discount Price/Shipping		

	Order #	Discount Price	Shipping
Multiplan (page 71)			
	ZMS031OS	$195.00	$4.50
Statpak (page 73)			
	ZNW027OS	$349.00	$4.50
Supercalc I (page 73)			
	ZSO026OS	$136.50	$4.50
Supercalc II (page 74)			
	ZSO038OS	$206.50	$4.50
Supercalc III (page 74)			
	ZSO039OS	$276.50	$4.50
SYSTEMS SUPPORT			
Quickcode (page 75)			
	ZFG012OS	$207.10	$4.50
WORD PROCESSING SYSTEMS & UTILITIES			
Final Word (page 76)			
	ZMU019OS	$228.00	$4.50
Word Plus (page 78)			
	ZOA015OS	$105.00	$4.50

SUPERBRAIN

I. EDUCATIONAL SOFTWARE

Secondary

TECHNOLOGY/PROGRAMMING LANGUAGES
MBASIC-80 (page 68)

	Order #	Discount Price	Shipping
MBASIC-80 (page 68)	ZMS008SB	$249.00	$4.50

Postsecondary
ACCOUNTING
Perfect Calc (page 72)

Perfect Calc	ZPS030SB	$175.00	$4.50

STATISTICS
Statpak (page 73)

Statpak	ZNW027SB	$349.00	$4.50

TECHNOLOGY/DATA BASE MANAGEMENT SYSTEMS (DBMS)
Perfect Filer (page 61)

Perfect Filer	ZPS003SB	$249.00	$4.50

TECHNOLOGY/PROGRAMMING LANGUAGES
CBASIC (page 67)

CBASIC	ZDR009SB	$115.00	$4.50
MBASIC-80 (page 68)	ZMS008SB	$249.00	$4.50

TECHNOLOGY/WORD PROCESSING
Perfect Writer (page 77)

Perfect Writer	ZPS017SB	$194.00	$4.50

II. APPLICATIONS SOFTWARE

DATA BASE MANAGEMENT SYSTEMS (DBMS)
dbase II (page 60)

dbase II	ZAT005SB	$455.15	$4.50
Infostar System (page 61)	ZMP007SB	$347.50	$4.50
Perfect Filer (page 61)	ZPS003SB	$249.00	$4.50
Personal Pearl (page 62)	ZPL006SB	$172.60	$4.50

PROGRAMMING LANGUAGES
CBASIC (page 67)

CBASIC	ZDR009SB	$115.00	$4.50
MBASIC-80 (page 68)	ZMS008SB	$249.00	$4.50

SPREADSHEETS/MANAGEMENT TOOLS
MBA Series (page 71)
3 in series

Accounts Receivable	ZMB032SB	$385.00	$4.50

	Order #	Discount Price	Shipping
General Ledger	ZMB1032SB	$385.00	$4.50
Payroll	ZMB2032SB	$385.00	$4.50
Multiplan (page 71)	ZMS031SB	$195.00	$4.50
Peach Pak (page 72)	ZPT037SB	$255.00	$4.50
Perfect Calc (page 72)	ZPS030SB	$175.00	$4.50
Realworld Series (page 73)			
4 in series			
Accounts Payable	ZMC029SB	$431.00	$4.50
Accounts Receivable	ZMC1029SB	$431.00	$4.50
General Ledger	ZMC2029SB	$431.00	$4.50
Payroll	ZMC3029SB	$431.00	$4.50
Star System I—General Ledger (page 73)	ZSC028SB	$305.00	$4.50
Statpak (page 73)	ZNW027SB	$349.00	$4.50
Supercalc I (page 73)	ZSO026SB	$136.50	$4.50
Supercalc II (page 74)	ZSO038SB	$206.50	$4.50
Supercalc III (page 74)	ZSO039SB	$276.50	$4.50
SYSTEMS SUPPORT			
Quickcode (page 75)	ZFG012SB	$207.10	$4.50
WORD PROCESSING SYSTEMS & UTILITIES			
Final Word (page 76)	ZMU019SB	$228.00	$4.50
Mailmerge (page 76)	ZMP021SB	$159.00	$4.50
Perfect Writer (page 77)	ZPS017SB	$194.00	$4.50
Spellbinder (page 77)	ZLS016SB	$275.00	$4.50
Spellstar (page 78)	ZMI022SB	$159.00	$4.50
Word Plus (page 78)	ZOA015SB	$105.00	$4.50
Wordstar (page 78)	ZMP020SB	$298.00	$4.50
Wordstar Professional (page 79)	ZMP023SB	$590.75	$4.50

TELEVIDEO

I. EDUCATIONAL SOFTWARE

Secondary
TECHNOLOGY/DATA BASE MANAGEMENT SYSTEMS (DBMS)
Personal Pearl (page 62)

Personal Pearl	ZPL006TV	$172.60	$4.50

TECHNOLOGY/PROGRAMMING LANGUAGES
MBASIC-80 (page 68)

MBASIC-80	ZMS008TV	$249.00	$4.50

Postsecondary
ACCOUNTING
Accounting Plus Series (page 69)
4 in series

Accounts Payable	ZAM035TV	$386.00	$4.50
Accounts Receivable	ZAM1035TV	$386.00	$4.50
General Ledger	ZAM2035TV	$386.00	$4.50
Payroll	ZAM3035TV	$386.00	$4.50
Perfect Calc (page 72)	ZPS030TV	$175.00	$4.50

Televideo (continued)

STATISTICS
Statpak (page 73)

ZNW027TV	$349.00	$4.50

TECHNOLOGY/DATA BASE MANAGEMENT SYSTEMS (DBMS)
Perfect Filer (page 61)

ZPS003TV	$249.00	$4.50

Personal Pearl (page 62)

ZPL006TV	$172.60	$4.50

TECHNOLOGY/PROGRAMMING LANGUAGES
CBASIC (page 67)

ZDR009TV	$115.00	$4.50

MBASIC-80 (page 68)

ZMS008TV	$249.00	$4.50

TECHNOLOGY/WORD PROCESSING
Perfect Writer (page 77)

ZPS017TV	$194.00	$4.50

II. APPLICATIONS SOFTWARE

DATA BASE MANAGEMENT SYSTEMS (DBMS)
dbase II (page 60)

ZAT005TV	$455.15	$4.50

Infostar System (page 61)

ZMP007TV	$347.50	$4.50

Perfect Filer (page 61)

ZPS003TV	$249.00	$4.50

Personal Pearl (page 62)

ZPL006TV	$172.60	$4.50

PROGRAMMING LANGUAGES
CBASIC (page 67)

ZDR009TV	$115.00	$4.50

MBASIC-80 (page 68)

ZMS008TV	$249.00	$4.50

SPREADSHEETS/MANAGEMENT TOOLS
Accounting Plus Series (page 69)
  4 in series

Accounts Payable	ZAM035TV	$386.00	$4.50
Accounts Receivable	ZAM1035TV	$386.00	$4.50
General Ledger	ZAM2035TV	$386.00	$4.50
Payroll	ZAM3035TV	$386.00	$4.50

MBA Series (page 71)
  3 in series

Accounts Receivable	ZMB032TV	$385.00	$4.50
General Ledger	ZMB1032TV	$385.00	$4.50
Payroll	ZMB2032TV	$385.00	$4.50

Peach Pak (page 72)

ZPT037TV	$255.00	$4.50

Perfect Calc (page 72)

ZPS030TV	$175.00	$4.50

Realworld Series (page 73)
  4 in series

Accounts Payable	ZAC029TV	$431.00	$4.50
Accounts Receivable	ZAC1029TV	$431.00	$4.50
General Ledger	ZAC2029TV	$431.00	$4.50
Payroll	ZAC3039TV	$431.00	$4.50

Star System I—General Ledger (page 73)

ZSC028TV	$305.00	$4.50

Statpak (page 73)

ZNW027TV	$349.00	$4.50

Supercalc I (page 73)

ZSO026TV	$136.50	$4.50

Supercalc II (page 74)

ZSO038TV	$206.50	$4.50

Supercalc III (page 74)

ZSO039TV	$276.50	$4.50

SYSTEMS SUPPORT
Quickcode (page 75)

ZFG012TV	$207.10	$4.50

WORD PROCESSING SYSTEMS & UTILITIES
Final Word (page 76)

ZMU019TV	$228.00	$4.50

Mailmerge (page 76)

ZMP021TV	$159.00	$4.50

Peach Text 5000 (page 77)

ZPT018TV	$254.50	$4.50

Perfect Writer (page 77)

ZPS017TV	$194.00	$4.50

Spellbinder (page 77)

ZLS016TV	$275.00	$4.50

Spellstar (page 78)

ZMI022TV	$159.00	$4.50

Wordstar (page 78)

ZMP020TV	$298.00	$4.50

Wordstar Professional (page 79)

ZMP023TV	$590.75	$4.50

TRS-80

I. EDUCATIONAL SOFTWARE

Secondary
  ENGLISH/COMPREHENSIVE
    Krell's College Board SAT Exam Preparation Series (page 53)

KS501TR	$254.95	$4.50

  MATHEMATICS/COMPREHENSIVE
    Krell's College Board SAT Exam Preparation Series (page 53)

KS501TR	$254.95	$4.50

TEXAS INSTRUMENTS

I. EDUCATIONAL SOFTWARE

Elementary
  MATHEMATICS
    Basic Number Facts: Practice (page 21)

School	CD214TI	$50.95	$4.50
Consumer	CD1214TI	$44.95	$2.50

    Decimals: Practice (page 23)

School	CD201TI	$50.95	$4.50
Consumer	CD1201TI	$44.95	$2.50

    Fractions: Practice (page 24)

School	CD202TI	$50.95	$4.50
Consumer	CD1202TI	$44.95	$2.50

    Whole Numbers: Practice (page 28)

School	CD203TI	$50.95	$4.50
Consumer	CD1203TI	$44.95	$2.50

Secondary
  FOREIGN LANGUAGE/FRENCH
    French Language Vocabulary Series
      Vocabulary Builder (page 37)

School	CD212TI	$50.95	$4.50
Consumer	CD1212TI	$44.95	$2.50

  FOREIGN LANGUAGE/GERMAN
    German Language Vocabulary Series
      Vocabulary Builder (page 38)

School	CD209TI	$50.95	$4.50
Consumer	CD1209TI	$44.95	$2.50

Texas Instruments (continued)

FOREIGN LANGUAGE/SPANISH
Spanish Language Vocabulary Series
  Vocabulary Builder (page 39)

School	CD205TI	$50.95	$4.50
Consumer	CD1205TI	$44.95	$2.50

SCIENCE/PHYSICS
Physics: Elementary Mechanics (page 48)

School	CD215TI	$59.50	$4.50
Consumer	CD1215TI	$50.95	$4.50

TECHNOLOGY/COMPUTER SCIENCE
Computer Literacy (page 51)

School	CD204TI	$59.50	$4.50
Consumer	CD1204TI	$50.95	$4.50

Postsecondary
SCIENCE/PHYSICS
Physics: Elementary Mechanics (page 48)

School	CD215TI	$59.50	$4.50
Consumer	CD1215TI	$50.95	$4.50

MISCELLANEOUS
French Language Vocabulary Series
  Vocabulary Builder (page 37)

School	CD212TI	$50.95	$4.50
Consumer	CD1212TI	$44.95	$2.50

German Language Vocabulary Series
  Vocabulary Builder (page 38)

School	CD209TI	$50.95	$4.50
Consumer	CD1209TI	$44.95	$2.50

Spanish Language Vocabulary Series
  Vocabulary Builder (page 39)

School	CD205TI	$50.95	$4.50
Consumer	CD1205TI	$44.95	$2.50

II. APPLICATIONS SOFTWARE

PROGRAMMING LANGUAGES
CBASIC (page 67)

	ZDR009TI	$115.00	$4.50

MBASIC-80 (page 68)

	ZMS008TI	$249.00	$4.50

SPREADSHEETS/MANAGEMENT TOOLS
CBASIC-86 (page 67)

	ZDR041TI	$168.00	$4.50

Learning Lotus 1, 2, 3 (page 70)

	AY001TI	$335.75	$4.50
Extra Manual & Backup disk	AY004TI	$63.75	$2.50

Learning Multiplan (page 70)

	AY002TI	$332.50	$4.50
Extra manual & Backup disk	AY005TI	$63.75	$2.50

Learning Visicalc (page 71)

	AY003TI	$250.75	$4.50
Extra manual & Backup disk	AY006TI	$44.95	$2.50

Lotus 1, 2, 3 (page 71)

	ZLD040TI	$346.50	$4.50

Multiplan (page 71)

	ZMS031TI	$195.00	$4.50

Visicalc (page 74)

	ZVC001TI	$190.00	$4.50

WORD PROCESSING SYSTEMS & UTILITIES
Easywriter II (page 76)

	ZIU024TI	$259.00	$4.50

Other Products
(Independent of Hardware Manufacturers)

COMPUTER LEARNING SYSTEMS INC.

The Computer Curriculum Guide (page 64)

	CC001	$335.75	$7.00

INFO DISC CORP.

College U.S.A. (page 79)

	ID001VD	$50.95	$4.50

NEA EDUCATIONAL COMPUTER SERVICE

The Yellow Book Subscription	NS004	$30.00	
Guide #1 Courseware	NS001	$5.00	
Guide #2 Applications Software	NS002	$3.50	
Guide #3 Combination Products	NS003	$5.00	

VIDEODISCOVERY

Bio Sci Videodisc (page 79)

	VD001	$420.75	$4.50

How to Order

Please fill in all the requested information. If your mailing address and shipping address differ, please provide both. To facilitate the ordering process, Cordatum will honor your purchase orders.

Make checks and money orders payable to Cordatum, Inc. If you prefer to charge your order, you may do so by filling in the necessary information or by phoning in your order to 301-652-5424.

Quantity discounts are available on some products, and organizational accounts are welcomed. Information on both will be furnished upon request.

Cordatum Inc.
4720 MONTGOMERY LANE • BETHESDA, MARYLAND 20814-5383 • (301) 652-5424

Return to:
Cordatum, Inc.
4720 Montgomery Lane
Bethesda, Maryland 20814

Ship Order To:

Name _____

Organization _____

Street _____

City _____ State _____

Zip _____ Phone ( ) _____

Bill Order To:

Name _____

Organization _____

Street _____

City _____ State _____

Zip _____ Phone ( ) _____

Quantity	Item No.*	Micro Make/Model And Disk Size	Name of Item	Unit Price	Unit Shipping	Total
	NS004		Catalog Subscription	$30.00		

*If no Item No. given, write in microcomputer make and model.

Total _____

_____

Total Enclosed _____
(Check or money order)*

- **Purchase orders honored:**
  Add $1.00 per order.
- **Maryland Residents Add**
  5% Sales Tax

Charge to my: (please check one) ☐ MasterCard ☐ VISA

Account Number _____ Card Expires: Mo._____ Yr._____

Signature _____

Product Warranties

All warranties of any kind relating to the goods listed in the Discount Price List are supplied by the manufacturer. Product warranties are not under any conditions or circumstances provided by Cordatum. Nor is Cordatum a party to any warranty that may be made by a manufacturer to the buyer or to any statement by the manufacturer concerning the suitability of the product for a particular age group or purpose.

Warranty Instructions

1. First, read carefully the warranty information that accompanies each product you buy since there are some differences from one manufacturer to another. In the event of a problem, be sure to follow the warranty instructions carefully.

2. All software manufacturers guarantee a "bootable disk," that is, a disk which, when properly inserted into an operating disk drive, will execute the program on the disk. If the disk does not fulfill this condition, it is defective.

3. Any disk determined to be defective may be exchanged for a replacement according to the specific provisions of the manufacturer's warranty.

4. If a disk is found to be defective, you may proceed to enforce your warranty either by shipping the re-packed product with an explanatory letter directly to the manufacturer or by shipping it to Cordatum who will follow through for you.

Cordatum, Inc.
4720 Montgomery Lane
Bethesda, Maryland 20814

Prices

Prices are subject to change without notice. Since Cordatum does not maintain its own inventory, and prices are subject to the manufacturer's changes, you may call toll-free at (800) 632-6327 for a current price quotation as of a particular date. The applicable price for any catalog item shall be determined on the date the manufacturer or author receives the order forwarded by Cordatum.

Discount and Billing

Any buyer who remits payment in full for an order received by Cordatum within 10 days of the date of the invoice shall be entitled to receive a 2% discount on the price of the goods ordered, not including applicable state and local taxes.

Payment is due in full within 30 days of the date of the invoice.

ADDITIONAL 5% DISCOUNT on total order
upon submission of this coupon with order

Business Education/Accounting (contiued)

STAR SYSTEM I — GENERAL LEDGER

See review, Applications, Spreadsheets/Management Tools, page 73.

Business Education/ Word Processing

BANK STREET WRITER

See review, Elementary, Technology/Word Processing, page 31.

EASYWRITER II

See review, Applications, Word Processing Systems and Utilities, page 76.

MASTER TYPE

Scarborough Systems

System Requirements

Tested on:
Apple II, 48K memory, disk drive, Applesoft, TV or monitor, (color recommended)
Apple IIe
Atari 800
IBM PC, 64K memory
Commodore 64

Also available (but not tested):
Atari 400, 1200 XL
Apple II +, 48K memory

Recommended Target Group
Technology/Word Processing, grades 3 and up.

Content
This package, in game format, is a well-organized, sequential, skill-building instructional program to introduce and improve keyboard (typing) skills. It contains a timing feature, provides a scoring report allowing the teacher to assess a student's progress, and provides an option for the teacher to create additional lessons.

Master Type (continued)

Comment
The space style game format is highly motivational, and the program is effective even with young children in the third grade, as well as older students who want to improve their typing skills. The option to create additional lessons is especially helpful. The manual is clearly written and easy for the beginner to follow. List Price: $49.95, IBM; $39.95, others.

PEACH TEXT 5000

See review, Applications, Word Processing Systems and Utilities, page 77.

English/Comprehensive

KRELL'S COLLEGE BOARD SAT EXAM PREPARATION

See review, Secondary, Miscellaneous, page 53.

OWLCAT SAT PREPARATORY COURSE

See review, Secondary, Miscellaneous, page 53.

PSAT/SAT ANALOGIES

See review, Secondary, Miscellaneous, page 53.

PSAT/SAT WORD ATTACK SKILLS

See review, Secondary, Miscellaneous, page 54.

BUILDING BETTER SENTENCES: COMBINING SENTENCE PARTS

See review, Elementary, Language Arts/Writing, page 16.

BUILDING BETTER SENTENCES: CREATING COMPOUND & COMPLEX SENTENCES

See review, Elementary, Language Arts/Writing, page 16.

INTRODUCTION TO POETRY

Edu-Ware Division/Peachtree Software, Inc.

System Requirements
Tested on:
Apple II +

Also available (but not tested):
Apple IIe, Franklin Ace

Recommended Target Group
English/Grammar-Composition, grades 7-12; miscellaneous, Post Secondary

Content
The programs teach the basics of scansion through word and verse introduction, examples and exercises. The teacher disk provides create and modify capabilities. Files can be transferred to student disks.

Comment
The program utilizes sound effectively to help the student understand and analyze the rhythm of various types of poetic lines. The program moves from word and verse examples to a series of required practices which effectively assure student progress. A definite plus is the program's capability to accept teacher input of additional easier or more challenging lines and verses to be scanned. Note that markers for poetic feet and stressed syllables flash and are not clear. List Price: $29.95.

LETTER WIZARD

See review, Applications, Word Processing & Utilities, page 76.

MASTER TYPE

See review, Secondary, Business Education/Word Processing, page 33.

PUNCTUATION SKILLS: COMMAS

See review, Elementary, Language Arts/Writing, page 17.

PUNCTUATION SKILLS: END MARKS, SEMICOLON, AND COLON

See review, Elementary, Language Arts/Writing, page 17.

THAT'S MY STORY

See review, Elementary, Language Arts/Writing, page 18.

VERBS

See review, Elementary, Language Arts/Writing, page 18.

WRITING IS THINKING

Kapstrom, Inc.

System Requirements
Tested on:
IBM PC, 64K memory, disk drive, TV or monitor, printer.

Recommended Target Group
English/Composition, grades 7-12

Content
The user is guided through an organized process of writing re-examining, and rewriting a 500-word paper. The program supplies examples, directions, and questions to force the user to work through an idea. A student lab manual, two computer disks, and a teacher's manual are the components of this four chapter interactive writing program. Exercises aid the student to develop, revise, edit, and print a thesis sentence, rough and final drafts. These exercises include brainstorming, differentiating between fact and opinion, limiting a topic, outlining distinguishing between narrative and expository writing, and

English/Grammar and Composition
(continued)
Writing Is Thinking (continued)

understanding the basic structural patterns of each type. The importance of unity, vivid details, clear order, smooth idea flow, introductions, and conclusions, as well as sentence structure, parallel structure, grammar, and mechanics, are stressed in the process.

Comment

This program is highly recommended as a useful supplement to a process-oriented writing program. The computer becomes an exacting task master compelling the student not only to put down ideas, but to reorganize and re-examine them in order to bring the writing to a whole, complete result. With the supervision of a teacher, a conscientious student can benefit greatly from the use of this program. The documentation is excellent. The approach is based on accepted theories and is developed in a logical, easily understood way. The interaction of lab book and teacher's manual with the courseware is well-planned. It should also be noted that this program is compatible with word processing software that will accept ASCII files, enabling the writer to produce finished copy. List Price: $165.00.

WRITING SKILLS SERIES

(five titles in series)

Edu-Ware Division/Peachtree Software, Inc.

System Requirements

Tested on:
Franklin Ace 1000

Also available (but not tested):
Apple II, II+, IIe

Recommended Target Group

English/Grammar-Composition, grades 9-12; miscellaneous, Postsecondary

Comment

The five (5) volumes of this series pretest, tutor, drill, and test specific grammar, mechanics, and usage editing skills that are so important to correct writing. The program employs active, as well as interactive, student participation, feedback, and alternate drills and exercises. The teacher can monitor the work of up to 40 students on each volume disk. The accompanying program narrative could be more specific regarding objectives, format of exercises, and additional resources. Note, in particular, that the teacher should especially preview Volume 5 and instruct the students on the difficult concept of parallelism and the format involved before allowing them to use the program. List Price: $39.95 each.

VOLUME 1

Content

This program presents pretests on possessives and contractions, noun plurals, and possessives, and subject/verb agreement. Scores indicate areas for further study and follow-up instruction and testing is provided.

Writing Skills Series (continued)

VOLUME 2

Content

This program presents pretests on pronoun/antecedent agreement, commas, and sentence fragments. Scores indicate areas for further study and follow-up instruction and testing is provided.

VOLUME 3

Content

This program presents pretests on quotations, pronoun cases, and subject/verb agreement. Scores indicate areas for further study and follow-up instruction and testing is provided.

VOLUME 4

Content

This program presents pretests on pronouns/antecedent agreement, troublesome modifiers, and subject/verb agreement. Scores indicate areas for further study and follow-up instruction and testing is provided.

VOLUME 5

Content

This program presents pretests on pronoun/antecedent agreement, problems of case, and of consistency relevant to parallel structure and shifts of person and voice. Scores indicate areas for further study and follow-up instruction and testing is provided.

English/Reading

COMPU-READ

See review, Elementary, Language Arts/Reading, page 8.

SPEED READER II

Davidson and Associates

System Requirements

Tested on:
Apple IIe, disk drive, TV or monitor, Speed Reader II Program Disk, Speed Reader II Data Disk

Also available (but not tested):
Apple II, 48K memory, Applesoft
Apple II+, 48K memory
IBM PC
Commodore 64

Recommended Target Group

English/Reading; high school, college, adult

English/Reading (continued)
Speed Reader II (continued)

Content
This program provides six kinds of practice and ten sequential lessons in speed reading. It provides exercises designed to increase reading speed and opportunities to practice these skills. It tests reading speed and comprehension to measure growth.

Comment
The program is recommended as an effective speed reading course. By means of increasingly difficult exercises, the eyes are trained to read more quickly and more efficiently. A suggested schedule of study is provided. An edit option allows the user to insert an additional text. The teacher's manual is well-written and clearly explains the execution of the program. List Price: $69.95

VOCABULARY SKILLS: CONTEXT CLUES

See review, Elementary, Language Arts/Reading, page 11.

VOCABULARY SKILLS: PREFIXES, SUFFIXES AND ROOT WORDS

See review, Elementary, Language Arts/Reading, page 12.

WIZARD OF WORDS

See review, Elementary, Language Arts/Reading, page 12.

WORK ATTACK!

See review, Elementary, Language Arts/Reading, page 12.

English/Thinking Skills

ANALOGIES-TUTORIAL

See review, Elementary, Language Arts/Thinking Skils, page 13.

THE FOURTH (4TH) R — REASONING

See review, Elementary, Language Arts/Thinking Skills, page 13.

GERTRUDE'S PUZZLES

See review, Elementary, Language Arts/Thinking Skills, page 14.

IN SEARCH OF THE MOST AMAZING THING

Spinnaker Software

System Requirements
Tested on:
Apple II + , 48K memory, disk drive, TV or monitor, (color recommended), DOS 3.3

Also available (but not tested):
Atari, 48K, diskette
IBM PC, diskette

Recommended Target Group
English/Thinking Skills, mid-teens through adult

Content
This problem solving game presents students with a mysterious science fiction simulation. The players use skills of decision making, data organization, note taking, and map making to reach the solution.

Comment
The game is highly motivational for the student to use and strengthen thinking skills in solving the problem. Graphics, color, and sound are effectively used for motivation. The game allows the student to learn from collecting information, analyzing it, and using trial and error to find the "Thing." It should be noted that use in a classroom setting requires up to five hours to reach the solution. The manual diagrams start-up procedures, and gives helpful hints on how to run the program in BASIC. Also included is an adventure book to add interest to the computer program. List Price: $39.95

MOPTOWN HOTEL

See review, Elementary, Language Arts/Thinking Skills, page 14.

English/Thinking Skills (continued)

PERCEPTION 3.0

See review, Elementary, Language Arts/Thinking Skills, page 15.

REASONING: THE LOGICAL PROCESS

See review, Post Secondary, Logic, page 55.

ROCKY'S BOOTS

See review, Elementary, Language Arts/Thinking Skills, page 15.

SNOOPER TROOPS—CASE #1

Spinnaker Software

System Requirements

Tested on:
Apple II + , 48K memory, disk drive, color TV or monitor (recommended)

Also available (but not tested):
Apple IIe
Atari 400/800, all XL's
IBM PC
Commodore 64

Recommended Target Group
English/Thinking Skills, early teens through adult

Content
Using a game format, the program presents the objective of solving a mystery through taking notes, drawing maps, classifying and organizing information using graphics, color, and sound.

Comment
This program is highly recommended as an excellent educational game program that allows the user many options and methods to solve the mystery. It succeeds in helping the learner draw a street map, organize materials, classify information, and draw conclusions from information gathered while solving the mystery. The user's manual is helpful in presenting start-up procedures and hints on how to run the program. Also included is a story line and background on the suspects. List Price: $44.95

English as a Second Language (ESL)

ANALYZING AN AD

See review, Secondary, Personal Skills Development, page 43.

JOB SURVIVAL SERIES

(three titles available separately)

See review, Secondary, Personal Skills Development, page 44.

Foreign Language

FRENCH LANGUAGE VOCABULARY SERIES

(two titles available separately)

FRENCH — CLASSROOM WORDS
FRENCH — VOCABULARY BUILDER

Control Data Corporation

System Requirements

CLASSROOM WORDS
Tested on:
Apple II + , 48K memory, disk drive, TV or monitor, DOS up through 3.3

Also available (but not tested):
Atari 800, 48K memory, disk drive, DOS up through 2
Texas Instruments 99/4A, 32K memory, disk drive, Plato Interpreter Cartridge

VOCABULARY BUILDER
Tested on:
Apple II + (as above)

Recommended Target Group
French; secondary and postsecondary students: introductory level — *Vocabulary Builder;* intermediate level — *Classroom Words*

Content
See review of GERMAN LANGUAGE VOCABULARY SERIES, page 38.

Comment
See review of GERMAN LANGUAGE VOCABULARY SERIES, page 38. List Price Each: $60.00 School Version; $49.95 Consumer Version.

Foreign Language (continued)

exercise. List Price Each: $60.00 School Version; $49.95 Consumer Version.

GERMAN LANGUAGE VOCABULARY SERIES

(three titles available separately)

GERMAN — CLASSROOM WORDS
GERMAN — TRAVEL VOCABULARY
GERMAN — VOCABULARY BUILDER
GERMAN — VOCABULARY FOR SHOPPING USE

Control Data Corporation

System Requirements
CLASSROOM WORDS
Tested on:
Apple II +, 48K memory, disk drive, TV or monitor, DOS up through 3.3

Also available (but not tested):
Atari 800, 48K memory, disk drive, DOS up through 2
Texas Instruments 99/4A, 32K memory expansion, disk drive, PLATO Interpreter Cartridge

TRAVEL VOCABULARY
Tested on:
Apple II + (as above)

VOCABULARY BUILDER
Tested on:
Apple II + (as above)

Recommended Target Group
German; secondary and postsecondary students: introductory level — *Vocabulary Builder;* intermediate level — *Classroom Words* and *Travel Vocabulary*

Content
Five hundred foreign language words for each program divided into either nine or ten categories by subject are presented for drill and practice in vocabulary. The student may see the word list for each category or play one of the two quiz exercises. Two games, *Hangperson* and *Pyramid,* may be placed in a foreign language to English, English to foreign language, or combination format. *Pyramid* is multiple choice with a help option and an interesting scoring system. *Hangperson* allows six mistakes for each word. Because the computer does not store the scores on either game after it is played, score sheets that may be duplicated are provided.

Comment
Reviewers recommend the supplemental programs as having strong educational value in vocabulary building and reinforcement for which drill and practice are essential. The exercises are highly motivational. When using the programs, teachers should check for various punctuation, spelling, and translation errors in the printed manual, both in student worksheets and in vocabulary lists. (Errata sheets are provided by the manufacturer.) Any errors should be corrected before duplicating and distributing materials to students. The errors do not appear on the screen. Reviewers also noted that some vocabulary terms are so specific to the content area (i.e., classroom vocabulary) that they are more appropriately used with the more advanced student.

These programs are a good way to maintain a student's interest and attention in vocabulary drills — usually a tedious

LE FRANCAIS PAR ORDINATEUR

(three titles available separately)

D.C. Heath and Company

System Requirements
Tested on:
Apple II +, 48K memory, disk drive, TV or monitor

Also available (but not tested):
Apple IIe

Recommended Target Group
Foreign Language/French I, grades 7-12.

Comment
These programs are highly recommended as excellent drill and practice reinforcement for instruction in French I. Immediate feedback and positive reinforcement are provided. The computer praises correct responses. Students are encouraged to try again after one incorrect answer. After a second incorrect answer, the correct response is given. In addition, there are game activities. The animated graphics are artistic, attractive, and motivational. The programs not only extend students' mastery of basic vocabulary and structure, but also extend their awareness of French culture — a feature particularly attractive to language teachers. List Price Each: $81.00.

LE DEMENAGEMENT
Content
This package, consisting of two disks, provides drill and practice with: (1) French terms for family members, (2) French terms for the rooms and furnishings of a house, (3) use of the present tense forms of the verb ''Mettre,'' (4) use of the second person forms of the ''imperatif,'' (5) use of the forms of the ''adjectif demonstratif,'' (6) use of the ''complement d'objet direct,'' and (7) use of French prepositions.

PARIS EN METRO
Content
This package, consisting of two disks, provides drill and practice for: (1) becoming familiar with the subway system in Paris, ''le metro,'' (2) recognizing several important places of interest and knowing how to visit them by subway, (3) learning the present tense forms of the verb ''aller,'' (4) using the preposition ''a'' with definite articles, and (5) using ordinal numbers.

UN REPAS FRANCAIS
Content
This package, consisting of two disks, provides drill and practice with: (1) the names of some common French food items, (2) typical French dishes, (3) metric weights and the French monetary system, (4) forms of the ''partitif,'' and (5) present tense forms of the verbs ''vouloir'' and ''prendre.''

Foreign Language (continued)

SPANISH LANGUAGE VOCABULARY SERIES

(four titles available separately)

SPANISH — CLASSROOM WORDS
SPANISH — TRAVEL VOCABULARY
SPANISH — VOCABULARY BUILDER
SPANISH — VOCABULARY FOR SHOPPING USE

Control Data Corporation

System Requirements

CLASSROOM WORDS
Tested on:
Apple II +, 48K memory, disk drive, TV or monitor, DOS up through 3.3

Also available (but not tested):
Atari 800, 48K memory, disk drive, DOS up through 2.0
Texas Instruments 99/4A, 32K memory expansion, disk drive, PLATO Interpreter Cartridge

TRAVEL VOCABULARY
Tested on:
Apple II + (as above)

VOCABULARY BUILDER
Tested on:
Apple II + (as above)

VOCABULARY FOR SHOPPING USE
Tested on:
Apple II + (as above)

Recommended Target Group
Spanish; secondary and postsecondary students: introductory level — *Vocabulary Builder;* intermediate level — *Classroom Words, Vocabulary for Shopping Use, Travel Vocabulary*

Content
See review of GERMAN LANGUAGE VOCABULARY SERIES, page 38.

Comment
See review of GERMAN LANGUAGE VOCABULARY SERIES, page 38. List Price Each: $60.00 School Version; $49.95 Consumer Version.

Mathematics/Algebra

ALGEBRA SERIES

(five titles available separately)

Edu-Ware Division/Peachtree Software, Inc.

System Requirements

Tested on:
Apple IIe, 48K memory, disk drive, TV or monitor, (color recommended), DOS 3.3

Algebra Series (continued)

Also available (but not tested):
Apple II, 48K memory, Applesoft
Apple II +, 48K memory
IBM PC (Vol. I only)

Recommended Target Group
Mathematics/Algebra, grades 7-12

Content
This package is a first-year algebra course, covering everything from numerals to quadratic inequalities. The course is divided into six volumes, each with its own disk. Each volume is broken into two to five units, and each unit is broken into three to five concepts. Under each concept the student has the option of the following paths: (1) "Definition," (2) "Rules," (3) "Examples," (4) "Sample Problems." Posttests are available at the end of each unit and at the end of each disk.

Comment
The package is highly recommended both for tutorials and for class demonstrations. The program is so user friendly that in a short time students could be left on their own with this tutorial. The program is the same throughout. The student does not have to go through these in order and after a while may use the disks to satisfy their unique learning styles. The graphics and the instructional design are excellent, especially in coordinate geometry.

ADVANCED MATHEMATICS: ALGEBRA
Vol. 1: List Price: $39.95
Vol. 2: List Price: $39.95
Vol. 3: List Price: $39.95
Vol. 4: List Price: $39.95
Vols. 5&6: List Price: $49.95

ELEMENTARY ALGEBRA SERIES

(nine titles available separately)

Control Data Corporation

System Requirements

Tested on:
Apple IIe and Apple II +, 48K memory, disk drive, TV or monitor

Also available (but not tested):
Apple II, 48K memory, Applesoft

Recommended Target Group
Mathematics/Algebra I, grades 9-12.

Comment
Titles in this series are recommended as visual aids to use with a whole class or as reinforcement and remedial material to be used on an individual basis. The nine major topics of the course are consistent with an Algebra I curriculum. Each topic is divided into objectives, which are well done. Despite the overall excellence of the series, several minor points should be noted: (1) Because the material is supplementary, teachers will require their own hard copy testing to determine mastery of the series. (2) Reward responses vary and could on occasion be confusing. (3) Since the titles are sold separately, a teacher's guide is provided for each title and initial credits are provided on every disk.

Mathematics/Algebra (continued)
Elementary Algebra (continued)

List Price — Instructional Package — Each: $49.95
List Price — Testing Package — Each: $39.95
List Price — Comprehensive Testing Package — Each: $39.95
List Price — Set of Activity Guides — Each: $20.00

EQUATIONS AND INEQUALITIES
Content

This package contains one disk with a total of four lessons: (1) "Linear Equations, Part I," (2) "Linear Equations, Part II," (3) "Linear Inequalities, Part I," (4) "Linear Inequalities, Part II." Prerequisites include competency in performing the four basic operations with whole numbers, fractions, integers, and polynomials.

EXPONENTS, ROOTS, AND RADICALS
Content

This package contains two disks with a total of four lessons: (1) "Integer Exponents," (2) "Exponential Expressions: Multiplication and Divison," (3) "Radical Expressions, Part I," (4) "Radical Expressions, Part II." Prerequisites include competence in performing basic arithmetic operations with whole numbers, fractions, and integers. Since all exponential and radical expressions in these lessons are numerical, it is not necessary that students be competent in dealing with polynomials.

FACTORING
Content

This package contains one disk with a total of four lessons: (1) "Common Monomial Factors," (2) "Factoring Trinomials," (3) "Special Cases," (4) "Factoring by Grouping." Prerequisites include competency in performing the four basic operations with whole numbers, fractions, and integers, as well as the ability to add and multiply polynomials.

GRAPHING LINES ON A PLANE
Content

This package contains two disks with a total of four lessons: (1) "Points in a Plane," (2) "Graphing Linear Equations," (3) "Lines: Slope and y-Intercept," (4) "Equations: $y = mx + b$ Form." Prerequisites include competency in performing operations with rational numbers and polynomials, as well as the ability to solve linear equations.

POLYNOMIALS
Content

This package contains two disks with a total of six lessons: (1) "Addition of Polynomials," (2) "Subtraction of Polynomials," (3) "Multiplication of Polynomials, Part I," (4) "Multiplication of Polynomials, Part II," (5) "Division of Polynomials, Part I," (6) "Division of Polynomials, Part II." To complete these lessons, the student must be competent in performing basic arithmetic operations with whole numbers, fractions, and integers.

Elementary Algebra (continued)
QUADRATIC EQUATIONS
Content

This package contains one disk with a total of three lessons: (1) "Special Cases," (2) "The General Case," (3) "The Quadratic Formula." To complete these lessons, the student must be able to perform the four basic operations with polynomials, factor polynomials, and solve linear equations. Note: Development of the quadratic formula and treatment of verticle lines were considered by the developer to be outside the scope of this supplemental series.

RATIONAL EXPRESSIONS
Content

This package includes two disks with a total of five lessons: (1) "Basic Concepts," (2) "Addition and Subtraction: Common Denominators," (3) "Multiplication and Division," (4) "Addition and Subtraction: Monomial Denominators," (5) "Addition and Subtraction: Polynomial Denominators." Prerequisites include competency in performing the four basic operations with rational numbers and polynomials.

SIGNED NUMBER OPERATIONS
Content

This package includes two disks with a total of five lessons: (1) "Order of Operations," (2) "Addition," (3) "Subtraction," (4) "Multiplication," (5) "Division." Prerequisites include the ability to perform the four basic operations with both whole numbers and fractions. Note: The description of "How I Think" may be considered by some not to reflect the target audience's thought processes.

SYSTEMS OF EQUATIONS
Content

This package contains one disk with a total of three lessons: (1) "Graphic Method," (2) "Substitution Method," (3) "Addition Method." To complete the lessons, the student must be able to perform operations with polynomials, and be competent in solving and graphing linear equations. Note: This program is intended to test only the answer, not the method used for solving equations.

FACTORING MACHINE

Micro Power & Light

System Requirements
Tested on:
Apple II + , 48K memory, disk drive, TV or monitor, DOS 3.3

Also available (but not tested):
Apple II, 48K memory, Applesoft
Apple IIe

Recommended Target Group
Mathematics/Algebra I and above

Mathematics/Algebra (continued)

Factoring Machine (continued)

Content

This drill and practice program reinforces instruction on the distributive properties of numbers.

Comment

The program is highly recommended for remediation, review, and testing on the distributive properties of numbers. Features of the program that maintain students' interest include graphics, game format, sound, personalization, timing, variation of computer responses, and self-pacing. It should be noted that the vocabulary may be too advanced for some students. Also, there is very little documentation either for the student or for the teacher. However, the program meets its stated objectives in a manner appropriate to the learner, and it is mathematically sound. List Price: $34.95

THE FUNCTION GAME

Muse Software

System Requirements

Tested on:
Apple II +, 48K memory, disk drive, TV or monitor

Also available (but not tested):
Apple IIc
Apple IIe
Apple II, 48K memory, Applesoft

Recommended Target Group

Mathematics, grades 7-12

Content

This is a one-player game program to drill recognition of functions from their graphs. It is also a teaching program in which an instructor may plot one or more functions atop one another. Algebraic, logarithmic, and trigonometric functions are included. Functions are provided in table form and graph form for the player to identify. Once the form of the function is identified, the specific parameters are to be entered.

Comment

The program is recommended for remediation and review as well as for classroom instruction. The graphics are excellent. The program contains material from the simplest linear graphs through hyperbolic trigonometric functions. Hints can be requested as needed. Points are awarded; running average is kept; three errors end a game. One reviewer noted that the program is so time flexible that it could be used for over four hours without using all functions. List Price: $39.95.

RATIOS AND PROPORTIONS

Milton Bradley Company

System Requirements

Tested on:
Apple II, 48K memory, disk drive, TV or monitor, Applesoft, DOS 3.3

Also available (but not tested):
Apple II +
Apple IIe

Recommended Target Group

Mathematics/Algebra, grades 9-12

Content

This supplementary drill and practice program for the study of ratios and proportions progresses through five skills: (1) writing ratios in context, (2) writing proportions in context, (3) solving stated proportions, (4) solving proportions in context, (5) writing and solving proportions in context.

Comment

The program is recommended as particularly effective in breaking down a task into subtasks. To maintain students' interest, the program provides graphics, scoring, sound, personalization, animation, and variation of computer responses. Students' records are stored, but no print option is available. Software cannot be terminated except at the end of the lesson. Teacher interaction is required to progress from one phase to another. It should also be noted that the problem description disappears from the screen while the student is still in the process of solving the problem. Teacher's manual is readable and accurate. List Price: $49.95

Mathematics/Comprehensive

KRELL'S COLLEGE BOARD SAT EXAM PREPARATION

See review, Secondary, Miscellaneous, page 53.

Mathematics/General Math

ELEMENTARY MATHEMATICS

(two products available separately)

Sterling Swift

System Requirements

Tested on:
Apple II +, 48K memory, disk drive, TV or monitor, DOS 3.3, paddles, printer

Mathematics/General Math (continued)
Elementary Mathematics (continued)

Also available (but not tested):
Apple II, 48K memory, Applesoft

Comment
For both programs, the documentation provides a full description of the instructional design of the courseware. Instructions to the teacher are complete and easy to read. A diagnostic placement test determines the ability of each entering student, and the results of this test form the basis of a continuing lesson prescription for each student. A mastery test is given at the end of each lesson, the results of which update the learning prescription for each student. The teacher can view and/or print out the progress and learning prescriptions of students by using the management diskette provided. The management disk will provide for the records of five classes with up to 40 students each. All lessons begin by showing in detail how to solve at least one sample problem; then several drill problems are presented. An incorrect response results in a review of the teaching directions for the problem. A quiz and automatic check-off are provided to reward and record lesson mastery. Each lesson can be studied numerous times without fear of repetition. A game disk included with each product provides both an educational and a motivational review of the math skills treated in the package. Reviewers recommend these two products as among the best math programs available. Note that *the programs are available in a Spanish Language edition.*

Whole Numbers
Recommended Target Group
Math skills fall in a range for grades 2-5. Because this is a complete math review of whole numbers including a management program that promotes the use of individualized instruction, this group of programs may be most appropriate in a junior or senior high school remedial or special education math course. A multigrade or diverse elementary class may also be a good placement.
Content
Four programs contain 22 lessons in increasing levels of difficulty. They present the concepts and skills of addition, subtraction, multiplication, and division of whole numbers. They follow the same content and sequencing as the programs in *The Arithmetic Classroom* (See review, page 19). List Price: $495.95

Fractions and Decimals
Recommended Target Group
Math skills fall in a range for grades 7-9. Because this is a complete math review of fractions and decimals including a management program that promotes the use of individualized instruction, this group of programs may be most appropriate in a senior high school remedial or special education math course.
Content
Four programs contain 18 lessons in increasing levels of difficulty. They present the concepts and skills of addition, subtraction, multiplication, and division of fractions and decimals. They follow the same content and sequencing as the programs in *The Arithmetic Classroom* (See review, page 19). List Price: $495.95

Mathematics/Geometry

BUMBLE PLOT

See review, Elementary, Mathematics, page 21.

GOLF CLASSIC AND COMPUBAR

See review, Elementary, Mathematics, page 24.

RENDEZVOUS

Edu-Ware Division/Peachtree Software, Inc.

System Requirements
Tested on:
Apple II+, 48K memory, disk drive, TV or monitor, DOS 3.3, joystick (optional)

Also available (but not tested):
Apple II, 48K memory, Applesoft
Apple IIe

Recommended Target Group
Mathematics/Geometry, early teens through adult
Content
Simulating a space flight mission, the program uses mathematics and natural physics laws to guide the student through four phases of a mission: (1) "Earth Lift-Off," (2) "Orbital Rendezvous," (3) "Approach," and (4) "Alignment and Docking."
Comment
The program is recommended as supplementary material for high school math and physics courses and above, especially in the use of vectors and geometry as well as flight mechanics of the shuttle. For junior high students the program can be used as a game. The program can be saved and restarted. Function keys are clearly shown in the student guide. Cues are present in graph form on the screen. The student guide (flight manual) gives sufficient explanation on how to operate the courseware but is limited in the installation instructions. Objectives are implied, rather than stated. The computer provides the logical tool to reach the objectives through instant feedback and the use of graphics and color to motivate students. List Price: $39.95

Mathematics/Statistics

GOING TOGETHER

Micro Power & Light

System Requirements

Tested on:
Apple II+, 48K memory, disk drive, TV or monitor, DOS 3.3

Also available (but not tested):
Apple II, 48K memory, Applesoft
Apple IIe

Recommended Target Group

Mathematics/Statistics, high school or above

Content

This drill and practice program reviews statistical concepts and emphasizes scatterplots and correlation coefficients.

Comment

This courseware is highly recommended as extensive practice with scatterplot and correlation coefficients. The program checks understanding in different ways before introducing new concepts. Although the program is recommended as technically sound and useful for instruction, it should be noted that there is little documentation either for the student or for the teacher. List Price: $29.95

NORMAL DEVIATIONS

Micro Power & Light

System Requirements

Tested on:
Apple II+, 48K memory, disk drive, TV or monitor, DOS 3.3

Also available (but not tested):
Apple II, 48K memory, Applesoft
Apple IIe

Recommended Target Group

Mathematics/Statistics, high school or above

Content

For use with introductory statistics, this tutorial and drill and practice program explores the normal curve and standard scores, and their relationship to each other. It also includes experimentation with standard z scores.

Comment

The program is highly recommended for the introductory statistics student. The examples are relevant, clear, and mathematically sound. Students are given ample opportunity to perform at their own pace and with the option of review and/or testing. It should be noted that the teacher's manual is weak and that further documentation would be helpful. List Price: $29.95

OFF LINE

Micro Power & Light

System Requirements

Tested on:
Apple II+, 48K memory, disk drive, TV or monitor, DOS 3.3

Also available (but not tested):
Apple II, 48K memory, Applesoft
Apple IIe

Recommended Target Group

Mathematics/Statistics, high school or above

Content

The program presents a detailed, step-by-step, interactive approach to regression, how correlation and regression are related, how to use the regression equation for measuring xy relationships, and how to draw a regression line in a scatterplot of x and y score pairs.

Comment

This program is recommended as mathematically sound and thoroughly developed in meeting its instructional objectives. The language may be too advanced for some students unless they have had previous preparation in the required vocabulary. The program is especially recommended for graduate students taking a required statistics course. List Price: $29.95

Music/Art

PICTURE WRITER

See review, Elementary, Music/Art, page 29.

SONGWRITER

See review, Elementary, Music/Art, page 29.

Personal Skills Development

ANALYZING AN AD

MCE, Inc.

System Requirements

Tested on:
Apple IIe, 48K memory, disk drive, TV or monitor

Personal Skills Development (continued)
Analyzing An Ad (continued)

Also available (but not tested):
Apple II, 48K memory, Applesoft
Apple II +, 48K memory

Recommended Target Group
Personal Skills Development, ages 16 and up (special education)

Content
The program is designed to develop skills in reading and understanding advertisements. Types of ads and advertisers are presented, as well as steps to take in breaking down exactly what a given ad is attempting to accomplish. Following instruction, students may interact with the application phase of the program during which they design and critically analyze their own ads.

Comment
The program allows the teacher to choose a reading level of either grades 5-6 or grades 2-3. This option makes the program appropriate for special education, secondary level students, rather than for regular students. The program operates smoothly and interesting graphics support the program's intent. The teacher's manual is well-written and clear. The program is an effective use of the computer for individualizing instruction through the two reading levels. List Price: $44.95.

JOB SURVIVAL SERIES

MCE, Inc.

System Requirements
Tested on:
Apple II +, 48K memory, disk drive, TV or monitor (color recommended)

Also available (but not tested):
Apple IIe, 48K memory, Voice Input Module (if used by physically handicapped)

Recommended Target Group
Personal Skills Development, English as a Second Language (ESL), and Special Education, ages 16 and up.

Comment
All three programs in this series are recommended for the adolescent special education student preparing to seek a first job. The instructor can run the program at a fifth to sixth grade reading level or at a second to third grade reading level, and adjust the speed with which the words appear on the screen. In the lower reading level all difficult words (three or more syllables) are divided into syllables to assist the slow learner in comprehending the words. More material is provided for the lower reading level than for the higher reading level. The teacher's manual clearly explains the running of the program. There are excellent worksheets to aid the student in reading the words to be encountered in the programs. Two points should be noted: (1) The "First Day on the Job," partially a summary, may seem somewhat repetitive of the other two disks. (2) The suggested voice input module for physically handicapped students was not tested. The programs are most useful for two

Job Survival Series (continued)

groups of students: (1) special education, and (2) ESL (English as a Second Language) students just learning English. List Price Each: $44.95; List Price Series: $119.95.

FIRST DAY ON THE JOB
Content
This third disk in the series provides a summary of the preceding two programs. It offers both an instruction and an application phase in the higher reading level and an instruction phase to the lower reading level. The program is designed to provide information about how to prepare for and what to expect the first day on the job. Instruction covers: (1) ways to organize oneself before reporting to work; (2) information introduced and defined during the first days of work; (3) stressful situations that can occur in a work environment; (4) techniques for handling stressful situations.

PERSONAL HABITS FOR JOB SUCCESS
Content
This program allows the students to choose among four different jobs and interact with situations relating to these occupations. It provides information about and experience in making personal choices on the job. Through the selection of behaviors, students learn that job success is the result of many factors including proper dress, punctual attendance, attitude towards peers and supervisors, and job responsibilities.

WORK HABITS FOR JOB SUCCESS
Content
This program provides instruction and simulation designed to demonstrate the effect of work habits on performance and ultimate success. Student responses to typical job situations are discussed. The specific work habits defined, discussed, and exemplified in the program include: cooperation, appearance, accuracy, attitude, attendance, company politics, and job responsibility.

LEARNING IMPROVEMENT SERIES
(four titles available together or separately)

MCE, Inc.

System Requirements
Tested on:
Apple II, 48K memory, Applesoft, disk drive, TV or monitor

Also available (but not tested):
Apple II+

Recommended Target Group
Language Arts (English)/Thinking Skills, and Social Science; grades 5-9; grades 6-10 Special Education.

Comment
Each program is recommended as having a well-conceived instructional design. There is effective branching to easier or more difficult problems, depending on student responses. Directions are presented clearly and concisely in both the teacher's manual and the software program. The teacher's

Personal Skills Development (continued)
Learning Improvement Series (continued)

manual provides the option for two levels: Concept Development Level (CDL) and Simplified Concept Developmental Level (SCDL), which is especially appropriate for the slow learner. The level and the speed of presentation can be preselected by the teacher or the counselor. The teacher's manual also includes necessary vocabulary for introducing material, various teaching strategies, evaluation suggestions, and excellent supplementary worksheets for reproduction. The package is highly recommended both for teachers and for counselors. It should be noted that teacher assistance may be required with some younger students. List Price Series: $154.00; Back Up Disks: $60.00. List Price Each: $44.95; Back Up Disk: $17.50.

EFFECTIVE STUDY SKILLS: A LEARNING STYLE APPROACH
Content

This program covers auditory, visual and multisensory learning styles. Each user of this program can, via either level, learn to improve study efforts by using proven methods. In addition, the program is designed to determine the user's primary learning modality(ies) and teach effective techniques based on the assessed learning style.

FOLLOWING WRITTEN DIRECTIONS
Content

This program teaches the required skills and provides practice through a progressively more difficult series of games. It is designed to assist the student with reading, analyzing, and organizing information in order to follow directions accurately. While the Application Phase of this program is primarily designed for students with reasoning skills at the CDL level and above, the game is accessible to all the students who successfully complete the CDL Instructional Phase.

IMPROVING YOUR MEMORY
Content

This program teaches techniques of recall, visualization, and association with practice in memorizing words, numbers, and shapes. It is designed to assist the student in gaining knowledge in both general and specific memory methods, as well as to provide practice in using the methods presented in memorizing visual material.

STRATEGIES FOR TEST TAKING
Content

This program provides pointers and practice in taking true-false, multiple choice, fill-in-the-blank, short answer, and essay tests. It is designed to take the student from preparing and studying for a test through the actual skill and techniques required for successfully taking these various types of tests.

MANAGING YOUR TIME

MCE, Inc.

System Requirements
Tested on:
Apple II, 48K memory, Applesoft, disk drive, TV or monitor

Also available (but not tested):
Apple II+

Recommended Target Group
Language Arts (English)/Thinking Skills, and Social Science; grades 5-9; grades 6-10 Special Education

Content
This program provides instruction and experiential practice in effectively managing one's time. Topics include ways in which time is wasted; how to make a list of jobs to be done; how to prioritize and plan time use; and how to finish on time.

Comment
Directions are presented clearly in both the teacher's manual and the software program. The teacher's manual gives the option for two levels: Concept Development Level (CDL) or Simplified Concept Development Level (SCDL), which is especially appropriate for the slow learner. Level and speed of presentation can be preselected by the teacher. Graphics are used effectively for reward on CDL and for reinforcement on SCDL. The teacher's manual is written from the perspective of a teacher and is especially helpful. The student is made aware of objectives at the beginning of the program and reviews these objectives at the conclusion. The sequencing of skills necessary for schedule planning is well presented so that as a concluding activity a student can develop his/her own schedule for a day. List Price: $44.95; Back Up Disk, $17.50.

Science/Biology

BIOLOGY SERIES

(four titles available separately)

Thoroughbred/SMC Software Systems

System Requirements
Tested on:
IBM PC, double-sided disk drive, DOS 2.0, color monitor

Recommended Target Group
Science/Biology, grades 7-12

Comment
These programs are recommended as an excellent package to aid the teacher in high school biology. It can be used to supplement a course, or the teacher may wish to assign additional laboratory work and readings to supplement the package. Color and graphics are used with sound educational purpose. Time is user-controlled. Screen displays are neat, readable, and correct. The teacher's manual describes how to boot the diskette for the initial use, then how to run the program and how to

Science/Biology (continued)
Biology Series (continued)

shut down the computer system. The instructional design is sound: the program provides the learner with basic information; an experiment or demonstration provides further learning situations; a quiz is administered, and, if the student passes, the next section may be started. It should be noted that a color monitor and a double-sided disk drive are required. A final test will be included with an educational version, which is not yet available. List Price Each: $49.94.

EXPLORING THAT AMAZING FOOD FACTORY, THE LEAF

Content

This package consists of two diskettes: (1) "Looking Inside a Leaf" contains four topics: (a) "Exploring New Ideas," (b) "Transport in the Leaf," (c) "Structure in the Leaf," (d) "Measuring Your Progress." (2) "The Leaf as a Chemical Factory" contains four topics: (a) "Exploring New Ideas," (b) "Photosynthesis and the Leaf," (c) "Stomate Action in Gas Exchange," and (d) "Measuring Your Progress."

THE FASCINATING STORY OF CELL GROWTH

Content

This package consists of two diskettes: (1) "How Does Your Cell Grow?" contains four topics: (a) "Exploring New Ideas," (b) "Surface Area/Volume of Cells," (c) "Experimenting With the Size of Cells," (d) "Measuring Your Progress." (2) "One Cell — Presto! — Two Cells" contains four topics: (a) "Exploring New Ideas," (b) "Chromosomes in Cell Division," (c) "Stages of Mitosis," (d) "Measuring Your Progress."

HOW PLANTS GROW: THE INSIDE STORY

Content

This program consists of five topics on one diskette: (1) "Growth," (2) "Root Tip of the Plant," (3) "Stem Cross Section," (4) "Terminal Bud," (5) "Plant Hormones."

PHOTOSYNTHESIS: UNLOCKING THE POWER OF THE SUN

Content

This program consists of four topics on one diskette: (1) "Light as Energy for Plants," (2) "Variables and Controls," (3) "Characteristics of Lights," (4) "Wavelengths of Light Used by the Chloroplasts."

DATA LOGGING AND GRAPHICS DISPLAY SYSTEM

See review, Applications, Educational Formats/Multisubject. page 64.

NUTRI-BYTES

Center For Science In The Public Interest

System Requirements

Tested on:
Apple II+, 48K memory, disk drive, TV or monitor, printer (optional)
IBM PC

Also available (but not tested):
Apple II, 48K memory, Applesoft
Apple IIe

Recommended Target Group

General Science, Health, Biology, Home Economics; grades 6-12.

Content

This program provides supplementary instruction in nutrition. It consists of quizzes and questionnaires. The first exercise analyzes the individual user's diet. From this the program moves to current concepts about nutrition.

Comment

Rather than being a complete program in nutrition, this package provides an "awakening" in the user to apply some basic principles of nutrition to his/her own diet. Throughout, the program provides information in an entertaining, useful, and interesting manner. Both audio and video "extras" are unique and add interest. The individualized diet analysis is especially effective. It should be noted that the disk contains several programs, each of which requires about 35 minutes for an average middle school student to do. List Price: $39.95.

Science/Chemistry

CHEMISTRY SERIES

(two titles available separately)

Thoroughbred/SMC Software Systems

System Requirements

Tested on:
IBM XT, disk drive, color monitor

Also available (but not tested):
Other IBM computers, 64K memory

Recommended Target Group

Science/Biology, grades 9-12

Comment

These programs are outstanding in their use of graphics for concept development. The educational design used to instruct is excellent. After vocabulary words are introduced and an unscramble activity is accomplished for subsequent reinforcement, new information is graphically presented and illustrated, and then sets of review/application are presented. The review is extensive, and the user has the option to return to the menu. It should be noted that there is additional material for the teacher's manual supplied on an information sheet; it emphasizes program functions and educational intent. List Price Each: $49.95.

Science/Chemistry (continued)
Chemistry Series (continued)

THE HOW'S AND WHY'S OF MIGRATING MOLECULES

Content

The package consists of two diskettes: (1) The first is concerned with the concept of osmosis. An interactive tutorial allows the user to analyze osmosis-related graphs and gain facility with the vocabulary and concepts of osmosis. The program is divided into four parts, each with its own summary quiz: (a) vocabulary, (b) transport through a membrane, (c) equilibrium and osmosis, and (d) a summary exam. (2) The second diskette is concerned with the process of diffusion. The program contains four parts, each with its own summary quiz: (a) vocabulary, (b) the structure of molecules, (c) the process of diffusion, and (d) a summary exam. It should be noted that some teachers may wish to use diskette #2 before diskette #1.

MOLECULES AND ATOMS

Content

The package contains two diskettes: (1) The first is concerned with the atom and the concepts of protons, neutrons, electrons, orbits, formulas, atomic structure, and charges. The program is divided into five parts, each with its own summary quiz: (a) vocabulary, (b) the concept of atoms and molecules, (c) the Bohr model, (d) drawing atoms, and (e) a summary exam. (2) The second diskette develops and reinforces the concept and rules of ionic bonding. The program consists of four parts, each with its own summary quiz: (a) vocabulary and new concepts, (b) ions, (c) ionic bonding, and (d) a summary exam.

DATA LOGGING AND GRAPHICS DISPLAY SYSTEM

See review, Applications, Educational Formats/Multisubject, page 64.

INTRODUCTION TO GENERAL CHEMISTRY

COMPress Division/Wadsworth, Inc.

System Requirements

Tested on:
Apple II+, 48K memory, disk drive, TV or monitor, (color recommended)

Also available (but not tested):
Apple IIe

Recommended Target Group
Science/Chemistry, grades 9-12

Content
Eight disks provide lessons on almost every topic included in general chemistry: (1) "The Elements," (2) "Inorganic Nomenclature," (3) "Chemical Formulas and Equations,"

Introduction to General Chemistry (continued)

(4) "Atomic Weights," (5) "Percent Composition," (6) "Chemaze" (game), (7) "Ideal Gases" (gas laws), (8) "pH: Acids and Bases in Water."

Comment

Much flexibility in the program makes this package a strong, individualized review of basic general chemistry. The topics are consistent with most general chemistry courses and stress those areas that students seem to have the most difficulty with, i.e., memorization and problem solving. The ability of the program to accept most or all versions of the correct answer is a welcome feature. Teachers will appreciate that the program will only accept answers if both the number and the unit are correct. The most promising usage of this program will probably be for those students who need reinforcement in specific topics or students who were absent and need to make up instruction. Because each lesson is brief, this program will not take the place of the textbook but should prove to be a worthwhile supplement for instruction of general chemistry. List Price: $470.00.

Science/General

DATA LOGGING AND GRAPHICS DISPLAY SYSTEM

See review, Applications, Educational Formats/Multisubject, page 64.

ECO-PARADISE

Center For Science In The Public Interest

System Requirements

Tested on:
Apple II, 48K memory, disk drive, Applesoft, TV or monitor, printer (optional)
IBM PC

Also available (but not tested):
Apple IIe

Recommended Target Group
General Science, Social Science, Home Economics; grades 6-12.

Content
The program consists of a game and a test that rates the user on his/her impact on the environment. Through question and answer format, the user is presented with a wide range of ecological information with the objective of producing an ecologically aware and responsible citizen.

Science/General (continued)

Eco-Paradise (continued)

Comment

Reviewers found the program to be informative and interesting in the presentation of ecological issues and the evaluation of the user's personal effect on the environment. Some questions require pre-existing knowledge of the user; without that, considerable trial and error will be needed. Nevertheless, the format allows for some second tries. List Price: $39.95.

NUTRI-BYTES

See review, Secondary, Biology, page 46.

Science/Physics

APPLE PHYSICS

Micro Power & Light

System Requirements

Tested on:
Apple IIe, 48K memory, disk drive, TV or monitor, DOS 3.3

Also available (but not tested):
Apple II, 48K memory, Applesoft
Apple II+, 48K memory

Recommended Target Group

Science/Physics, secondary and postsecondary

Content

This program contains a simulation of the monkey-and-the-hunter problem, an illustration of simple harmonic motion, and a pendulum demo from which the pendulum length can be calculated.

Comment

The projectile motion simulation is particularly clear and entertaining. The simple harmonic motion illustration is clear and concise. The pendulum demonstration is good except for lack of directions for recovery and exit. Also note that the pendulum period, given as 18.5 seconds, is actually 17 seconds, and this affects the given answer. While recommending the package, reviewers noted that teacher instruction, objectives, and curriculum issues are treated very briefly. List Price: $34.95

DATA LOGGING AND GRAPHICS DISPLAY SYSTEM

See review, Applications, Educational Formats/Multisubject, page 64.

PHYSICS: ELEMENTARY MECHANICS

Control Data Corporation

System Requirements

Tested on:
Apple II+, 48K memory, disk drive, TV or monitor, DOS up through 3.3

Also available (but not tested):
Atari 800, 48K memory, disk drive, DOS up through 2.0
Texas Instruments 99/4A, 32K memory expansion, disk drive, PLATO Interpreter Cartridge

Recommended Target Group

Science/Physics, secondary and postsecondary

Content

Eight exercises provide practice in the reasoning skills necessary to solve problems in elementary mechanics. The student must determine what information and concepts are necessary to answer the question posed in the exercise. The program provides a calculator function to assist in computations, a help function, a list of formulas, and answers to students' typed-in questions.

Comment

Reviewers recommend this very easy-to-use supplementary program for students with a background in basic physics. Teachers should be aware that student documentation materials are very abbreviated, particularly in relation to operating the computer program.

Educational Version: List Price: $70.00
Consumer Package: List Price: $59.95

RENDEZVOUS

See review, Secondary, Mathematics/Geometry, page 42.

Social Science

ECO-PARADISE

See review, Secondary, Science/General, page 47.

GAME OF THE STATES

See review, Elementary, Social Science, page 29.

Social Science (continued)

MEDALIST SERIES:

(four programs available separately)

Hartley Courseware, Inc.

System Requirements

Tested on:
Apple IIe, 48K memory, disk drive, TV or monitor, DOS 3.3

Also available (but not tested):
Apple II, 48K memory, Applesoft
Apple II+, 48K memory
Franklin ACE 1000 48K memory

Recommended Target Group

Social Science; optimal, grades 7-9; remedial, grades 10-12; enrichment, grades 5-6.

Comment

These programs have value as support in courses involving an overview of the subject. The gaming technique is effective in motivating and challenging learners. Pace is user-controlled in a timeframe that would be realistic for school use. Feedback is provided, and the programs are user friendly. An attractive feature is the program's adaptability, allowing the teacher to program additional clues and information. This compensates for some content that teachers might find trivial or unimportant, the one major flaw reviewers found. List Price: $39.95.

BLACK AMERICANS

Content

The game requires a student to identify Black Americans from clues, such as dates, background, and achievements. It can be used to reinforce a unit on Black history or a larger course in American history.

CONTINENTS

Content

The game requires a student to identify a continent or an ocean. It reinforces knowledge about world geography. Student uses clues until the correct identification can be made.

STATES

Content

The game requires a student to identify a state by using such clues as shape, date of entry into the union, major agricultural products, etc.

WOMEN IN HISTORY

Content

The game requires a student to identify great women in world history. It can be used for collecting research information about women in history.

Special Education

ANALYZING AN AD

See review, Secondary, Personal Skills Development, page 43.

FINANCING A CAR

MCE, Inc.

System Requirements

Tested on:
Apple II+, IIe, 48K memory, disk drive, TV or monitor

Also available (but not tested):
Apple II, 48K memory, Applesoft

Recommended Target Group

Special Education, grades 9-12

Content

This tutorial program is designed to teach the basics of credit purchasing. At the Concept Development Level (CDL), the student is expected to compare various annual percentage rates and terms and to evaluate their effects on monthly and total car payments. The lower Simplified Concept Development Level (SCDL) stresses a basic understanding of credit financing. The application phase assists students in making decisions about car financing.

Comment

This program is recommended for special education high school students who are preparing to buy their first car. The CDL level is designed for a reading level of grades 5-6; the SCDL level for grades 2-3. There is a clear progression from concept development to application. The manual is clear and useful, and there are useful suggestions for the teacher. All information necessary to run the program is on the disk except for a teacher option to control speed and set level. It should be noted that a teacher may wish to provide additional information about Blue Book value and to teach information about repossession. List Price: $44.95.

Comment

The space style game format is highly motivational, and the program is effective even with young children in the third grade, as well as older students who want to improve their typing skills. The option to create additional lessons is especially helpful. The manual is clearly written and easy for the beginner to follow. List Price: IBM, $49.95; others, $39.95.

JOB SURVIVAL SERIES

See review, Secondary, Personal Skills Development, page 44.

Technology/ Computer Science

A COMPUTER IS:

Micro Power & Light Co.

System Requirements

Tested on:
Apple II + , 48K memory, disk drive, TV or monitor, DOS 3.3

Also available (but not tested):
Apple II, 48K memory, Applesoft
Apple IIe, 48K memory

Recommended Target Group
Technology/Computer Science, grades 7 and above

Content
This tutorial program illustrates terms, devices, shapes, and sizes of computers. It provides basic definitions, describes computer architecture (how to build a computer), peripheral devices, and useful configurations.

Comment
The program is recommended as a useful introduction to computers and related vocabulary. A user ID number allows a student to put aside the program and then restart it later. The program is menu-driven with all instruction presented on the screen rather than in printed documentation. It should be noted that the program is a basic introduction with no test of mastery provided. Although its tutorial mode is similar to a paper text, it is appropriate to introduce the learner to the computer with the use of the computer's sound, color, and graphics for motivation. List Price: $34.95

COMPUTER CONCEPTS SERIES

(four titles in series)

Control Data Corporation

System Requirements

Tested on:
Apple II + , 48K memory, disk drive, TV or monitor, (color recommended), Applesoft, printer (optional)

Recommended Target Group
Technology/Computer Science, grades 8-adult.

Comment
This package of four modules can be used together or separately. Each module contains disks and a user's guide. There is also a teacher's manual containing technical operation information, course outlines, objectives, extension activities, and supplemental worksheets for some disks. This package is recommended as professionally programmed and packaged and educationally balanced. Screen displays are well presented and easy to read. Color graphics are appropriately used. The soft-

Computer Concepts (continued)

ware can be saved, restarted, or menu recalled. Help and review options are available, as are cues and prompts when needed. The instructional design is interactive throughout in a tutorial approach for individual, self-paced instruction. The programs are exceptionally user friendly. Two minor problems should be noted: (1) The delay between file loads, a programming language problem with Apple Pascal, is somewhat distracting. (2) There is an inconsistency from disk to disk in the required response, which was a conscious strategy of the publisher — initially to use a yes/no response and later to use Y/N responses. List Price Series: $180.00.

THE COMPUTER KEYBOARD
Content
The program guides the user step by step through the learning of the computer keyboard. In addition, computer-generated designs, designing and printing stationary, graphics, and animation are taught.

DATABASES
Content
This program presents the concept of using a database to store and handle information. The user is presented with visual displays and then is guided through the program. Terminology and applications of databases and database searches are presented.

FILES AND EDITING
Content
This program teaches the user how to create, name, add to, and delete files. It also teaches various editing features. The user will learn fundamental concepts of using files and fundamental tasks in word processing, including editing.

STORAGE AND MEMORY
Content
This program teaches the user how to introduce and store variables in the computer, as well as how to retrieve information from it. This instruction is accomplished by screen presentations with excellent graphics.

THE COMPUTER CURRICULUM GUIDE

See review, Applications, Educational Formats/Multisubject, page 64.

Technology/Computer Science (continued)

COMPUTER LITERACY

Control Data Corporation

System Requirements

Tested on:
Apple II + /IIe, 48K memory, disk drive, TV or monitor, DOS up through 3.3

Also available (but not tested):
Atari 800, 48K memory, DOS up through 2
Texas Instruments 99/4A, 32K memory expansion, PLATO Interpreter Cartridge

Recommended Target Group

Technology/Computer Science, junior and senior high students

Content

This historical introduction to computer literacy explores the evolution of computers, their applications, and their impact on people and society. It stresses objectives and vocabulary, and it maintains student records.

Comment

This program is highly interactive and recommended for the beginner. It contains a variety of examples, animated diagrams, questions, and games placed in a well-organized, interesting sequence. Qualified teacher guidance is needed to assist students in running the program.

Educational Version: List Price: $70.00
Consumer Package: List Price: $59.95

Technology/Data Base Management Systems (DBMS)

PERSONAL PEARL

See review, Applications, Data Base Management Systems, page 62.

Technology/ Programming Languages

THE COMPUTER CURRICULUM GUIDE

See review, Applications, Educational Formats/Multisubject, page 64.

DISCOVER BASIC

Sterling Swift

System Requirements

Tested on:
Apple IIe, 48K memory, disk drive, TV or monitor, DOS 3.3, printer (highly recommended)

Also available (but not tested):
Apple II, 48K memory, Applesoft
Apple II + , 48K memory

Recommended Target Group

Technology/Programming Languages; high school, college, and adult; also gifted and talented younger than high school

Content

This is a complete BASIC programming course. In eight units the programming concepts include: (1) "Output"; (2) "Input and Numeric Variables"; (3) "Decisions, Counting, Accumulating, and Error Checks"; (4) "Loops"; (5) "String Variables and Graphics"; (6) "Simulation"; (7) "Low Resolution Color Graphics"; and (8) "Lists and Arrays."

Comment

This self-timed course is so thorough and clear and is presented in so positive a manner that the learner should master BASIC. Complete instructions are given for user operation, and rewards and errors are noted and prompts given. The manual covers the use of the computer, disk, printer, and all software. The instructional design is computer tutorial with additional work recommended. A solution disk is provided for the teacher. The course can be used with equal success by students in classes and by independent learners (including teachers).
List Price: $74.95
Workbook: List Price: $5.95

HANDS ON BASIC

Edu-Ware Division/Peachtree Software, Inc.

System Requirements

Tested on:
Apple IIe, 48K memory, disk drive, TV or monitor, DOS 3.3

Also available (but not tested):
Apple II, 48K memory; Applesoft
Apple II + , 48K memory

Recommended Target Group

Technology/Programming Languages; postsecondary students who are not majors in computer programming, adults at the home computer, and selected high school students.

Content

This computer tutorial in BASIC is a complete course (one semester) in BASIC programming for the person inexperienced with computers. It covers both operating commands (computer) and program commands (writing program). It progresses through chapters on: (1) "Automatic Arithmetic," (2) "Computer Variables," (3) "Looping Around in HOB," (4) "Limited Looping," (5) "The READ/DATA/RESTORE Command Set," (6) "Inputs and Interactive Programming,"

Technology/Programming Languages
(continued)
Hands On Basic (continued)

(7) "Arrays," (8) "Other Ways of Branching," (9) "Getting Functional," (10) "Program Planning," (11) "Getting the Bugs Out." Also included are Appendices on various other items.

Comment

The manual is very helpful to the learner. If the student has the self-motivation to learn BASIC, this course can be the answer. The program is controlled by the user, who can take as much time as necessary to enter lines. The student may exit or start up the program at the beginning of any section (practice program). The student manual acts as a menu. Sound is used as a cue for some errors. Each output is compared with the manual for the correct answer. The program is strong in content and deals well with curriculum issues. List Price: $79.00

KRELL'S LOGO

See review, Elementary, Technology/Programming Languages, page 30.

KRELL'S TURTLE PAK

See review, Elementary, Technology/Programming Languages, page 31.

LET'S EXPLORE BASIC

Milton Bradley Company

System Requirements

Tested on:
Apple II +, 48K memory, disk drive, TV or monitor, DOS 3.3

Also available (but not tested):
Apple II, 48K memory, Applesoft
Apple IIe

Recommended Target Group

Technology/Programming Languages, junior high to adult

Content

This tutorial program provides both an overview of BASIC and instruction in how to program in BASIC. Additional practice is provided on side 2. Instruction progresses through "How To Talk To Computers," "Making Computers Remember," "Storing Words and Numbers," and "Putting It All Together."

Comment

The program is recommended as excellent instruction in BASIC. The tutorial design allows the user to control time by adjusting to the screen display and problem solving situations.

Let's Explore Basic (continued)

The manual provides instructions for the student to operate the program. Sound may be on or off, and function keys are clearly noted. Although the manual is brief, it does cover the content and objectives that the student is expected to master. List Price: $39.95

MBASIC-80

See review, Applications, Programming Languages, page 68.

THE TERRAPIN LOGO LANGUAGE

See review, Elementary, Technology/Programming Languages, page 31.

Miscellaneous

GO TO THE HEAD OF THE CLASS

Milton Bradley Company

System Requirements

Tested on:
Apple II +, 48K memory, disk drive, TV or monitor

Also available (but not tested):
Apple II, 48K memory, Applesoft
Apple IIe

Recommended Target Group

Miscellaneous, general information; Ages 8-adult; family play, school/peer group play

Content

This program is a computer version of a well-known popular board game in which up to three players move from desk to desk by correctly answering questions on general information, until they reach the head of the class.

Comment

This game is an interesting format for acquiring and testing general information. Three levels afford family play in which young members can compete with older at minimum disadvantage. The inexperienced user can run this game easily. The instructions are clear, and the program is user friendly. Note that no save, terminate, or restart options are provided. The unit is one game of approximately 15 minutes. List Price: $39.95

Miscellaneous (continued)

KRELL'S COLLEGE BOARD SAT EXAM PREPARATION

Krell Software Corporation

System Requirements

Tested on:
Apple II+, 48K memory, disk drive, TV or monitor, DOS 3.3, paddle

Also available (but not tested):
Apple IIe
Apple II, 48K memory, Applesoft
Acorn, 48K memory
TRS-80 Models III & IV
Atari 800XL, 48K memory
Commodore 64

Recommended Target Group

Miscellaneous, grades 11-12; "Test of Standard Written English" (TSWE) disks suitable for younger students; math, vocabulary, verbal skills

Content

The package consists of six disks with 1,000 questions per disk, covering math, vocabulary, verbal skills, and TSWE. Questions are provided in SAT format.

Comment

Reviewers recommend this package as meeting, with one exception, the stated aims of the series. These aims are to enhance performance on SAT Exams by providing both substantive experience with mathematical and verbal knowledge and practice with genuine mastery of the test taking skills provided. The major exception is that one-third of the math section, geometry, has no graphs. These would be necessary for thorough review. A management system would be highly desirable but will not be ready before the end of 1984. With these exceptions, the reviewers note major strengths. First, the manual and the program work well together to make accessing, understanding, and using the program an easy task. Second, the format of the user's manual and the layman's language are easily understood by the student. Third, the design of the program and the format of the material work to the benefit of the user by focusing on both content and skills needed for the SAT. List Price: $299.95

OWLCAT SAT PREPARATORY COURSE

Owlcat / Digital Research

System Requirements

Tested on:
IBM PC

Recommended Target Group

General (Mathematics and English); high school students preparing to take the SAT examination.

Content

The package includes all the areas in mathematics and English that a student will need in preparation for the SAT: (1)

Owlcat SAT Preparatory Course (continued)

"Synonyms," (2) "Theme Words and Antonyms," (3) "Analogies and Sentence Completion," (4) "Reading Comprehension," (5) "Algebra," (6) "Geometry," (7) "Geometric Figures and Quantitative Comparison," (8) "Diagnostic Disk," (9) "Standard Written English Disk."

Comment

This course is recommended for all students preparing for the SAT examination. It will work best when administered by a teacher, but can be used as a private tutor for students who must or want to work alone. Each disk is self-contained and provides simple operating instructions and content information. The user can operate the program without technical assistance; no additional instructions other than those provided are needed. It should be noted that there are certain errata, such as in the manual, page 111, #3, where the word "trapezoid" is incorrectly used; the correct word is "rectangle."

Some of Owlcat's unique and important features are as follows. The Learning Mode and the Drill Mode options allow for the creation of a desired learning atmosphere. A Time-Arrow Clock provides time constraint when selected. A particularly attractive option is the Review-of-Missed Question, which recalls incorrectly answered questions at the end of the lesson or test and demands that the student answer the question correctly on review. Dictionary and Manual options provide instant accessibility of background and supportive information. Encouragement Responses or Cheers provide motivation along the way. Additional motivation is provided by utilizing a gaming device in the Buddy Study feature, which allows a student to compete with another. The program asks questions alternately to each player, keeps score and time, and declares one person a winner. An electronic Scoreboard charts progress and graphically portrays percentile ranking. List Price: $249.95.

PSAT/SAT ANALOGIES

Edu-Ware Division/Peachtree Software, Inc.

System Requirements

Tested on:
Apple II+

Recommended Target Group

Miscellaneous, preparation for PSAT and SAT examinations in analogies; grades 9-12

Content

This preparatory courseware for the analogies section of the PSAT/SAT tests presents instruction on word relationships, word meanings, and testing conditions. A pretest, 2 post tests, and a record of scores aid the student in ascertaining his continuing deficiencies and/or progress. An appendix lists short definitions of the vocabulary tested in the program.

Comment

This well-written, easy to operate program offers the student significant help on analogy test items. Of particular effectiveness is the simulated times test section, the print-out of test results, and suggestions for additional work. Note that the diagram on page 9, however, is not what is seen on either disk under lesson selection. List Price: $49.00.

Miscellaneous (continued)

PSAT/SAT WORD ATTACK SKILLS

Edu-Ware Division/Peachtree Software, Inc.

System Requirements

Tested on:
Apple II+, 48K memory, disk drive, TV or monitor

Also available (but not tested):
Apple II, 48K memory, Applesoft
Apple IIe

Recommended Target Group
Miscellaneous, preparation for PSAT and SAT examinations in Word Attack; grades 10-12

Content
The student is presented with a series of multiple choice exercises grouped by roots or affixes for which either antonyms or synonyms can be chosen. The student selects either instructional or test mode. Review lessons follow each topic.

PSAT/SAT Word Attack Skills (continued)

Comment
The program is recommended as excellent for college bound students preparing for the PSAT/SAT examinations. The help, hints, rewards, and follow-up reinforce or restate the principle involved.
PSAT: List Price: $49.00
SAT: List Price: $49.00

WRITING SKILLS SERIES

See review, Secondary, English/Grammar-Composition, page 35.

POSTSECONDARY

Accounting

ACCOUNTING PEARL

(two titles available separately)

See review, Applications, Spreadsheets/Management Tools, page 68.

ACCOUNTING PLUS SERIES

(four titles available separately)

See review, Applications, Spreadsheets/Management Tools, page 69.

DATA LOGGING AND GRAPHICS DISPLAY SYSTEM

See review, Applications, Educational Formats/Multisubject, page 64.

FINANCIAL MANAGEMENT SERIES

See review, Applications, Spreadsheets/Management Tools, page 69.

PERFECT CALC

See review, Applications, Spreadsheets/Management Tools, page 72.

PERSONAL ACCOUNTING

See review, Applications, Spreadsheets/Management Tools, page 72.

STAR SYSTEM 1 — GENERAL LEDGER

See review, Applications, Spreadsheets/Management Tools, page 73.

Logic

REASONING: THE LOGICAL PROCESS

MCE, Inc.

System Requirements

Tested on:
Apple IIe, 48K memory, disk drive, TV or monitor

Also available (but not tested):
Apple II, 48K memory, Applesoft
Apple II+, 48K memory

Recommended Target Group
English/Thinking Skills, grades 9-Adult.

Content
This program is designed to help students develop and refine their reasoning skills to solve problems, make decisions, and analyze statements critically. Responses cover: (1) asserting a property, a relationship, and a pattern; (2) inductive and deductive reasoning; (3) hypotheses, probability, formal logic, premises, and conclusions.

Comment
This program is recommended as a supplement to a course on reasoning and logic. It is not a "stand alone" program because there are various concepts that would need teacher clarification. The instructional design is effective and uses graphics to clarify concepts. The documentation is very well-organized and clearly written. It should be noted that the concepts included in this package are difficult. Teachers should be aware of the necessity for class discussion and instruction required prior to use of the software. The vocabulary is especially difficult. List Price: $44.95.

Science/Chemistry

MOLECULAR ANIMATOR

COMPress Division/Wadsworth, Inc.

System Requirements

Tested on:
Apple IIe, 48K memory, disk drive, TV or monitor, (color recommended)

Recommended Target Group
Science/Chemistry, college chemistry and professional chemists.

Content
This program enables the advanced chemistry student to view, create, and manipulate three dimensional molecular structures. It contains three tutorials: (1) "Displaying a Shape,"

Molecular Animator (continued)
(2) "Cartesian Coordinate Files," (3) "Internal Coordinate Files." The first tutorial introduces the display routines along with the general features of the master menu. The second and third tutorials provide exposure to the two types of coordinate entry; in the second the file editor is introduced in detail.

Comment
The manual is complex and requires careful reading. The tutorials are very helpful in providing practice with program functions for advanced chemistry students. The program could also be useful as a demonstration tool for general chemistry students. However, the teacher using this program as a demonstration tool would need to spend several hours reading and reviewing the program as well as feeling competent with the subject matter of molecular structure. The user should be aware that the program is very useful and equally complex. List Price: $85.00.

Science/Physics

APPLE PHYSICS

See review, Secondary, Science/Physics, page 48.

DATA LOGGING AND GRAPHICS DISPLAY SYSTEM

See review, Applications, Educational Formats/Multisubject, page 64.

PHYSICS: ELEMENTARY MECHANICS

See review, Secondary, Science/Physics, page 48.

Statistics

GOING TOGETHER

See review, Secondary, Mathematics/Statistics, page 43.

Statistics (continued)

NORMAL DEVIATIONS

See review, Secondary, Mathematics/Statistics, page 43.

OFF LINE

See review, Secondary, Mathematics/Statistics, page 43.

STATPAK

See review, Applications, Spreadsheets/Management Tools, page 73.

Technology/Data Base Management Systems (DBMS)

PERFECT FILER

See review, Applications, Data Base Management Systems, page 61.

PERSONAL PEARL

See review, Applications, Data Base Management Systems, page 62.

Technology/ Programming Languages

CBASIC

See review, Applications, Programming Languages, page 67.

COMPUTER CONCEPTS SERIES

See review, Secondary, Technology/Computer Science, page 50.

DISCOVER BASIC

See review, Secondary, Technology/Programming Languages, page 51.

HANDS ON BASIC

See review, Secondary, Technology/Programming Languages, page 51.

LET'S EXPLORE BASIC

See review, Secondary, Technology/Programming Languages, page 52.

MBASIC-80

See review, Applications, Programming Languages, page 68.

"M" PASCAL COMPILER

See review, Applications, Systems Support, page 74.

MICROSOFT C COMPUTER SYSTEM AND PROGRAMMING LANGUAGE

Microsoft, Inc.

Uses in an Educational Environment
A person familiar with programming in C could use this program to write operating systems, text processing, and data base programs for purposes of educational administration. It can also be used for instruction in programming languages at the postsecondary level.

Technology/Programming Languages (continued)

Microsoft C Computer System and Programming Language (continued)

Experience Level
The documentation and manuals assume some familiarity with fundamental programming concepts, such as variables, assignment statements, loops, and functions. A computer beginner would find this a difficult language to learn with only the supplied documentation.

Content
C is a general purpose, high level programming language.

Comment
Programs written in C are often compatible, with few or no changes, with a variety of computers, including many mainframe computers. List Price: $500.00

Exceptions For IBM and other MS-DOS computers only. Call for availability on your equipment.

PERSONAL PEARL

See review, Applications, Data Base Management Systems, page 62.

Technology/Word Processing

EASYWRITER II

See review, Applications, Word Processing Systems and Utilities, page 76.

MULTITOOL WORD

See review, Applications, Word Processing Systems and Utilities, page 77.

PEACH TEXT 5000

See review, Applications, Word Processing Systems and Utilities, page 77.

PERFECT WRITER

See review, Applications, Word Processing Systems and Utilities, page 77.

Miscellaneous

FRENCH LANGUAGE VOCABULARY SERIES

Classroom Words
Vocabulary Builder

See review, Secondary, Foreign Language/French, page 37.

GERMAN LANGUAGE VOCABULARY SERIES

Classroom Words
Travel Words
Vocabulary Builder

See review, Secondary, Foreign Language/German, page 38.

INTRODUCTION TO POETRY

See review, Secondary, English/Grammar-Composition, page 34.

LE FRANCAIS PAR ORDINATEUR SERIES

See review, Secondary, Foreign Language/French, page 38.

SPANISH LANGUAGE VOCABULARY SERIES

Classroom Words
Travel Words
Vocabulary Builder
Vocabulary for Shopping Use

See review, Secondary, Foreign Language/Spanish, page 39.

SNOOPER TROOPS—CASE #1

See review, Secondary, English/Thinking Skills, page 37.

Applications Software

The Applications Software described in the Yellow Book will operate on all the computers listed below unless otherwise noted as an "EXCEPTION" in the product description:

CP/M based machines

Altos	Hewlett-Packard
Apple*	Northstar
Cromemco	Osborne
Epson	Superbrain
Heath/Zenith	Televideo

*Apple requires CP/M capability card, such as Microsoft's Softcard (see below), in order to use the applications software listed in this Catalog).

Applications Software (continued)

MS-DOS based machines

IBM PC	IBM compatible
TI Pro	

Other operating system based machines:

Apple	Commodore
Atari	Franklin Ace

Important: All products listed are available for other popula computers. If your computer is NOT listed, call: 800 632-6327. Be sure to include the make, model, and disk size c your microcomputer with your request.

Authoring Languages

An authoring language is computer software which allows a user who is not a programmer to develop educational programming on the computer. Through a series of formats, prompts, and parameters which are displayed to the user in English rather than a programming language, the software executes computer commands which in turn construct a learning sequence for a student. The purpose of an authoring language is to enable a teacher to develop his or her own computer-based educational (CBE) programs, without the necessity of first becoming an expert programmer.

PILOT

Commodore Business Machines, Inc.

Uses in an Educational Environment

Educators who have curriculum design skills but who do not have adequate programming skills can, with *Pilot*, increase

Pilot (continued)

their programming skills to a level required to autho courseware.

Experience Level

Prior experience in programming is not essential to operate th program; however, the greater the programming and cur riculum design skills of the user, the easier the learning and us of *Pilot* will be.

Content

Pilot is an authoring system (language) designed to assis educators to produce interactive computer lessons for use i their classes.

Comment

The Commodore version of *Pilot* contains features that use th unique capabilities of the Commodore 64. Users should b prepared to spend the time necessary to learn to use the systen prior to attempting the production of lessons for students. It i strongly recommended that a new user read the manual first then do the tutorial sequentially. List Price: $49.95

Exceptions For Commodore Only (color recommended)

TELE TALK

Datasoft, Inc.

Uses in an Educational Environment
Advanced computer students and instructors can find a whole world of information to retrieve and use for classroom work and individual research. Libraries can become more sophisticated in the quantity and quality of information they could provide students and staff.

Experience Level
This program is intended for "experts" who have a background in computer jargon and have a modem hookup to a computer network.

Content
This is a communication program that will connect one computer with another or with an information utility or data base through a modem. Through this program the computer, via telephone lines, can interact with information networks and

Tele Talk (continued)

communicate with other users. It permits the user to transmit, receive, store data, and even print out information. This provides access to information services, such as newspapers, magazines, electronic mail, banking, reservations, libraries, etc.

Comment
The scope of this product brings many outside information banks within easy grasp of one's own personal computer. By subscribing to a computer information service, the user extends the computer beyond the home, the classroom, the library, or the school. This package does permit an easy hookup and convenient menu-driven directions on the screen. It should be noted that although a glossary is provided, the terms are technical. Even the menu contains words like "BAUD," "Baud rate," "duplex," "time and cash clocks," and "host download." The beginner could become lost. List Price: $49.95.

Exceptions For Atari only

DATA BASE MANAGEMENT SYSTEMS

Data Base Management Systems (DBMS)

A DBMS provides the user with a sophisticated system capable of storing and retrieving records. These records can be changed or deleted, searched for particular information, and used to generate reports. Records can be individually found, examined, changed, and re-saved. Records can also be sorted for presentation on the screen or on a printer by a specially designed screen format.

Personnel files, equipment inventories, order invoices, mailing lists, and bibliographies are typical uses for a DBMS.

CLASS RECORDS

Learning Technologies

Uses in an Educational Environment
This applications software is a teacher utility for monitoring class attendance records and individual student progress in various subjects, especially in conjunction with *Supermath II* (see abstract page 28).

Experience Level
Computer beginner.

Content
This utility program is designed to be used with *Supermath II* and other programs yet to be developed by the manufacturer. With *Supermath II*, it can be used to offer drill and practice

Class Records (continued)

and problems to the student, to remediate based on answers, to quiz at the appropriate time, to prepare a student file on the disk concerning progress, grade, etc. The software then permits the teacher to retrieve the information. It can also be used with educational software designed by the individual teacher to interface with the utility package.

Comment
The documentation that is included is clearly written and easily understood by the computer beginner. Using the utility package also may not be practical for teachers who already have available a satisfactory computerized system of maintaining records. The program will be more valuable when the publisher has produced other educational software to use with it, or if teachers develop their own educational software to use with it. List Price: $89.95

Exceptions For Apple IIe only

COLLEGE SELECTION GUIDE

Peterson's Guides, Inc.

Uses in an Educational Environment
This package is useful for parents and students who are beginning to work on the college selection process. It can also be used as a team teaching project by a guidance counselor, who would provide an overview of the college selection process and

College Selection Guide (continued)

how to use the program, and by an English teacher, who could reinforce instruction in writing with exercises from the package.

Experience Level

Because of the clearly written instructions, simple commands, and the self-prompting nature of the program, it is very easy to use and is appropriate for users both experienced and inexperienced with computers.

Content

This data base includes a computer program for students and parents to help speed the college selection process by narrowing down from a pool of 1,700 colleges to 40 or fewer colleges. The program allows the user to select criteria that are important to her/him, such as location, cost, admission requirements, etc. As each criterion is entered, the list of remaining colleges is reduced. When the list of colleges is reduced to 40 or fewer, the user can get a hard copy of the schools with pages referenced to *Peterson's Guide* (print), where the list can be further reduced or refined after researching the referenced pages.

Comment

The program is easy to use and very helpful in the college selection process. Step-by-step instructions in the Counselor/Student manual are clearly written. Simple commands appear at the bottom of each screen to prompt the user about what the computer requires to continue running the program. Several features are particularly attractive: (1) the option of using the ''I'' (for information) while running the program, or reading the same information in the Counselor/Student Manual; (2) the fast speed at which the program runs; (3) the interactivity between the program and the printed *Peterson's Guide;* (4) the use of the printed guide after completion of the computer program to further narrow down college choices. Two cautions should also be noted: (1) an ''end message'' should appear at the top of the page after completing the last criterion, but it does not; (2) some invalid entries can result in either no computer response or a nonsense screen, which can only be corrected by turning off the machine and reloading the program. List Price: $145.00.

Exceptions For Apple II, II +, IIe only

THE COMPLETE IEP MANAGER STORAGE SYSTEM

Rocky Mountain Education Systems

Uses in an Educational Enviroment

The program can be used to determine the need for special education services, to develop and print staffing forms, and to develop and print finished Individualized Educational Plan (IEP) documents with goals and objectives.

Experience Level

The program requires little computer experience to operate. The manual is a clear tutorial of the features and their operation.

The Computer IEP Manager Storage System (continued)

Content

The user enters the desired IQ results, standardized test data, criterion reference results, and/or teacher estimate in one or more of 15 academic and social skill areas. The program will then chart and graph the assessment data and, by a preselected formula (one of five), determine in which tested areas a significant difference exists between the student's ability and performance. The program also suggests the starting level for the selection of the goals and objectives to be accomplished. At this point the user can print a four-page Staffing Guide to be used at an IEP development conference, annual review, or team meeting. A bank of 1600 measurable objectives is divided into 15 academic and social areas. The objectives are leveled from preschool to grade 6, with 16 objectives in each academic or social area. After the goals are selected, the program will print an IEP containing the federally required information.

If the user so chooses, the program will store the information on a blank floppy disk. A single disk will hold the IEP records of approximately 20 students for a six-year period. An exact amount of storage per disk cannot be stated because each IEP varies in length. This storage system also has an additional program for retrieving the data using an index that has the student's last name, first name, and grade on it.

Comment

The program is flexible, as it allows for the rewriting of the existing goals and for the addition of goals for each student. Levels of proficiency can also be added to the goals. The user can select the desired goals from as many of the academic and social areas and levels as desired. Customized IEP formats can be obtained from the publisher. The program executes well and contains many useful features. Adequate storage and records update capability make this program particularly useful for special education teachers and administrators. List Price: $439.50.

Exceptions For Apple II, II +, IIe only

dBASE II

Ashton-Tate

Uses in an Educational Environment

A school or small school district could use the program for such administrative functions as accounting, inventory control, job costing, order entry and invoicing, and mailing labels.

Experience Level

The documentation is clear and easily followed. Those who have had some programming experience or have previously used text editors will best be able to use the system.

Content

dBASE II is an interactive data management tool for constructing and manipulating numeric and character information files. It has its own program-building language. Records can be sorted, edited, and displayed directly, or menus and programs can be written to prompt operators.

Comment

dBASE II is best for an educator who works with large numbers

dBASE II (continued)

of records and will train support personnel to use the system. List Price: $700.00
Exceptions Not for Atari, Commodore, Osborne

EASYFILER

Information Unlimited Software

Uses in an Educational Environment
Administrative functions include creating and maintaining billing records, inventory records, and any other files.
Experience Level
Because the documentation is somewhat technical, *EasyFiler* will require a computer beginner to invest some time before being able to utilize the system fully.
Content
This data base management system provides rapid data entry/retrieval, multi-key record search, and a report generator. Records of up to 50 numeric or alphanumeric fields can be maintained with the system.
Comment
The program is menu-driven and has several tutorials to aid the beginner. To get full use of the program, a user needs a printer and a hard disk. List Price: $400.00
Exceptions For IBM Only

IMMUNIZATION DATA MANAGER (IDM)

Rocky Mountain Educational Systems

Uses in an Educational Environment
Schools or school districts can use this software to keep immunization records of students.
Experience Level
A person inexperienced with computers can operate this program.
Content
The program allows the recording of immunization data for up to 300 students per disk. The program will print non-compliance letters and yearly reports, and it can update reports.
Comment
The compliance requirements are placed in the program by state. The letters are standard. The program operates exactly as described in the manual. It should be noted that the program allows very little flexibility in the manipulation of the data in the files. Nevertheless, it is recommended for users who need the capability of this program. List Price: $125.00.
Exceptions For Apple II, IIe, only

INFOSTAR SYSTEM

Micropro International Corporation

Uses in an Educational Environment
For a school building or a school district not large enough to warrant the purchase of a mainframe computer but needing the power of a sophisticated data base management and reporting system.
Experience Level
This is not a program appropriate for a data base beginner because of the complexity and extent of documentation. Considerable time will be required to gain proficiency with the various features. The design of the forms requires understanding of the workings of a computer. However, once the form is designed, almost anyone who can use a keyboard can enter the data.
Content
The *InfoStar System* is a combination of two data base management and reporting programs, *DataStar* and *ReportStar,* which are also available separately. The combination of these two programs into one package is very useful because their true power comes from their combination. The *DataStar* program permits a user to set up a ''form,'' enter and manipulate various types of data. The *ReportStar* program creates a report designed by the user from any one or combination of fields. Extensive documentation in two notebooks and a training manual are included.
Comment
Reviewers note that in today's world of inadequate documentation this set of programs is refreshingly different. The documentation is several hundred pages long, filling three half-sized two-inch thick notebooks, and it is extremely comprehensive and readable. The *InfoStar System* is a superior product that nearly gives mainframe power to a microcomputer. After a bit of practice by the user, the *InfoStar System* should be able to meet virtually any data base need of a school district. List Price: $495.00
Exceptions Not for Altos, Atari, Commodore, Heath/Zenith, Hewlett-Packard

PERFECT FILER

Perfect Software, Inc.

Uses in an Educational Environment
Administrative uses for schools include creating and maintaining an inventory of equipment, student records, etc.
Experience Level
The tutorials, the command summary, and the menu-driven format make this program usable for the computer beginner after a few hours of practice.
Content
PERFECT FILER allows the user to create and modify data records and to add and delete individual data records to and from a data base. The program also allows the transfer of individual record data between data bases, as well as the genera-

Perfect Filer (continued)

tion of form letters, mailing labels, sorted lists, and reports. The system will do up to five consecutive sorts and allows 20 selective subsets for a single data base.

Comment

Users of *PERFECT WRITER* will find this program attractive because of the similarities between the programs. List Price: $595.00

Exceptions For Apple, Epson, IBM, Northstar, Superbrain, Televideo

PERSONAL PEARL

Pearlsoft Division/
Relational Systems International Corporation

Uses in an Educational Environment

This program can be used as a data base for individual schools to monitor inventory, cash distribution, attendance, or any other activity in which a large quantity of data needs to be monitored or recalled in an orderly fashion. It would also be appropriate for use in a vocational school setting or in a unit on data base use and implementation in a computer literacy course.

Experience Level

Computer beginners as well as advanced computer users.

Content

The program is a data base management system with three manuals. The *Easy Tutorial* presents everything the computer beginner needs to know to get started. First, one learns to set up an Address Book. As a result of doing this, the user will learn how to operate the system, design a data base form, design a report using the information entered into the data base, and produce a report. The *Advanced Tutorial* assists the user to construct a client information and appointment calendar. In the process, more advanced functions of the data base are discussed, including setting up a unique index, developing labels, sorting information, performing computations, locating information in a range, and updating data disks with program changes. The *Reference Manual* provides additional information for both tutorials.

Comment

The thorough documentation in the two manuals for beginners and advanced computer users makes this program useful for a wide range of groups within the educational setting. The manuals are written so well they can be used in lieu of a textbook. This package is very highly recommended. List Price: $295.00

Exceptions Not for Atari, Commodore, Heath/Zenith, Osborne, TI Pro

PHI BETA FILER

Scarborough Systems

Uses in an Educational Environment

This program can be used by administrators or by teachers as file management system for up to 250 files, and as a qui generator.

Experience Level

The documentation is easy to read, easy to follow, and com plete. It enables the program to be used by either a compute beginner or a computer expert.

Content

This package is a filing system that will hold up to 250 record per file and that contains a quizzing option for the teacher t use with students in any subject area. The program allows th user to select, add, delete, sort, print, find, and edit record and files.

Comment

This package is recommended as a versatile and easy to use too for keeping track of data or objects, and the quiz option is ver helpful. Graphs are in color; sound is available; and scree print is easy to read. List Price: $49.95.

Exceptions For Apple II, II+, IIe only

PUPIL INFORMATION PROFILER

Electronic Tabulating Corporation

Uses in an Educational Environment

This utility package permits student information to be entered into the computer for the purpose of generating reports. This i not a teacher directed package, but an administrative o counselor's package for monitoring a student's address schedule, advisor, etc.

Experience Level

The program can be used by and is designed for a compute beginner.

Content

This package is a restricted database system with predeter mined number and types of fields. It permits student informa tion to be entered and, upon request of the user, generate reports based on the student information.

Comment

The program is well-conceived and executed. The documenta tion is very easy to follow. The program is designed to interfac with the *EasyWriter* word processor, which enables the user t utilize all the word processor capabilities to enter/edit the stu dent data. (This feature has not been tested.) Also note tha the same functions can be performed with a data base manage ment system that is broader in scope than keeping studen records. List Price: $2,450.00

Exceptions For IBM Only

VISIFILE

Visicorp

Uses in an Educational Environment
Administrative functions include equipment inventories, class lists, etc.

Experience Level
Some experience using data base management systems and the IBM PC would be helpful.

VisiFile (continued)

Content
This package is a comprehensive electronic filing system to organize and maintain data. It will store, search, sort, retrieve, display, and calculate. It can also be used to print reports and mailing labels.

Comment
There is no tutorial program for beginners included. There is a VisiFile user group, which publishes a bulletin. List Price: $300.00

Exceptions For Apple, IBM only

EDUCATIONAL FORMATS/MULTISUBJECTS

Educational Formats/Multisubject

These programs are essentially highly structured, single purpose data bases. They allow the teacher to input data, such as words, letters, numbers, problems, colors and patterns, as well as questions and answers. The data base is applicable to a single purpose, such as testing, a particular game, or other structure of data presentation. The content which can be used within this structure is highly variable.

The purpose of these "educational formats" is to provide a teacher a very simple-to-use method for supplementing instruction with "customized" CBE (computer-based educational) exercises.

CLASSMATE

Davidson and Associates

Uses in an Educational Environment
This program is appropriate for the teacher who wants a computerized means to record and average grades, record attendance, and save comments.

Experience Level
This program can be used by a person inexperienced with computers.

Content
Classmate is a computerized replacement for the standard grade book. It allows the teacher to record and recall grades in both letter grade and percentage formats; to maintain and report attendance; and to save and recall brief comments using a predetermined set of abbreviations, original abbreviations, or written comments. Information may be recalled either for individuals or for entire classes; it may be called up for one entry or an entire set.

Comment
This program offers an advantage over most other programs, which operate by recording raw scores and thus predetermining

Classmate (continued)

weights for entries as they are recorded. Instead, *Classmate* allows the teacher to record either letter grades or percentages and to determine the weight of various entries after they have been accumulated. There is the further advantage of maintaining attendance and behavior records to be included with reports at the teacher's option. The program is user friendly, and one or two uses with the easily understood manual should suffice to make the user fully conversant with the various options. It is recommended that the program be used with a printer, and that two disk drives be used for ease and speed. List Price: $49.95.

Exceptions For IBM PC, Franklin ACE 1000, Apple II +, IIe only.

COLLEGE U.S.A.

Info-Disc Corporation

System Requirements
Tested on: Pioneer LD-V4000 laser videodisc player, color TV

Suggested Target Group
Counselors, students, parents; grades 11-12.

Content
This collection is a library of laser discs containing college recruiting messages, financial aid information, and other topics of interest to college-bound students. The disc contains scenes of college campus life not available in brochures and handbooks, interviews with college students and faculty, as well as tours of classrooms, dormitories, libraries, and laboratories. The information has been transferred to videodiscs from colleges' current recruiting films, video tapes, or slide shows. Presentations are from one to five minutes per college.

Comment
Student viewers of the system can request additional informa-

College U.S.A. (continued)

tion on any college in the country by completing and returning a postage-paid response card provided by the manufacturer. A two-track audio feature permits the message to be recorded and heard in two languages. The system is recommended for high school students and their parents in the college selection process. It assists colleges and universities in reaching large numbers of potential students through laser technology. A test group of selected high schools currently using the *College U.S.A.* system is available without charge. List Price Each: $59.95.

THE COMPUTER CURRICULUM GUIDE

Computer Learning Systems

Uses in an Educational Environment
This print package can be used as a curriculum guide or as a valuable resource for developing a curriculum. It can be used with a variety of computers.

Experience Level
The teacher is required to have very little computer experience to implement this fundamental curriculum about computers and programming in BASIC.

Content
This package is a curriculum guide for teaching computer literacy and BASIC programming at the beginning level. It has information for Apple, Commodore, and TRS 80 computers.

Comment
The curriculum guide is well done and easy to follow. It provides sample lesson plans, objectives, student and teacher glossaries, BASIC programs, related activities, student lesson materials, evaluation procedures, graphics, and a curriculum grade level matrix. The teacher would need to consider the grade level matrix in view of the students' readiness and available time. Implementation time lines would need to be set up. List Price: $395.00.

CREATE — INTERMEDIATE

Hartley Courseware, Inc.

Uses in an Educational Environment
This program enables teachers to develop multiple choice tests and CAI lessons of up to 20 questions. It is applicable to almost any subject area, with the exception of a subject requiring symbols not available on the computer.

Experience Level
Any teacher who has some computer experience should have little difficulty in implementing this program. Those already "computer shy" might not find it sufficiently user friendly.

Content
The program provides the format for the teacher to develop tests and lessons. It does not contain preprogrammed lessons with subject content.

Create-Intermediate (continued)

Comment
Documentation is presented in clear English, with no technical jargon, and directions are clear. The major limitation to be noted is the time required to input the data for the questions and responses, which may be greater than the teacher is willing to commit for the value it produces. This is a matter of individual choice. The program is highly recommended for teachers of small groups, e.g., tutorial, mentally or physically handicapped. List Price: $29.95.

Exceptions For Apple II +, 48K memory

DATA LOGGING AND GRAPHICS DISPLAY SYSTEM

Ohaus Scale Corporation

Uses in an Educational Environment
The program is best suited to the needs of a high school or college level, laboratory oriented chemistry or advanced biology course, where accuracy to the 1/100 of a gram is necessary. It is designed to store data and print results in graphic form.

Experience Level
Setting up a computer that does not already contain the necessary firmware (real-time clock and serial interface) requires moderate computer background since the installation of these boards is not covered in the software manual. Once the computer is set up, the one-time installation of the software is relatively easy. Although the user is guided through the execution of the various programs by a series of menus on the screen, much of this information is not included in the printed manual.

Content
This package contains three programs that are used in conjunction with a series "B" or "C" Ohaus Electronic Balance: (1) the "Big Digit Scale Program" displays the weight of the sample in 2 cm high characters (on a 12" monitor); (2) the "Sample/Graph Program" allows for the collection and bar-graphing of up to 15 data entries from the balance; (3) the "Time-Plot Program" will collect and graph data from the balance at time intervals (seconds to days) selected by the user.

Comment
This package is recommended as very useful for the indicated science classes. The most useful components are considered to be the continuous weight and time plot for conducting experiments and reporting the results. The display is updated about every five seconds, which is enough time for the balance to stabilize if the sample weight is changed. It should be noted that the display of the "Big Digit Scale" could be larger for easier reading. List Price: $155.00.

Exceptions For Apple II +, IIe, 64K memory, disk drive, TV or monitor, graphics printer (optional), real-time clock, serial interface card, "B" or "C" series Ohaus Electronic Balance.

DELTA DRAWING

Spinnaker Software

Uses in an Educational Environment
The program allows the user (teacher or student) to write programs using different designs, shapes, and/or patterns for a variety of purposes. It can be useful in art; mathematics, such as geometry; science, such as physics, organic chemistry, earth sciences; geography; and other subjects.

Experience Level
The manual leads the computer beginner step by step through the program, while an expert can use the summary as a text to complete the desired designs.

Content
The software allows the user to write a program to draw pictures involving different designs and patterns in color.

Comment
This program invites creativity. It enables the user to draw both simple and complex pictures (such as cartoons). It is highly recommended as a very useful tool in a variety of subjects. List Price: $49.95

Exceptions For IBM, Apple II, color TV or monitor only

DRILL BUILDER SERIES

(six titles available separately)

DLM Teaching Resources

Uses in an Educational Environment
Although each of the titles provides a sample drill and practice game with preprogrammed content in a particular subject area, the principal value of each program is in drill and practice created by the teacher to individualize instruction in different subject areas for students ages 8-11.

Experience Level
The documentation is so well written that a teacher who is a computer beginner can program the individualized content, and students inexperienced with computers can operate the programs easily.

Comment
These six packages provide a variety of game formats for highly motivational drill and practice exercises. The program design for each package is instructionally sound, as it allows the teacher to create a large variety of drill and practice activities. Work time and difficulty levels can be adjusted in a matter of seconds. A printout of all created programs and drill questions is easy to create and proves to be very helpful. List Price Each: $44.00.

ALIEN ACTION

Content
The sample game provided in the program assists students in practicing addition facts. During an invasion, alien spaceships containing problems move down the screen and attack the base station. The station's laser-equipped cannon at the bottom of the screen can shoot the answer at the spaceship. This program

Drill Builder Series (continued)
can also be programmed for other math activities, as well as language arts and other subjects.

ALLIGATOR ALLEY

Content
The sample game assists students in matching answers to the appropriate addition and subtraction facts. An apple with an addition or subtraction moves across the screen. The student tries to match an alligator containing the correct answer with the apple. Content can be programmed for other subject areas.
Exceptions For Apple II+, IIe, IBM PC only.

IDEA INVASION

Content
The sample game assists students in recognizing words representing the major parts of speech. "A.O." uses her magic ring to zap invading words descending from above her. The player must identify the word representing the part of speech for "A.O." to use. The teacher can program content for other subject areas.

MASTER MATCH

Content
The sample game provided in the program is a language arts/reading activity. It assists students in recognizing pairs of words representing antonyms. The word scope, a large diamond in the center of the screen, contains a word. The word is to be matched with one of the eight words in blue word stations in the four quadrants of the screen. This format can be used for other language arts activities, as well as math, social science, etc.

METEOR MISSION

Content
The sample game assists students in practicing multiplication facts. Eight large meteors containing problems come from all around the screen toward the star station. The player must aim the star station gun at a meteor and fire the correct answer to disintegrate the meteor. The program can be adapted to other subject areas.

WIZ WORKS

Content
The sample game assists students in spelling words most frequently misspelled. The wizard uses his magic wand to zap missing letters into a word that appears at the top of the screen. The player must select the letter that correctly completes the spelling word for the wizard to fire it into the word. The program can be adapted to other subject areas.

THE GAME SHOW

Computer Advanced Ideas

Uses in an Educational Environment
This package is basically a "shell" program, with which, through appropriate prompts, a teacher enters questions, correct answers, possible wrong answers, and responses which the

The Game Show (continued)

computer should give to students based on their answers. The format is adaptable to virtually any subject area.

Experience Level

A teacher who has had no previous experience with a computer could succesfully program new information because the instructions are so clear and complete.

Content

Within the established format, several sample games on the disk provide ''Password'' type clues for words in such subjects as: (1) ''Advanced Vocabulary,'' (2) ''Animals,'' (3) ''Algebra I,'' (4) ''Computer Terms,'' (5) ''Sailing Terms,'' (6) ''Constitution.''

Comment

The program is recommended because it allows the teacher to program the game to suit the needs of any subject and class. Some technical problems should be noted: (1) Conflicting instructions for start-up are given; turn on computer before inserting disk. (2) Program accepts some incorrect and rejects some correct answers if spacing is not perfect. List Price: $39.95

Exceptions For IBM, Commodore 64, Apple IIe only

GO TO THE HEAD OF THE CLASS

See review, Secondary, Miscellaneous, page 52.

MASTER MATCH

Computer Advanced Ideas

Uses in an Educational Environment

Content can be programmed into an existing format for games. Teachers of elementary grades can use this program with any subject area.

Experience Level

A computer beginner could follow the instructions to program new content in any subject area.

Content

The program is a one- or two-player game in which players select two-numbered boxes from a set of 6, 12, 18, 24, or 30 boxes, in the effort to match like boxes.

Comment

Simple problem solving and object relations skills are used along with memory of locations to earn points in a game based on matching an item with its counterpart. Success produces fireworks. It is recommended as an interesting game for young children. Detailed documentation explains how to run the program and how to create extra sets for any subject desired. Examples are given. Free back-up and one-year replacement are provided. List Price: $39.95

Exceptions For Apple only

MEDALIST: CREATE

Hartley Courseware, Inc.

Uses in an Educational Environment

Teachers inexperienced in the use of computers can use this shell program to create, in game format, an instructional program to teach facts and concepts for any subject at any grade level.

Experience Level

Both computer beginners and experienced computer users can use this program.

Content

This package is a shell program in the same game format as Hartley Courseware's series *THE MEDALIST*. (See review, page 00 in Educational Software.)

Comment

Teacher reviewers were enthusiastic about this program as something teachers are looking for because it allows them to create programs easily. The program is easy to operate, and the teacher's manual provides clear instructions for creating a program. The teacher may pick any topic, select categories, and then generate clues. The program can be used in any area of the curriculum in which the student needs to learn facts or concepts. List Price: $39.95.

Exceptions For Apple only

TIC TAC SHOW

Computer Advanced Ideas

Uses in an Educational Environment

Teachers can use this shell program to provide content for students in different subjects at different levels; for example, Language Arts, Social Science, or Mathematics, among others.

Experience Level

Both computer beginners and experienced computer users can use this program.

Content

This package is a shell program based on the game of Tic Tac Toe, in which the teacher programs the desired content.

Comment

The documentation is accurate and easy to read. The instructional design is sound. Unfortunately, there are no suggestions to the teacher for class activities or follow-up, no feature to help students review missed items, and no report feature to the teacher. The shell enables the program to have more than one-time use in all subject areas. This program is recommended highly as fun, motivating, and entertaining. List Price: $39.95

Exceptions For IBM, Commodore 64, Apple IIe only

WORD MATCH, WORD SCRAMBLE, WORD SEARCH

(Three titles available separately)

Hi Tech

Uses in an Educational Environment
Each of these programs is a useful learning activity to help students build vocabulary and word recognition skills in a variety of subject areas and grade levels.

Experience Level
Containing easy-to-read documentation, each of these pro—grams can be used easily by teachers who are inexperienced with computers; however, the user should be familiar with using the printer and initializing DOS 3.3 diskettes.

Comment
Each program is recommended as an excellent tool for building word skills and can be used for a variety of grade levels in a variety of subject areas. The program allows a user to add a name, date, and instructions to a puzzle. Completed word activities can be stored and re-used. The user also has the option to change, delete, hand place, and relocate words in a puzzle.

Word Match, Word Scramble, Word Search (continued)

Puzzles can be printed with or without clues, and an answer key can also be printed out. List Price Each: $24.95.

WORD MATCH
Content
This program enables the teacher to produce word match curricular activities of up to 20 words (two columns of 10 each), with a maximum of 25 letters per word.
Exceptions For Apple II, II+, IIe only.

WORD SCRAMBLE
Content
This program enables the teacher to produce anagram puzzles of up to 20 words each, with a maximum of 16 letters per word.

WORD SEARCH
Content
This program is a fast and easy way to produce word search puzzles of up to 100 words each in a grid of from 5 to 20 rows and columns.

PROGRAMMING LANGUAGES

Programming Languages

The interface between the computer's operating system software and the actual programs executed by the user is called a programming language. In order to write programs on the computer, the user must be able to write computer code in a programming language such as the ones listed below.

CBASIC

Digital Research

Uses in an Educational Environment
Educators could use *CBASIC* for record keeping and file maintenance if they have the needed operating system. Advanced classes or independent study students in computer math and/or data processing could probably use the package.

Experience Level
The manual is not as tutorial as most programming guides. The serious beginner could, however, use the documentation to learn BASIC programming.

Content
This program is a comprehensive and versatile programming language for developing professional microcomputer software.

CBASIC (continued)
Comment
CBASIC combines the power of a structured, high level language with the simplicity of BASIC to provide a serious development tool that is easy to learn and to use. A prior familiarity with BASIC is recommended. Such users will find their capabilities greatly enhanced with this system. List Price: $150.00
Exceptions Not for IBM or IBM compatible

COMMODORE LOGO

See review, Elementary, Technology/Programming Languages, page 30.

DISCOVER BASIC

See review, Secondary, Technology/Programming Languages, page 51.

HANDS ON BASIC

See review, Secondary, Technology/Programming Languages, page 51.

KRELL'S LOGO

See review, Elementary, Technology/Programming Languages, page 30.

KRELL'S TURTLE PAK

See review, Elementary, Technology/Programming Languages, page 31.

LET'S EXPLORE BASIC

See review, Secondary, Technology/Programming Languages, page 52.

MBASIC-80

Microsoft, Inc.

Uses in an Educational Environment
Administrative uses include enhancing record management. Instructional uses include upgrading present systems with

MBASIC-80 *(continued)*
CP/M and standardizing MBASIC in computer, math, science, and data processing courses.
Experience Level
The user should have some experience with computer systems and file management to use this package.
Content
This is a powerful interactive version of BASIC, which is ANSI compatible and combines ease of use with versatile features. Some of the features are: chaining, variable length file records, four variable typefaces, and error trapping.
Comment
This package will help equip a user who has a casual knowledge of BASIC to do serious programming. List Price: $350.00
Exceptions Not for Atari, Commodore

MICROSOFT C

See review, Postsecondary, Technology/Programming Languages, page 56.

THE TERRAPIN LOGO LANGUAGE

See review, Elementary, Technology/Programming Languages, page 31.

SPREADSHEETS/MANAGEMENT TOOLS

Spreadsheets/Management Tools

For those who need to develop budgets or do any other kind of financial planning, electronic spreadsheets provide a capability unimagined by those still using a calculator and pencil. Calculations anywhere on the grid can be instantly changed for any variable the user enters. Spreadsheets typically incorporate extensive math capabilities, and reports can be easily edited, saved, and printed.

ACCOUNTING PEARL

Pearlsoft Division/
Relational Systems International Corporation

Uses in an Educational Environment
This program is appropriate for a small school system's accounting needs although it is perhaps too sophisticated for a single school's financial record keeping. It can also be used in an advanced, postsecondary accounting course.

Accounting Pearl (continued)

Experience Level:
Although the program can be used by a person inexperienced with computers, the manual, which is several hundred pages long, will require much reading and practice. The program is not recommended for someone inexperienced with accounting procedures.

Content
The software contains five separate but interdependent programs: "General Ledger," "Accounts Receivable," "Accounts Payable," "Payroll," and "Inventory." There are also several other programs on the disks that allow for disk file maintenance, initialization of disks and programs, etc.

Comment
Accounting Pearl is a complete accounting package. The system's manual is well-written, comprehensible, and extensive. There is a tutorial on the disk to guide the user through the use of the programs, but it is not a tutorial on accounting. Throughout the documentation there are many supports, such as sample printed pages and step-by-step instructions. When the package is purchased, it is configured to use two 5.25 inch floppy disk drives. However, instructions are provided for the user to adapt these programs to a hard disk drive system, provided the user has access to at least one 5.25 inch drive. List Price: $745.83.

Exceptions   For IBM only

ACCOUNTING PLUS SERIES

Ask Micro

Uses in an Educational Environment
This is a complete accounting package for administrative use by a school or a school district. Because the documentation is so thorough and well-designed, the program can be used in a comprehensive accounting course.

Experience Level
The clear documentation makes the program usable by a computer beginner who has familiarity with accounting procedures.

Comment
The high quality of the documentation makes this program useful for a wide variety of users. The manual is a formal tutorial that leads the user step-by-step through both the computer operation and the accounting procedures. It should be noted that there are three additional titles in the series, but they have not been reviewed: (1) "Sales Order," (2) "Purchase Order," (3) "Inventory Control." List Price Each: $595.00

General Ledger
Content
Nine units present the functions and use of a general ledger: (1) "General Ledger Maintenance," (2) "Account/Department Listing," (3) "Journal Voucher Entry," (4) "Recurring Voucher Maintenance," (5) "Post Outstanding Journals," (6) "Print Financial Reports," (7) "Print Budget Reports," (8) "Prior Year Reporting," (9) "General Ledger Utilities."

Accounting Plus Series (continued)

Accounts Payable
Content
Seven units present the accounts payable system: (1) "Vendor Maintenance/Listing," (2) "Automatic A/P Maintenance," (3) "Accounts Payable Entry," (4) "Select Invoices for Payment," (5) "Check Generation (Printing)," (6) "Accounts Payable Reports," (7) "Accounts Payable Utilities."

Accounts Receivable
Content
Seven units present the accounts receivable system: (1) "Customer Maintenance/Listing," (2) "Automatic Customer Billing," (3) "Invoicing/Billing," (4) "Cash Posting and Miscellaneous Entry," (5) "Customer Statements," (6) "Accounts Receivable Reports," (7) "Accounts Receivable Utilities."

Payroll
Content
Eight units present the payroll system: (1) "Employee Maintenance," (2) "Employee Listing," (3) "Payroll Hours Entry," (4) "Payroll Select and Calculations," (5) "Check Generation," (6) "Payroll Posting," (7) "Payroll Tax Deposit," (8) "Payroll Utilities."

Exceptions   For Apple, Altos, Epson, IBM, and Televideo only

FINANCIAL MANAGEMENT SERIES

(three titles in series)

Information Unlimited Software

Uses in an Educational Environment
These programs are useful primarily in accounting departments of school districts. They are also useful in a college level bookkeeping/accounting course.

Experience Level
The programs are best executed by a user with experience both in accounting and with computers. However, it is tutorial and can be run by a computer beginner.

Comment
The manuals are well-documented and very readable. The package is recommended for those having specifc needs for this specialized material. List Price Series: $2,250.00

Payroll
Content
Included are operating procedures needed to process a payroll and to keep necessary records.

General Ledger and Financial Reporter
Content
The program covers company profile, general ledger accounts, transaction batch maintenance, and posting and listing.

Financial Management Series (continued)

Inventory Control and Analysis

Content

The program covers inventory record layout, categories, cost, formatting, year-end processing, inventory, receipts, shipments, and adjustments.

Exceptions: For IBM only

FINANCIAL PLANNER

Ashton-Tate

Uses in an Educational Environment

The budget planning features will be valuable for administrative purposes.

Experience Level

The documentation assumes an understanding of common computer terminology. Its language and format can be confusing to those not familiar with business applications.

Content

This electronic spreadsheet program is designed to customize financial planning needs. Information can be easily accessed, analyzed, and manipulated, and complex reports constructed. A model can be structured, previewed, and edited before producing presentation-quality reports. Some key features are: budget planning, cash flow management, capital investment analysis, product evaluation, and real estate analysis.

Comment

Users should have a clear understanding of their financial needs before using this program. List Price: $700.00

Exceptions Not for Atari, Commodore, IBM, TI Pro

GRADE AAA GRADE BOOK

The Soft Warehouse

Uses in an Educational Environment

The program can be used by teachers to record, store, average, and report students' grades.

Experience Level

This program is easily understood and operated by a person inexperienced with computers.

Content

The program allows the teacher to store, change, add, or delete student grades and/or classes. It will, at any point in the process, average and report grades to date. Information can be retrieved and printed for individual students, for classes, or by topics. The spreadsheet format of reporting class performances simulates the traditional gradebook and provides the user an all-at-once overview of class performance.

Comment

The spreadsheet format is particularly impressive and useful. The manual is thorough, well-ordered, and presented for easy

Grade AAA Grade Book (continued)

learning and reference for even the most inexperienced of computer users. The program will be appreciated by teachers as a great advance over a traditional gradebook. It should be noted that, like most computer gradebooks, loading subprograms is slow, and there are places where revisions would help; however, user friendliness is the cause of this situation and the benefits far outweigh the problem. List Price: $65.00.

Exceptions For Apple II + , IIe only.

LEARNING LOTUS 1-2-3

Arthur Young

Uses in an Educational Environment

This program can be useful in conducting in-service training on *Lotus 1-2-3* without using a consultant. The videotapes might also be used independently for group sessions.

Experience Level

The lessons are self-instructive. The program is useful for both experienced and inexperienced users.

Content

The package consists of a training manual, a floppy disk, and a series of video tapes to be used in conjunction with *Lotus 1-2-3*. The video tapes present lesson modules on the features and uses of *Lotus 1-2-3*. The manual further explains the videotaped lessons and provides problem sets for the user to work out. The software consists of examples to be loaded into *Lotus 1-2-3*. (This packages does not include *Lotus 1-2-3*.)

Comment

This series begins at a very basic level and progresses through the major features of *Lotus 1-2-3*. The program works well. The manual provides the information in a clear and straightforward manner. The package is recommended for anyone who wants a video-based training program. List Price: $395.00; Extra manual and backup disk: $75.00.

LEARNING MULTIPLAN

Arthur Young

Uses in an Educational Environment

This package can be useful in conducting inservice training on *Multiplan* without using a consultant.

Experience Level

The lessons are self-instructive. The package is useful by persons both experienced and inexperienced with computers.

Content

The package consists of a training manual and a series of video tapes. The video tapes present lesson modules on the features and uses of *Muliplan*. The manual further explains the video taped lessons and provides problem sets for the user to work out.

Learning Multiplan (continued)

Comment

The series begins at a very basic level and progresses through the major features of *Multiplan*. The program works well. The manual provides the information in a clear and straightforward manner. The package is recommended for anyone who wants a video based training program. List Price: $350.00; Extra manual and backup disk: $75.00.

LEARNING VISICALC

Arthur Young

Uses in an Educational Environment

This package can be useful in conducting inservice training on *Visicalc* without using a consultant.

Experience Level

The lessons are self-instructive. The package can be used by persons both experienced and inexperienced with computers.

Content

The package consists of a training manual and a series of video tapes. The video tapes present lesson modules on the features and uses of *Visicalc*. The manual further explains the video taped lessons and provides problem sets for the user to work out.

Comment

The series begins at a very basic level and progresses through the major features of *Visicalc*. The program operates well. The manual provides the information in a clear and straightforward manner. It should be noted that the video tapes use an Apple computer for the demonstrations and that users of other microcomputers would need to make the necessary adjustments. The package is recommended for anyone who wants a video based training program. List Price: $295.00; Extra manual and backup disk: $50.00.

LOTUS 1-2-3

Lotus Development Corporation

Uses in an Educational Environment

Schools and school districts can use this package for spreadsheeting, data management, and graphing. Users can prepare and manage budgets, inventories and graph relationships of data in both the data management and spreadsheet programs.

Experience Level

While knowledge of the desired operations is essential, the inexperienced user can adequately operate the programs with the very detailed documentation, the help screens, and the on-disk tutorial.

Content

Lotus 1-2-3 is a system containing a spreadsheet of 255 columns and 2048 rows, a graphing program providing five types of graphs in color, and a data base management program that operates with a spreadsheet format.

Lotus 1-2-3 (continued)

Comment

Lotus 1-2-3 is a powerful package for the individual needing to coordinate the data from the spreadsheet or from the data management program in graphs. The program is flexible with excellent documentation and on-screen help at each command level. The spreadsheet size is much larger than most of the competition. List Price: $495.00.

Exceptions For use with IBM-PC or TI Pro

MBA SERIES

(three titles available separately)

Micro Business Applications

Uses in an Educational Environment

The programs are recommended for an individual school or small school system, not for instructional purposes.

Experience Level

The package will best be used by someone experienced both in accounting and in the use of computers.

Content

This set of programs covers three areas of accounting: general ledger, payroll, accounts receivable. Each of the documents for the three areas contains needed information for computer operation and for the accounting principles and practices covered.

Comment

The documentation is not thorough enough to guide an inexperienced user either through the computer operation or through the accounting. However, it is adequate for the user who is sufficiently experienced. The appendix contains helpful information sheets for determining the number of records a particular computer system can accommodate and a listing of the programs on the disks, as well as blank forms. List Price Each: $595.00

Exceptions For Apple, Epson, IBM, Superbrain, Televideo

MULTIPLAN

Microsoft, Inc.

Uses in an Educational Environment

The program would be useful for the central or business office of a school where the budget planning feature would be attractive.

Experience Level

The documentation is well-organized and attractively presented, but the user must have a basic understanding of the functions of the computer and a solid background in business planning and statistics.

Content

Multiplan is an electronic financial worksheet. It is helpful in budget analysis for forecasting and financial planning. It is also

Multiplan *(continued)*

useful to home computer users who have to manage intricate budgets that include stocks and other investment projects. Engineers can use this package for formula analysis and statistical research.

Comment
Note that no softcard is required. List Price: $250.00

Exceptions For Apple, Epson, IBM, Osborne, Superbrain, TI Pro

PEACH PAK

(three titles in series)

Peachtree Software, Inc.

Uses in an Educational Environment
The package is recommended for an individual school or small school system needing a comprehensive accounts payable program. It is not recommended for instructional purposes.

Experience Level
The documentation is written well enough for a person inexperienced with computers to use it easily. The accounts payable section is so thorough and clear that one does not need to be a trained accountant to use it, but the user should know accounting principles.

Content
The package contains thorough documentation both of computer operation of the program and of accounting practices that are covered. Instructions are given for configuring the disks, with special assistance for a user inexperienced with computers. Use of the computer program with all commands presented is illustrated by sample screens. Special cases are described and appendices for terms, forms, data file structures and layouts, subprograms, and sample reports are provided.

Comment
The documentation is well-organized and easy to follow. Though not written specifically as a tutorial, it serves that purpose. It is unusually helpful both with operation of the program and with assistance in implementing the accounting practices. (General Ledger, Accounts Receivable, Accounts Payable) List Price: $395.00

Exceptions For Apple, IBM, Northstar, Televideo

PERFECT CALC

Perfect Software, Inc.

Uses in an Educational Environment
This program is useful to administrators needing financial applications for budgets and inventories. The only classroom use would be in business education courses teaching spreadsheet analysis.

Perfect Calc *(continued)*

Experience Level
The tutorials included with the system make it an appropriate choice for either a computer beginner or an experienced spreadsheet user.

Content
This package is an electronic spreadsheet that organizes numeric data for easy calculation and presentation. It has a sophisticated "what if?" capability, which allows the user to postulate changes in the data of the spreadsheet and to see the results of those changes immediately.

Comment
Users experienced with *Perfect Writer* may find this program particularly attractive because the commands are similar to those used in that word processing program. List Price: $295.00

Exceptions For Apple, Epson, IBM, Northstar, Superbrain, Televideo

PERSONAL ACCOUNTING

BPI Systems

Uses in an Educational Environment
Classroom uses include secondary and postsecondary bookkeeping/accounting courses. It is useful for maintaining school accounts in a school business office.

Experience Level
The manual is detailed and complete. It anticipates problems, questions, errors, and discoveries that the most inexperienced user may have. Because of the many operations, variations, and types of accounts that are necessary for an accounting system as complete as this, users should be prepared to spend time learning the system both before and as they implement the many applications available.

Content
Although the audience specified by the publisher is the individual user for home/family purposes, a school with a maximum of 200 accounts, several checking accounts, and multiple ledgers can use the program. It can make double entries and write checks when used with a printer.

Comment
This system was written and programmed by professionals who know the system and understand the problems of even the rank amateur. It demands only time and practice for mastery. The system is complete, easily understood, and most useful in the classroom and in the business office. List Price: $195.00

Exceptions For IBM only

REALWORLD SERIES

(four titles available separately)

Micro Business Software

Uses in an Educational Environment
These programs would be useful to a school district needing a comprehensive and powerful accounting package for a microcomputer.

Experience Level
The programs can be used by a computer beginner because the documentation is remarkably complete, thorough, and well-written. However, the programs are not intended for a person inexperienced in accounting.

Content
The four programs, available separately, are comprehensive accounting packages that perform necessary computation, make appropriate reports, and print pertinent informaton on blank forms available from RealWorld at additional cost.

Comment
Reviewers judge that these programs incorporate all features desired in these types of packages, including being menu-driven, containing a maintenance program on the disk, printing two-part check forms, etc. If a school system already has a formal accounting procedure that is working successfully but is getting difficult to manage due to an increase in the amount of paper work, these programs will be very beneficial. List Price Each: $670.00

Exceptions Not for Atari, Commodore, Cromemco, Heath/Zenith, Osborne, TI Pro

STAR SYSTEM 1 — GENERAL LEDGER

Star Computer Systems, Inc.

Uses in an Educational Environment
The program can be used to teach accounting or accounting procedures to business education or vocational education students. It is a fine accounting applications program for a school or school system that is not large enough to warrant the purchase of a mainframe computer system yet would like to computerize all of its financial transactions.

Experience Level
The program and documentation are acceptable for a user experienced both with computers and with accounting principles and practices.

Content
The package is a complete general ledger program.

Comment
The documentation is adequate for an experienced user. If it were clearer and more thorough in presenting installation procedures, especially with the computer/printer interface, the entire program could be used by a person inexperienced with computers. It would have been helpful if the documentation had given examples of what to enter for various computer/printer combinations or even provided an ASCII chart with explanation. The disk drive configuration is very vague in

Star System 1 — General Ledger (continued)
the documentation. List Price: $400.00
Exceptions For Altos, Cromemco, Hewlett Packard, Northstar, Superbrain, Televideo

STATPAK

Northwest Analytical

Uses in an Educational Environment
The primary use of *Statpak* is for testing and counseling in schools and school systems. A large department could use it when preparing standardized tests. The program would also be useful in an advanced statistics course.

Experience Level
Experience with file structure, programming, and word processing is needed. The documentation is directed to the experienced computer user and programmer. Some knowledge of statistics is also desirable.

Content
This package is a library of statistical and probability calculation programs that allow an analyst to manipulate data. *Statpak's* utilities handle large numbers of data items, expedite file creation, provide file editing and merging, and select data subsets and data scaling. Features include: probability calculations, discrete distribution functions, regression analysis, means testing, survey data, and contingency tables.

Comment
Statpak is a very useful research tool. List Price: $495.00
Exceptions Not for Atari, Commodore, Heath/Zenith, TI Pro

SUPERCALC

Sorcim Corporation

Uses in an Educational Environment
Administrative applications include developing budgets and other financial planning.

Experience Level
Users should be familiar with financial applications, but no previous computer experience should be necessary.

Comment
Financial planners will find this package invaluable. List Price: SuperCalc I, $195.00; SuperCalc II, $295.00; SuperCalc III, $395.00

SUPERCALC I
Content
This package is an electronic spreadsheet. It is designed to use the minimum number of commands and is self-explanatory. A help key is available when assistance is needed. Reports can be generated combining portions of previously created spread-

SuperCalc (continued)

sheets. It also has powerful editing capabilities, and all data can be protected from new manipulation.

SUPERCALC II

Content

This package offers additional capabilities to SuperCalc I: consolidation, sorting, and more format choices such as floating dollar signs and variable decimal places. It also allows the user to hide confidential information.

SUPERCALC III

Content

This package goes beyond SuperCalc II and helps the user solve modeling and forecasting problems through the presentation of quality graphics. It produces line, bar and stacked bar graphs, pie and exploded pie graphs, as well as H-Y, H-Lo, and area graphs.

Exceptions Not for Altos, Atari, Commodore, Hewlett-Packard, TI Pro

VISICALC

Visicorp

Uses in an Educational Environment

Educators who plan budgets or use other business-type applications will find *VisiCalc* useful.

Experience Level

The documentation is well-organized, and a computer beginner will be able to follow the step-by-step instructions. However, a clear understanding of business and financial concepts is necessary.

Content

This package is an electronic spreadsheet for business and financial management. It will calculate revenue projections, cost estimates, budgets, financial rates, etc. It offers split-screen viewing, fast row/column reformatting, and block moves. By inserting or changing a value at one location of the spreadsheet, the user can instantly recalculate all values.

Comment

A user with the required financial knowledge will find this package very helpful. List Price: $250.00

Exceptions For Epson, IBM, Apple, TI Pro

SYSTEMS SUPPORT

Systems Support

Included in this grouping are computer languages and utility programs. These software packages are helpful to those who write their own computer programs. Many microcomputer languages and their documentation are easy to use and are designed for beginners; other are designed for experienced programmers. The utility programs enhance the language's capabilities, perhaps by adding some feature, such as a debugging aid, or the generation of a program for the user based on information he or she inputs in response to screen prompts. Utilities are used in conjunction with the support of another software package.

M PASCAL COMPILER

Microsoft, Inc.

Uses in an Educational Environment

Educators could use the compiler to implement the Pascal programs for a class in Pascal programming language.

Experience Level

The compiler manual states, "The manuals in this package provide complete reference information for your implementa-

M Pascal Compiler (continued)

tion of the "M" Pascal Compiler. They do not, however, teach you to write programs in Pascal." This is not a program for a computer beginner. It should be used by persons who can program in Pascal.

Content

The program is for use with machines having MS DOS and MS-Link (IBM compatible machines). Most Pascal compilers compile to a P-code, which is then taken to machine language. This compiler goes to the machine language and skips the P-Code.

Comment

The two-part manuals for the package are detailed, well-written, clear, and well-indexed. They are excellent manuals for compiler information. List Price: $350.00

Exceptions For Apple, Epson, IBM, Northstar, Superbrain, Televideo

MOUSE

Microsoft, Inc.

Uses in an Educational Environment

The *Mouse* should be a valuable tool for teachers and administrators. It is used in conjunction with a word processing

Mouse *(continued)*

program to edit text. The *Mouse* can also be used to create and move graphic symbols and manipulate data in programs.

Experience Level

The user should have some experience with an IBM PC prior to using the *Mouse*. A computer beginner should plan to spend several hours of practice with the tutorials to become familiar with the *Mouse* capabilities.

Content

This complete program package contains both hardware and software. The program provides two tutorial/learning programs and a mouse with 16 different functions.

Comment

This is a complete mouse system that provides fast and easy manipulation of text, graphic symbols, and data. It is a complete and powerful tool for controlling the cursor and manipulating screen data. The packaging of this product is well-conceived. A tutorial provides a practical method for the user to become familiar with the features of the program. List Price: $195.00

Exceptions For IBM Only

QUICKCODE

Fox and Geller

Uses in an Educational Environment

Administrative applications include such items as schedules, newsletters, calendars of events, and financial reports that need to be regularly retrieved, updated, and mailed out.

Experience Level

Those with previous data base or word processing experience should find the documentation satisfactory. The documentation assumes some familiarity with programming.

Quickcode *(continued)*

Content

Quickcode is a screen-oriented program generator for Ashton-Tate's *dBASE II.* It can write almost any type of application program using the *dBASE II* programming language, or it can write a program to transfer any part of a *dBASE II* data base to *Wordstar.*

Comment

Note that there are technical hardware configurations with which the user must be familiar. List Price: $295.00

Exceptions Not for Atari, Commodore, Heath/Zenith, TI Pro

SOFTCARD

Microsoft, Inc.

Uses in an Educational Environment

This system is needed by schools or school systems wanting to run CP/M based programs, such as *VisiCalc* or *Wordstar,* on the Apple II.

Experience Level

Any Apple II user, whether a computer beginner or an expert, will need this or a similar system for the required purpose.

Content

The *Softcard* system is a hardware/software combination for the Apple II computers that adds the ability to run software written for the thousands of educational, scientific, business, and system applications that run on the popular CP/M operating system.

Comment

Apple users must have such a card to run CP/M based packages. List Price: $345.00

Exceptions For Apple II Only

WORD PROCESSING SYSTEMS AND UTILITIES

Word Processing Systems & Utilities

A word processor can do nearly everything that you can do with a typewriter but more easily and with infinitely more options. Any kind of text formatting such as memos, letters, tests, research papers, articles, resumes, and lists, can be entered, modified, saved, and printed an unlimited number of times. Headings, paragraphs, columns, etc., can be reformatted, deleted, or changed easily at any time. Additional utilities can perform such tasks as spelling checks and personalized mailing lists. Word processing systems are among the most useful tools available to educators.

BANK STREET WRITER

See review, Elementary, Technology/Word Processing, page 31.

EASY WRITER II

Information Unlimited Software

Uses in an Educational Environment
The program is useful for teachers and administrators needing a word processing program.
Experience Level
The documentation is clear and easy to follow. This is a good word processing system for the beginner.
Content
This powerful word processing program is page-oriented, which means that a user can see a page before printing it. A single keystroke will communicate commands without any complicated control key combinations. The editor is very flexible, and the system stores up to ten documents.
Comment
This program is for IBM only. Note that it requires the use of only one disk drive. List Price: $350.00
Exceptions For IBM Only

FINAL WORD

Mark of the Unicorn

Uses in an Educational Environment
This package is too complicated to be used in a classroom, but it can be used in lieu of a dedicated word processor for administrative applications. The program can also be used by teachers in composing tests and worksheets.
Experience Level
Familiarity with computers and with word processing would be helpful. Although the first section of the documentation is intended for the computer beginner, it would take a great deal of time for a beginner to learn how to operate the program effectively, and the program would require constant use for one to maintain competency with it.
Content
This program is a high-powered word processing package. The lengthy documentation contains three sections: (1) step-by-step lessons for the user to enter textual data and manipulate it; (2) the technical section with information, alphabetically arranged, about the features of the word processor; (3) appendices including additional instruction on file swapping, error messages, and a glossary of terms.
Comment
This program is recommended for use with the IBM PC. Many of the commands required to manipulate the textual information are extremely complicated and require as many as four simultaneous keyboard entries. However, with the IBM PC many of these complicated entries are reduced to single function key entries, or, at most, a two-key entry. List Price: $300.00
Exceptions None (available for many systems not listed in catalog)

LETTER WIZARD ·

Datasoft, Inc.

Uses in an Educational Environment
This program has multiple uses. It can be used by the teacher to create lessons and tests for students, and to generate reports. It can be used in place of a typewriter. Students with teacher guidance can also use the program to do creative writing and reports.
Experience Level
The manual is well written for adult use. Because some technical jargon is used, the teacher with some computer experience (particularly with the Atari) would find the program easier to use and operate than a computer beginner. Nevertheless, it does not require experience in any way comparable with that needed to operate professional word processing programs such as *Wordstar*. As the features become more complicated, so do the directions. Simple typing and editing would be no problem for the inexperienced computer user.
Content
All the features of a desirable word processor are included: one mode operation for writing and editing; relatively simple but numerous commands; easy cursor movements; adding, deleting, and moving text; file management functions; printing functions; and good documentation.
Comment
The program has more options than a teacher or home user will ordinarily need, but they are useful to have. An adult user can successfully use the manual to learn how to use the program. A handy reference card explains all the features in an abbreviated form. The program contains more features and is more difficult to use than such elementary programs as *Bank Street Writer*, but it is far simpler than professional word processing packages for office use. If high school students use the program, teacher guidance will be needed. List Price: $49.95.
Exceptions For Atari only

MAILMERGE

Micropro International Corporation

Uses in an Educational Environment
The program is useful to administrators who need to add the production mailing capability to *Wordstar* word processing.
Experience Level
Although documentation is not as well written as for some other similar packages, the computer beginner will still be able to use this utility.
Content
This is a utility program that enables *Wordstar* to perform production mailing of personalized form letters or other documents. It provides the interface between word processing and data base management. It permits merging data from two or more files at print time, chained and nested printing, printing multiple copies automatically, and printing data in report formats.

Mail Merge (continued)

Comment

Since *Mailmerge* will not hold mailing lists, a data base system must be used for this purpose. List Price: $250.00

Exceptions Not for Altos, Cromemco, and Osborne

MULTITOOL WORD

Microsoft, Inc.

Uses in an Educational Environment

Teachers can use this word processing program to produce and maintain quality letters, tests, and reports. Administrators can use it to produce professional quality documents. Postsecondary courses in word processing that use the IBM PC may find this program useful for instruction in word processing, though it is complex.

Experience Level

The user should have experience with an IBM PC before using *Word.* A beginner should plan to spend several hours of practice to become familiar with the program. Proficiency may take several weeks of part-time use.

Content

This is a powerful tool for producing quality documents from memos to manuscripts. Command options are presented at the bottom of the screen, and a help command will explain the command or feature. Microsoft also markets a *"Mouse,"* which will make editing easier.

Comment

The packaging of this product is well-conceived. A tutorial and getting started section provide a practical method for the user to become familiar with the features of the program. The program will allow the user to have up to eight different "windows" on the screen at the same time. These can be parts of one document or from different documents.

See review of *Microsoft Mouse,* page 44. List Price: $395.00

Exceptions For IBM Only

PEACH TEXT 5000

Peachtree Software, Inc.

Uses in an Educational Environment

The package is useful for administrators needing word processing and for business education courses in word processing.

Experience Level

Peach Text 5000's documentation contains easy-to-read progressive tutorials. It is useful for both computer beginners and experts.

Content

In addition to the progressive tutorial in lesson format, this word processing package also contains a summary of commands and a help menu, which is always available.

Peach Text 5000 (continued)

Comment

Since *Peach Text 5000* has a complete complement of word processing features, the beginner should plan to spend several hours with the program lessons in order to become familiar with the program. Proficiency may take several weeks of part-time use. List Price: $395.00

Exceptions For Apple, Epson, IBM

PERFECT WRITER

Perfect Software, Inc.

Uses in an Educational Environment

Teachers and administrators needing a word processing package will find this product useful.

Experience Level

The documentation is organized and easy to follow. A computer beginner will find the examples clear, but may have some difficulty using the many function keys and commands.

Content

Perfect Writer is a word processing package that also includes *Perfect Speller,* a program that corrects spelling mistakes and typing errors. This package can be used for the standard word processing tasks of creating, storing, editing, and retrieving documents.

Comment

This program has a sophisticated formatting capability that allows the user to create attractive documents easily. List Price: $495.00

Exceptions For Apple, Epson, IBM, Northstar, Superbrain, Televideo

SPELLBINDER

Lexisoft, Inc.

Uses in an Educational Environment

Teachers and administrators could use this program for any communications requiring word processing.

Experience Level

Computer beginners should be able to use the program quickly because of the excellent tutorial manual. The other documentation assumes familiarity with computer and word processing terms.

Content

This full-feature word processing system contains office management capability. Some of the features are: automatic word wrap, full cursor movement, horizontal scrolling, forms creation, zip code sorting, and others. Users will find the various search capabilities extremely useful. *Spellbinder* also allows variable interword spacing and printing with special character treatments, such as shadow print and slash overstrike.

Spellbinder (continued)

Comment
Users needing both word processing and office management capabilties will find this package particularly helpful. List Price: $495.00
Exceptions Not for Atari, Commodore, Hewlett-Packard, Osborne

SPELLSTAR

Micropro International Corporation

Uses in an Educational Environment
The program is useful for teachers or administrators using *Wordstar.*
Experience Level
Computer beginners will be able to use *Spellstar* easily.
Content
Spellstar, used with *Wordstar,* automatically checks the spelling of a document against its 20,000 word dictionary. It flags all errors and depends on the user to change, ignore, leave marked, or add the word to the dictionary.
Comment
The program is very helpful to *Wordstar* users. List Price: $250.00
Exceptions For Apple, Cromemco, Epson, IBM, Northstar, Superbrain, Televideo

SPELL WIZARD

Datasoft, Inc.

Uses in an Educational Environment
This program can be used in conjunction with a word processing program to correct spelling errors, or it can be used separately. The teacher can use the program to proofread a document already written with a compatible word processing program. With instruction, the student could also use the program for this purpose. The teacher can also use the program to create a spelling lesson for students to use without a word processing program.
Experience Level
This program can be used as a word processing utility by the computer beginner, although the manual is written more for the adult than for the secondary level student. The documentation is easy to follow, but with the use of two or more disks, it can become confusing for an inexperienced user. Students can learn how to use the program with teacher guidance.
Content
The package contains a dictionary of spelling and a user-created dictionary. It does not include word meanings, pronunciations, parts of speech, or proper nouns. The user must type in the correct spelling of the word. The program does not correct spelling without user input. The dictionary can be used on its own.

Spell Wizard (continued)

Comment
This package itself contains two disks. The addition of a word processing program means that three pieces of software must be used interchangeably. This makes the program more usable by an adult than by a child. Text can be scanned at 600 words per minute to identify misspelled words and allow the user to correct them. Other features allow for printout of any part of the 33,000+ word dictionary or for writing one's own customized dictionary. To be used to its fullest, a compatible word processing program* is necessary. (*See *Letter Wizard.*) List Price: $49.95
Exceptions For Atari only

THE WORD PLUS

Oasis Systems

Uses in an Educational Environment
Teachers and administrators can use this program with word processing packages to check spelling.
Experience Level
Any user of word processing packages is experienced enough to use this program. Documentation is simple, clear, and complete.
Content
This is a program that checks spelling. It also makes a list of all words in the document that are not in its dictionary. It then permits the user to view each word. If a word is spelled correctly but is not in the disk dictionary, it can be added to the main dictionary or to any number of special dictionaries the user may choose to create. If a word is misspelled, the program allows the user to make any spelling correction(s).
Comment
The program displays the particular word in only one line of context; display of the line above and the line below would be more helpful. Otherwise, the program is strongly recommended. List Price: $150.00
Exceptions For Apple, IBM, Northstar, Osborne, Superbrain

WORDSTAR

Micropro International Corporation

Uses in an Educational Environment
Teachers and administrators needing word processing capability will find this program useful.
Experience Level
The documentation's language and format are difficult for the beginner to use. Some familiarity with word processing systems is desirable.

Wordstar (continued)

Content

This word processing package is screen-oriented. Automated margins, justification, and pagination allow high speed text entry. Editing commands are complete and powerful. One file can be printed at the same time another is being edited.

Comment

This system is complex and not as easy to learn as some more recently developed products. List Price : $495.00

Exceptions Not for Altos, Atari, Commodore, Hewlett-Packard, Osborne, TI Pro

WORDSTAR PROFESSIONAL

This package includes *Wordstar, Mailmerge and Spellstar*. List Price: $695.00

Exceptions For Apple, Epson, IBM, Northstar, Superbrain Televideo

VIDEODISC

One of the most interesting new teaching technologies is the videodisc. The videodisc stores audiovisual materials in a similar manner to videotape. Not only is the disc far more compact and durable than tape, it also gives the user more control to stop, start, freeze, slow and speed the A-V sequence. Laser videodisc adds the capability of random access to any of the over 50,000 images on each side of the disc. When connected to a computer, a technology called "computer-interactive videodisc" (CIV), the teaching potential is extremely promising.

BIO SCI VIDEODISC

Videodiscovery, Inc.

System Requirements

Pioneer videodisc player (models 8210, LD-V1000 and 4000), color TV

Recommended Target Group

Science/Zoology; postsecondary and gifted and talented high school biology.

Content

The *Bio Sci Videodisc* is an excellent library of over 6000 high-quality photographic slides and several time-lapse movie sequences that are most important in college zoology or high school biology classes. Content areas include invertebrate and vertebrate zoology, taxonomy, biochemistry, cell biology, developmental biology, and ecology.

Comment

This excellent disc allows the instructor to use a single slide or many slides in a sequence during a presentation to a large group. An add-on cassette (not tested) recorder allows for individualized instruction. The disc system may be used as part of a multimedia presentation. An image directory with hierarchical listing that assists in easy slide access is available with the system. Through the use of modern technology, this system provides the instructor a wide range of subject matter stored on

Bio Sci Videodisc (continued)

a single disc. Its use saves considerable class preparation time. Using the slides, the instructor can adjust the lecture to class questions. This system also saves money compared to the purchase of individual slides. List Price: $495.00.

Exceptions N/A

COLLEGE U.S.A.

Info-Disc Corporation

System Requirements

Tested on: Pioneer LD-V4000 laser videodisc player, color TV.

Suggested Target Group

Counselors, students, parents; grades 11-12.

Content

This collection is a library of laser discs containing college recruiting messages, financial aid information, and other topics of interest to college-bound students. The disc contains scenes of college campus life not available in brochures and handbooks, interviews with college students and faculty, as well as tours of classrooms, dormitories, libraries, and laboratories. The information has been transferred to videodiscs from colleges' current recruiting films, video tapes, or slide shows. Presentations are from one to five minutes per college.

Comment

Student viewers of the system can request additional information on any college in the country by completing and returning a postage-paid response card provided by the manufacturer. A two-track audio feature permits the message to be recorded and heard in two languages. The system is recommended for high school students and their parents in the college selection process. It assists colleges and universities in reaching large numbers of potential students through laser technology. A test group of selected high schools is currently using the *College U.S.A.* system without charge. List Price Each: $59.95.

PRODUCING INTERACTIVE VIDEODISCS

3M Corporation/Optical Recording Project

System Requirements

laser videodisc player, TV

Recommended Target Group

Experienced curriculum developers with knowledge of television production

Content

This course is designed to teach curriculum developers and teachers how to develop and produce a videodisc for instruction in virtually any subject.

Comment

If the course is to be used for actual production of the instructional videodisc, video production facilities will be required. The course is not intended for persons inexperienced with curriculum development or with video production. The technical content is well-presented and uses various instructional techniques to maintain interest. The interactive capabilities of the videodisc are used effectively. There is a self-instructional manual reinforcing the videodisc. The course contains much useful and well-organized information about videodisc production. List Price: $495.95

How to Choose and Use Courseware for the Learning Disabled Student

by Karen Marshall and Mary Rogers

(Editor's Note: The subject of this feature is an exciting new area for computer-based instruction (CBI). The authors are practitioners of the new art they describe below. They are teachers, rather than scholars or writers, but their experience carries an authority of its own. Perhaps someday they will also be known as pioneers).

Learning disabled students have difficulty acquiring new skills. Often they are discouraged by the learning process and are fearful of repeated failures. Their learning styles and needs are varied. Finding appropriate techniques to meet these varying styles and needs has offered a continuing challenge to educators. Microcomputers can provide a new and exciting vehicle to meet this instructional challenge.

Computer-based instruction offers some unique advantages in educating the learning disabled student. It provides individual instruction, giving the child its "undivided attention." Lessons are structured to ensure success, while allowing the student to work at his or her own rate. Computer-based instruction provides many opportunities for repetition and review. Praise or reinforcement is immediate and frequent. Errors are corrected in a nonthreatening manner. Even drill and practice can become exciting through color, sound, animation, and learning games. The computer can provide the student a medium for self-expression through art, music, writing, and programming. Even the most reluctant learner finds the computer to be a highly motivating instructional tool.

In choosing microcomputer software to meet the instructional needs of learning disabled students, educators should consider the following features:

1. The level of vocabulary and sentence complexity should be appropriate for the intended learner.

2. The visual presentation should be clear and uncluttered with a limited amount of material presented at one time.

3. The presentation should include multisensory stimulation through text, graphics and sound presentations.

4. The material should reflect a logical progression of skills with opportunities for review.

5. The time allowed for response to material should be student-controlled.

6. There should be immediate and frequent positive reinforcement of student responses.

7. The error correction procedure should be written in positive, simple, and concise language.

8. The presentation should involve a high level of student interaction with the computer to help maintain attention on the desired task.

9. The software program should provide options which allow the teacher to insert his or her own material, turn sound on or off, change letter types (upper to lower case), and control the speed of presentation of the materials.

Most of the existing software was not designed specifically for learning disabled students. Despite this fact, it is possible to find quality software programs that have instructional value in a learning disabilities setting. The learning disabilities specialist may need to employ some of the following adaptive strategies to ensure successful computer interaction:

1. Provide a reader for instructional screens when the language is too difficult.

2. Follow up computer instruction with related tasks to ensure transfer of learning.

3. Explain directions for software use and skip wordy introductory instructions.

4. Use finger pointing on the screen to maintain visual awareness of cursor location.

5. Encourage the student to "talk through" the instructional procedure. This will add a multisensory dimension to the learning process.

The potential for the computer's use with learning disabled students is mind boggling. Computing may offer a new context in which these students begin to think, read, write, calculate, and solve problems.

Following are several examples of how to use standard products with learning disabled students.

Building Better Sentences: Combining Sentence Parts, Milton Bradley
(See review, Elementary, Language Arts/Writing, pg. 16).

This program teaches students the process of combining sentence parts to develop more effective skills in written expression. The systematic development of sentence expanding exercises makes this program effective for use with learning disabled students at the secondary level. The interactive nature of the program provides the stimulus to keep students working on the task. In order to use this program, the student should be able to comprehend material at the junior high level or above. After initial teacher instruction, the program can be used with a minimum of teacher interaction. The inclusion of a pretest, practice, and a posttest makes the program easy to incorporate into a student's I.E.P.

Building Better Sentences: Creating Compound and Complex Sentences, Milton Bradley
(See review, Elementary, Language Arts/Writing, p. 16).

This program exmphasizes the skills of combining clauses to create more effective compound and complex sentences. The concepts presented are often quite difficult for learning disabled students to comprehend. Nevertheless, the interactive nature of the program does assist the student to stay on the task while trying to master these advanced language concepts. In order to use the program, the student should be able to comprehend material at the junior high level, but due to the abstract content of this program, frequent teacher assistance is necessary to clarify concepts presented. The inclusion of pretests, practice, and posttests makes this program easy to incorporate into the student's I.E.P.

Division Skills, Milton Bradley
(See review, Elementary, Mathematics, p. 23).

Milton Bradley's **Division Skills** is an excellent instructional program for learning disabled students. The visual presentation is well-designed with screens that clearly focus on the problem to be solved. The highlight of this program for use with learning disabled students is the step by step approach in the Instruction mode. In this mode, the program guides the student with carefully selected cues that teach the division process. In the Practice mode, the student can transfer skills learned to paper and pencil tasks. If the student becomes confused, he or she can solicit help from the computer by simply pressing the letter "H". The program can be used with a minimum of teacher interaction and thus can encourage student independence. This comprehensive division program is appropriate for learning disabled students, elementary through high school age.

Game of the States, Milton Bradley
(See review, Elementary, Social Studies, p. 29).

This game program is fun and an easy way for learning disabled students to learn state names, state capitals, state abbreviations, major cities, and neighboring states. The program provides two levels of play: easy and challenging. The easier level gives the player more clues. Each level allows the player a second chance if the first response is incorrect. The player receives credit for correct answers on the first or second try. There is no penalty for incorrect answers. Success is almost guaranteed. Memorizing information such as state names is often difficult and frustrating for learning disabled students. This program makes an otherwise dull task exciting!

Percents, Milton Bradley
(See review, Elementary, Mathematics, p. 27).

This program provides the learning disabled student with a sequential approach to learning how to use percents in mathematics. A readiness section provides practice in prerequisite skills, which also helps the teacher to determine whether the student is ready for the new concept. The main body of the program provides the learner with a choice of using either proportions or equations to solve problems. This is especially helpful for the learning disabled student since the program allows the use of the method that makes the most sense to the student. The lessons are all reinforced with instruction and practice worksheets. Word problems are provided to help the student apply skills. This program is recommended for use with learning disabled students who can comprehend written material above the sixth grade level.

Progressive Phonics, Comp-Ed
(See review, Elementary, Language Arts/ Reading, p. 10).

Comp-Ed **Progressive Phonics** has many features that make it attractive for use with learning disabled students. The visual presentation of material is clear and utilizes enlarged letters. The program

employs good use of pictures to aid the development of letter-sound associations. Correct answers are immediately reinforced. Errors are corrected in a clear and concise manner. The program has several teacher options. The teacher may choose to turn off sound for distractable students or change the speed of presentation to a comfortable rate for the individual learner. This program would be best used with elementary learning disabled students in need of review and repetition of these basic phonics skills. Because examples and practice words are sometimes too difficult for the level of instruction, it should not be used to introduce these phonetic concepts. Also, introductory statements and directions are too advanced and need to be read or explained to the student.

Punctuation Skills: Commas, Milton Bradley
Punctuation Skills: End Marks, Semicolon, and Colon, Milton Bradley
(See reviews, Elementary, Language Arts/ Writing, p. 17).

Commas and **End Marks, Semicolon, and Colon** are interactive programs that reinforce difficult concepts in grammar. Both programs involve and motivate the student by using a student-controlled device to insert punctuation into example sentences. This feature helps to keep the distractible student on task and learning. In order to use these programs, the student should be able to comprehend material at the junior high level or above. After initial teacher interaction, the program can be used with a minimum of teacher assistance. The format of pretest, instruction, practice, and mastery test is easy to incorporate into a student's I.E.P. These programs would be easily integrated into a remedial English curriculum.

Ratios and Proportions, Milton Bradley
(See review, Secondary, Mathematics/ Algebra, p. 41).

This program is an excellent instructional tool for use with learning disabled students. It provides a logical, sequential approach to learning the troublesome mathematical concepts of ratio and proportion. The program includes a readiness section that covers the skills of writing a fraction in lowest terms and solving simple equations, and provides the learning disabled student practice in prerequisite skills. This activity is very important for students who have gaps in their mathe-

matical knowledge. The three levels of presentation — instruction, practice, and mastery — ensure successful student-computer interaction and allow for individualizing the program to suit a student's needs. Off-computer worksheet activities help the student to transfer what has been learned on the computer to paper and pencil tasks. The total package is well-designed and educationally sound. It is an excellent choice for use with learning disabled students in grades 7-12.

Vocabulary Skills: Context Clues, Milton Bradley
(See review, Elementary, Language Arts/ Reading, p. 11).

This program provides an effective, sequential approach to learning the use of context clues. It is appropriate for use with high school learning disabled students, especially those with disabilities in the area of reading comprehension. It provides this type of student an additional tool to aid in sentence and passage comprehension by analysis of word meaning. The five skill levels are sequential in development although each skill can be taught independently. This feature allows the teacher to match the skill level with the student's educational needs.

Vocabulary Skills: Prefixes, Suffixes, and Root Words, Milton Bradley
(See review, Elementary, Language Arts/ Reading, p. 12).

This drill and practice program teaches the concept of using basic word parts to cause change in sentence meaning. The program is clearly presented and provides the learning disabled student with concrete exercises from which to build vocabulary skills. These skills are essential for developing reading comprehension skills; they provide a foundation for building structural analysis skills critical to the decoding process in reading. The inclusion of pretests and mastery tests makes this program easy to incorporate into a student's I.E.P.

ADMINISTRATIVE SOFTWARE. Applications software designed to solve administrative problem(s).

APPLICATIONS SOFTWARE. A program written to serve a function or solve a problem not related to the operation of the computer system.

ARITHMETIC/LOGIC UNIT. The unit of a computer that performs the arithmetic and logical operations.

AUTHORING SOFTWARE. Computer programs which enable a courseware developer (author) to generate computer-assisted instruction and/or computer-managed instruction.

BILINGUAL EDUATION. Intended for persons whose primary language is not English. It provides instruction in academic subjects in the student's native language until the student has achieved sufficient mastery of English to use it for the study of the curriculum.

BRANCHING. A computer operation where a selection is made between two or more possible courses of action depending upon user input.

BREAK POINTS. Stopping points designed into the courseware to allow for termination of a session before the actual conclusion of a unit of instruction.

CATHODE RAY TUBE (CRT). An output device that gives a visual display of text and graphics from a computer (similar to a television screen).

CENTRAL PROCESSING UNIT (CPU). A control unit of a computer that directs information in and out of the different parts of the computer.

CODE. The symbolic text of a program. This is the form in which programs are written and read by programmers.

COMPUTER. A device that can input, store, manipulate, and output data. A computer has five main parts: Input Device(s), Memory, Arithmetic/Logic Unit, Central Processing Unit (CPU) and Output Device(s).

COMPUTER ASSISTED INSTRUCTION (CAI). A computer software application in which a computer is used to conduct instruction using techniques such as text screens, graphics screens, etc.

COMPUTER INTERACTIVE VIDEO (CIV). An integrated system using the capabilities of the computer and audiovisual media for instruction. User input enables the computer program to select both the appropriate audiovisual sequences and the appropriate computer responses.

COMPUTER MANAGED INSTRUCTION (CMI). A computer software application in which a computer is used to sequence, branch, test, prescribe, and track progress and report on user input, but not to conduct instruction.

COURSEWARE. Educational applications software used for teaching and learning.

CURSOR. The graphic notation on the screen identifying the user's point of entry for any input into the computer.

DATA. A collection of information, facts, etc., for processing.

DATA BASE. A collection of information (Data), large or small, about any particular subject or groups of subjects.

DELETE/BACK SPACE. A key that is used to erase commands and correct typing mistakes before RETURN is hit.

DIGITAL SCREEN. Monitor screen displaying text generated by a computer program.

DISKETTE. A magnetically coated, record-shaped object used to store data. (Also called a FLOPPY DISK).

DOCUMENTATION. A collection of written or printed materials that aid in the understanding of a computer system or program.

DRILL AND PRACTICE. Computer programs to reinforce learning through repeated examples and questions relating to a particular subject being taught.

DUBBING. Reproduction of visual or audio images from one source or medium to another.

ENGLISH AS A SECOND LANGUAGE. Intended for non-English speaking students or for non-native students who lack English proficiency. For them it provides instruction to achieve proficiency in English speaking, reading, and writing.

EXTERNAL SOFTWARE. Software, other than the operating system, required to use the computer system for a particular purpose.

FEEDBACK. The computer's response to the particular input of the user.

GRAPHICS. Output displayed in representational or pictorial forms, such as histograms, maps, or graphs.

HARD COPY. A printed copy of machine output in a visually readable form, such as printed reports, listings, documents, and summaries.

HARDWARE. The actual machinery or physical parts of a computer (mechanical, magnetic, electrical, or electronic devices).

HELP FUNCTION. The capability within the computer program for the user to call up and receive assistance in operational instructions for the program.

INPUT. The data that go into the computer to be processed.

INPUT DEVICE. A mechanical device used to transmit the input to the computer.

INTERACTIVE CAPABILITY. A computer system or program designed to allow an interchange (dialogue) between the user at a terminal and the computer during the execution of a program.

INTERACTIVITY. The integration of two or more separate elements in a manner that enables them to respond to each other. This can be in a computer program for response between the program and the user, or it can be in computer interactive video (CIV) for the response among the program, the videodisc, and the user.

INTERFACE. The peripheral devices which connect the computer to the videodisc player and enable the interaction required for computer interactive video (CIV).

INTEGRATED SYSTEM. Two or more components forming a working whole, in which all the components are essential for operation, each fulfilling a different function.

LIGHT PEN. A hand-held, light-sensing device that detects the CRT beam when pointed toward a portion of the screen.

LOCK OUT CODES. That portion of a computer program that requires a code to access parts of the computer program and records stored on it from various aspects of the content, scores, and/or other information that the instructor wishes to protect from outside tampering.

MACHINE READABLE. Data that are directly readable by the machine, such as from disk and tape, or documents specifically prepared for Optical Character Recognition (OCR).

MAGNETIC MEDIUM. A magnetically coated medium such as a disk, diskette, or magnetic tape used to store data.

MENU. A list of the features and/or segments of a program which is displayed on the screen and from which the user can select the next program option.

MICROCOMPUTER. A computer designed primarily for use by one person at a time.

MONITOR. See CATHODE RAY TUBE.

MOUSE. A special device that allows the user to move a cursor on the computer screen in any direction—up or down, diagonally, left or right, or in a circle. When the cursor is properly positioned on the screen, the user can then designate his/her selection.

NEA TEACHER CERTIFIED. Software which has passed through the Assessment Procedure of the NEA Educational Computer Service and has qualified for the NEA Teacher Certified Trademark.

OPERATING SYSTEM. Software which controls the execution of computer programs and which may provide scheduling, input/output control, data management, and related services.

OPTICAL CHARACTER RECOGNITION. The process of reading characters or other symbols through the use of light sensitive devices.

OUTPUT. Data that have been processed in a computer and are transferred to an external device (e.g., printer, screen).

PERIPHERAL. Any piece of equipment, distinct from the computer itself, that allows the computer to communicate with the "outside" world.

PRINTOUT. Information or output from the computer printed on paper.

PRODUCTION VALUES. Technical qualities and standards required for the resulting product, whether that is a video product, a computer program, a filmstrip, or any other product requiring expertise for its production.

PROGRAM. A set of instructions written in sequence that tell the computer what to do.

PROGRAMMING CODE. See CODE.

RANDOM ORDER. Questions and problems presented by the courseware appear in a different (random) sequence during each session using the courseware.

RECORD KEEPING. The computer's capability to remember (store) the user's responses to questions, score them, and have them available for retrieval.

REPORT GENERATION. The computer's capability to produce reports based on the records (i.e. student performance) that it has stored.

RETURN. A key on the terminal keyboard which completes a user entry and transmits it to the computer for processing.

SCREEN DISPLAY. Use of a CRT for display of output from the computer, including instructional text, questions, and responses.

SIMULATION. A type of computer assisted instruction which imitates a real operation or scenario of some type such as the operation of a control panel on an aircraft.

SOFTWARE. A (set of) program(s) written to process data and solve problems.

SOURCE LISTING. A print copy of the code. See. CODE.

SPECIAL DEVICES. Special purpose peripheral equipment. See PERIPHERAL.

SPECIAL EFFECTS. Sound or visual additions to the primary material presented, whether on the computer program or on the visual image. These can be computer-generated still or moving graphic displays, overlays, or various other audio or visual additions to attract attention to or emphasize the primary material.

STORAGE CAPACITY. The amount of data and code that can be stored in the computer system usually expressed in kilobytes (k) or thousands of bytes.

TEACHER'S MANUAL. Documentation provided to the teacher containing information concerning the operation of the software (how to run the program) and its instructional design and characteristics.

TECHNICAL MANUAL. Documentation provided to the reviewer which describes the functions of the software and indicates how to use the software.

TERMINAL. A device, usually equipped with a keyboard and some kind of display, capable of sending and receiving information over a communication channel.

TEST DATA. Data organized to aid in the testing of the software allowing for all features to be exercised.

TOUCH SCREEN. A CRT screen equipped with a position sensor so that finger contact causes the coordinates of the point touched to be transmitted to a computer.

TRACKING. The computer's capability to remember the input and course of the user through the computer program.

TUTORIAL. A type of computer assisted instruction (CAI) which presents a question, judges the student's response, and "tutors" the student when an incorrect response is received. In tutorial CAI, an attempt to diagnose the source of the student's problem is frequently made; the tutoring is thereby customized.

USER. A person or organization that utilizes the hardware and/or software components of a computer system.

VIDEODISC (LASER). Audo visual material prerecorded on a durable plastic disc. A single disc can store one hour of continuous play video images (108,000 frames) and up to two sound tracks. A videodisc player allows quick, random access to any one of the discs' 54,000 frames per side or to a series of frames. It will search forward or reverse, and play at standard speed, in slow motion, or frame by frame.

VOICE INPUT. Voice communication with the computer system. Voice transmission of data to be processed.

VOICE OUTPUT. Audio transmission of output from the computer system.

EDUCATIONAL SOFTWARE

PUBLISHER INDEX